T0196389

A Comprehensive Situation-by-Situation Guide Whether your Daughter is a
Pubescent 10-year-old or a 20-year-old Adolescent,
This book will Guide you through the
Turbulent Teenage Years in a Changing World

PARENTING
TEEN
GIRLS
24/7

MERYL FISHMAN

Author will donate 10% of her proceeds
in memory of Dr. Jack Fishman to
not-for-profit organizations that help
prevent and treat teen drug addiction

ARCHWAY
PUBLISHING

Archway Publishing books may be ordered through booksellers or by contacting:

Archway Publishing
1663 Liberty Drive
Bloomington, IN 47403
www.archwaypublishing.com
1 (888) 242-5904

Because of the dynamic nature of the Internet, any web addresses or links contained in this book may have changed since publication and may no longer be valid. The views expressed in this work are solely those of the author and do not necessarily reflect the views of the publisher, and the publisher hereby disclaims any responsibility for them.

Any people depicted in stock imagery provided by Thinkstock are models, and such images are being used for illustrative purposes only.
Certain stock imagery © Thinkstock.

This book is a work of non-fiction. Unless otherwise noted, the author and the publisher make no explicit guarantees as to the accuracy of the information contained in this book and in some cases, names of people and places have been altered to protect their privacy.

ISBN: 978-1-4808-5693-6 (sc)
ISBN: 978-1-4808-5694-3 (e)

Library of Congress Control Number: 2018900177

Print information available on the last page.

Archway Publishing rev. date: 02/15/2018

AUTHOR'S NOTE

The author disclaims any professional knowledge with respect to the matters discussed herein which are based solely on her experiences as a mother and grandmother and those of friends and acquaintances. When professional or outside counseling is recommended or suggested, it doesn't mean you need to immediately send your daughter to a psychiatrist but that the assistance of a third party is advisable. Check with your daughter's doctor, school counselor, religious official or local library for information on services that would be appropriate to the situation. Parent-child confrontations during adolescence are similar whether the authority figure is male or female, parent, step-parent or guardian. The terms "mother" or "parent" are used herein for convenience.

CONTENTS

1. INTRODUCTION

Despite the ever-increasing dangers of life in today's changing world, you and your daughter *can* enjoy her journey to adulthood. You *can* help her appreciate herself. You *can* help her become a responsible adult. This book will explain how not to over- or under-react to your daughter's often outlandish and even rude adolescent behavior. This book will also show you how and when to loosen the reins so that as her path takes her further and further from home and your protective guidance, her inner compass will serve her well along life's journey. While you may find some of the suggested responses too permissive, keep in mind that the overall tenet of this book is for you to reserve your "No's" for issues of your daughter's safety and well-being or for her behavior that you find particularly irritating.

Though individual physical and emotional development from girlhood to womanhood varies greatly, most girls will exhibit most of the behavior described herein sometime during their second decade of life. However, the need for ever-increasing education and advanced skills may extend the period of adolescence even longer. One mother reported that her 24-year-old daughter (a doctoral student) still behaved like an adolescent around her. Apparently, the extended period of the daughter's dependency necessitated by the cost of graduate school and the amount of studying and preparation needed for her PhD thesis, had left no time or energy for the daughter to move past typical teen disdain at even the slightest suggestion by her mother. At the other end of the spectrum are ten-year-olds who have already begun to menstruate, or because of modern technology, are repeatedly exposed to issues that were only whispered about a decade ago. Thus, while being a parent is difficult even in the best of times, today's parents face even greater challenges considering not only the longer period of adolescence but the dangers of social networking, easily obtainable addictive drugs, and worries about an uncertain future for themselves and their children in our ever-changing and more dangerous world.

Regardless of the current trend celebrating Diversity over The

Meryl Fishman

Melting Pot, most families share similar values and want their children to grow up in a safe and clean environment, receive a quality education, and have an opportunity to follow their dreams. Intruding on these desires though is that due to globalization and modern technology the work shift is no longer an 8-hour, Monday-Friday workweek but can be any time, any day, in our 24/7 world. Consequently, many families are unable to eat dinner or spend any quality time together. Our 24/7 culture and education system add to the complication since they each now emphasize self-fulfillment rather than patience and sacrifice—words seemingly unheard of or unheeded by today's children. Not surprisingly, today's parents are not immune to the drumbeat of a "me first" culture even if only on a minimal level. Consequently, today's parents often parent on the fly or pursuant to advice garnered from the worldwide web or other social media. Using such tools as a source for information though creates the danger that discussing private issues in a public forum will come back to haunt you.

Be assured that that there is no "right" way to bring up an adolescent— only a way that is right for you and your daughter. Adolescence is not the time for a test of wills or the time for you to try to change your daughter into a different person. Instead, it is the time for your daughter to begin to find out who she is and how to live a life that is best for her. In the meantime, not to worry if your daughter no longer speaks a civil word to her siblings or treats you with disdain (at best!).

2. CHANGING TIMES

Because of social networking and a myriad of high tech gizmos intruding 24/7 on parents and children and a general relaxation of mores, a parent's task is now much more difficult than in the past. Children are exposed to messages about racial and ethnic hatred, wanton violence, pornography, bullying, wild rumors, and misinformation about almost any topic. Also dangerous are the purveyors of child pornography and drugs and the ease with which such predators and other exploiters of children can reach out to your daughter. Less obvious but also dangerous is the subliminal media encouragement of drinking and drug use by featuring characters (even doctors) in starring roles who suffer little or no consequences from such self-inflicted bodily onslaughts.

Further, our current over-protective, child-centered milieu coupled with the ever-expanding dangers from technology and increased government intrusion into family matters, rightly or wrongly, limit a parent's ability to create opportunities for their children to learn self-reliance and how to choose for themselves. Thus, today's parents need to walk a thin line between being over-bearing or too Pollyannaish in guiding their children toward proper choices on their road to maturity.

While the times are different, children are still children. Each generation of teenagers suffer the pangs and insecurities of adolescence. Each generation of teenage girls will argue with their parents about curfews and homework and worry about pimples and boys and each generation of teenage girls will want to assert their independence—against their parents and against convention. However, before discussing the delightful (and other) idiosyncrasies of your daughter, I've chosen to first discuss the really tough stuff since they involve areas that can bring serious harm to her.

3. TODAY'S DANGERS

Bullying — Depression/Suicide
Domestic Abuse
Drugs, Alcohol & Cigarettes
Hitching a Ride — Sexual Predators
STDs/AIDS

BULLYING

Cyberbullying. It used to be that the mantra *sticks and stones will break my bones but words will never hurt me* was heard in every schoolyard. Unfortunately, given the advent of social media and its ever-increasing use among teenagers, cyberbullying— bullying via malicious postings on social media or via texts and tweets, etc.— has become a serious national problem and a huge concern for parents of teenagers.

The typical school and playground bullying incidents of yore are chicken feed compared to the damage that can be done by venomous social media and instantaneous communication. Your daughter's addiction to tech gizmos that put her in constant touch with her friends can also make her a target of malicious gossip and physical threats. To protect your daughter from cyberbullying, you must do several things. First and foremost, you must become familiar with the gadgetry that your daughter uses. Ideally you too should know how to blog, to chat, to text, to tweet, to snap-chat, to attach and transmit pictures, to use Instagram, to download U-tube videos and whatever else has been developed by the time you read this book and thereafter. If you're clueless about modern communication technology, take a tour of your local box-store's computer and electronics section so that you have at least an over-view of what's out there and how it is used. Determine which if any Internet or social media sites you wish to block or lock and learn how to do so. Some smart phones and the like also have programs that allow parental monitoring. Also, just like you tell your daughter not to open the door to strangers, remember to advise her not to open any "spam" or e-mails or any texts or tweets, etc. from unknown senders and not to answer her phone unless the caller is on her contact list.

While I believe it is important that you respect your daughter's privacy, since we all now live in an electronic fish bowl, you should know what's swimming around in hers. Thus, you should have access to your daughter's Facebook page and whatever other sites or electronic devices she signs on to or uses for communication. While the foregoing sounds contradictory to respecting your daughter's privacy, it need not be. Simply explain to your daughter that you will be monitoring her Internet and social media use from time to time because it is your job to do so in the same way that when she goes somewhere with her friends, you need to know where she's going and when she'll be home. Tell her you will behave no different than a Secret Service agent guarding a President's child. Assure your daughter that your sole purpose in monitoring is to keep an eye out for danger to her but that you will keep mum about and ignore harmless gossip or simple foolishness. *And keep your word!* (*See also* Chapter 8 at "Spying.")

Middle and high school girls often form cliques, most of which are innocuous. However, some clique members go beyond cattiness and pettiness and are downright mean and dangerously so. For these girls, any non-clique classmate is a potential target for malicious and salacious gossip regardless of race, religion, ethnicity or sexual orientation or whether the target be thin or fat, tall or short, freckled or not, disfigured or not, native born or immigrant, a loner or a Special Needs student, or just some girl who ticked off a clique member way back in first grade. Thus, you cannot protect your daughter from capricious teen girls who believe the nastier or more vicious their postings, the more popular they will become.

If your daughter becomes a target of media postings disparaging her because of race, ethnicity, religion or gender or imply even a hint of physical harm to her or your family, or encouraging her to harm herself, immediately notify the police and let them guide you as to your next steps. Let your daughter know that you've reported the incident. Also, have a lawyer at the ready in case the matter becomes public as it would be best for your family to stay out of public view and have someone else speak and act on your family's behalf. It's also a good idea to meet with a counselor to help your family through this troubled time particularly if your daughter was hesitant about reporting the matter to the police out of embarrassment. I don't mean to make light of any backlash against you or your family as a result of going to the police, but in doing so, you and your family should consider yourselves heroes, particularly your daughter. Reporting the matter will not only help your daughter and others from being bullied in the future but could also forestall the bullies from getting into the kind of trouble that could lead to jail time for them.

If the postings are from classmates spreading malicious or salacious gossip, true or untrue about your daughter, also report the matter to your daughter's school and again let your daughter know that you are doing so. Even if you know the parents of the bullies, it's best that the school and/or the police take the lead on this. Be aware too that while all hateful postings are hurtful to your daughter, they may not rise to the level where police action is warranted. Thus, while reporting the situation may lead to the cessation of the maliciousness, it may also exacerbate the situation by leading to more frequent and more vicious postings. While a change of schools may seem like a good idea, it's a risky move. The same wrongdoers may continue their cyberbullying and there's no guarantee that your daughter would not become the target of a new clique of cyberbullies at the new school. Again, allow yourself to be led by guidance from the police, the school, and a counselor.

Whether or not the postings were actionable resulting in their cessation or are ongoing, your daughter's self-esteem likely took a big hit. Thus, after reporting the matter, you must concentrate your efforts on enabling your daughter to withstand the resultant onslaught. First, compliment your daughter on her good judgment if it was she that reported the bullying to you. (If it was you that discovered the bullying, do not criticize your daughter at this time for not telling you—your disappointment about not being trusted can be addressed at a later date.) Second, nix any teasing of your daughter by family members be it about her looks, her grades, her friends, whatever.

Next, assure your daughter that she is a lovable and valuable person not just with soothing words but by validating her concerns and respecting her opinions. As to remedying the reason your daughter was targeted, save that for another time if in fact the basis for her being targeted is remedial such as her being over-weight. You do not want to imply that she was in any way at fault. Best to put the onus squarely back on the wrongdoers where it belongs and just say that some children have not yet learned to follow "The Golden Rule"—that is, *to treat others as they would like to be treated.*

Lastly, help your daughter get involved in an activity where she can make a positive difference even if it's something as simple as walking an elderly neighbor's dog. The important thing during this ordeal is that your daughter become busy in an activity where she feels safe, valued, and needed. Keep in mind though that despite your kind and caring concern and actions designed to enable your daughter to move on, and while learning to hold one's head high in times of adversity is a good lesson to learn, it may be a lesson that your daughter is just not yet ready for. Thus, if your daughter has trouble moving past the incident, consider engaging a counselor to ensure that her positive self-esteem returns.

You must also remind your daughter often and loudly that the world is now one large fishbowl and that anything she transmits, even to a trusted friend, will very likely be forwarded to classmates who will in turn forward her message to others. Further, the more gossipy or sexual her transmission, the more likely it will be sent around making her a target for cyberbullying. Raging teen hormones cloud judgment and a teen girl who engages in "sexting" (sending text messages containing nude photographs or descriptions of sexual acts engaged in or planned) is no different than a three-year old who plays with matches. Unfortunately, while you can hide matches from a toddler, you cannot prevent your pubescent daughter from sending a nude photo of herself to her boyfriend via her cell phone if she is determined to do so. Somehow you must convince your daughter that doing so, or texting messages describing her sexual wishes or acts to anyone, can not only make her a subject of malicious gossip that can easily ruin her teen years but her adult years as well.

Sadly, some teens have committed suicide as a result of malicious cyber gossip or media exposure of their nudity or sexual acts or thoughts. (*See* this Chapter below at "Depression/Suicide.") Your daughter must understand that no matter how much she may trust someone, she is not, under any circumstances, to send anything via any media that could be used to harm her or her family or someone else's reputation. Once it's out in cyberspace, it's out there—photos and text messages still exist in cyberspace even when delete and erase buttons are pressed. You should also instruct your daughter that if she receives any sexual pictures or sexual or malicious messages, she should not only not forward them to anyone else but should also tell you about them. Contact the police if any such messages contain even a hint of violence to anyone; as for the others, use your judgment as to whether to report such messages to the sender's parents and/or the school.

Cyberbullying by Your Daughter. If you suspect that your daughter is transmitting malicious messages, either on her own or with friends, trust your instincts and be as nosey as the situation warrants and take action. Whether your daughter was the instigator or just joined the others because of peer pressure, save the reprimands for later and do what's necessary—notify the school, and if warranted, the police, so that the malicious transmissions cease and obtain whatever counseling your daughter needs to get past her foolishness before her actions become criminal.

Physical Bullying. Schools nowadays usually have written policies as to what constitutes bullying and procedures to be followed in such event; assumedly such procedures also call for police involvement when warranted. Also, many schools have programs where children act out scenarios as to what student bystanders should do when witnessing actions of bullying. You too should encourage your daughter to interfere (as long as her personal safety is not seriously jeopardized) when seeing others being bullied. However, school anti-bullying programs may only be moderately effective in thwarting bullies who threaten physical harm or launch direct in-school verbal attacks against another student. In such event, all a school can do is take appropriate action as dictated by local law. Such actions may include a good talking-to, require that the bully attend special programs, excluding the bully from school-related activities, and/or suspending or expelling the bully from school. However, school actions and peer interference do not always stop a bully from bullying. In my view, bullies know exactly what they are doing and enjoy the power rush they get at someone else's expense just as if they were high on an illicit drug. Thus, you must be on guard if your daughter seems fearful of going to school.

If your daughter has told you that she is being physically threatened at school, or you think she is, immediately advise the school authorities (and police if warranted). If appropriate action is not taken resulting in a cessation of the bullying so that your daughter can safely attend school without fear of physical harm, try to send her to another school. If this is not possible, perhaps your daughter can be switched out from the classes where she has the greatest fear or her schedule can be rearranged so she need not be one of the last ones in the hallways during class breaks.

DEPRESSION/SUICIDE *(see also Chapter 4 at "Techitis")*

Sadly, some teens who feel unloved or unworthy or, in their mind horrifically embarrassed by their own or a parent's action, may try suicide as a way out. They feel pressures they cannot cope with—from school, for social acceptance, from their parents, from cyberbullying, or from real or imagined deficiencies in themselves. Also worrisome is that suicide pacts among teenage girls are on the rise. Current statistics show an almost 50% increase in suicide among teen girls aged 15-19 and that the more time a teen girl spends on social media, the more likely she is to be depressed or attempt suicide.

If your daughter has attempted suicide, be grateful that her attempt failed. Don't be embarrassed by it. Don't try to cover it up or pretend it didn't happen. Instead, seek outside help immediately so as to determine the cause of her despair and to heal her psyche. (If medication is prescribed to help with your daughter's depression, keep a watchful eye out for possible side effects, particularly potentially addictive ones.) In any case, it's imperative to remain non-judgmental. You may think it's no problem for her to be an A student; she may think otherwise. You may think that gymnastics is a fun and healthy activity; she may think it too competitive. Listen and validate her fears and make sure she knows that it is she that you love, not her accomplishments.

If your daughter's attempt was the result of cyberbullying, even if she was the underlying cause by posting sexually explicit photos of herself on social media or sending them to her boyfriend, you must still be non-judgmental. Your daughter's acts were foolish but the only person she hurt was herself. You must not add to her hurt by blaming her. She feels bad enough already. Instead, contact the bullies and/or their parents, the school, and the police if necessary, and do what else you've been advised to do to protect your daughter from suffering further from her foolish act—even sending her to Aunt Betsy's to finish out the school year if plausible. Regardless, you can help her through her embarrassment by reminding her that foolishness regarding nudity and sex has been around since Adam and Eve. Your daughter needs to acknowledge her lack of good judgment and move on from there. She needs to understand that everyone makes stupid mistakes from time to time but such mistakes are not a reason to punish oneself let alone kill oneself. Ditto if your daughter's suicide attempt arose from her being the bully and causing harm to another. Her having definitely known better is still not a reason to commit suicide. She is after all still a child.

If your daughter threatens suicide and life does not seem to be going too well for her in general, don't automatically pooh-pooh her threats and ignore her despondency as typical teenage behavior. Studies have shown that teenage girls suffer from depression to an alarming degree. Threatening to die if she doesn't get tickets to the next pop concert is not the same as *if you don't let me go out Saturday night, I'll kill myself...then you'll be sorry*, or *if I wasn't around, you wouldn't need to support me or have so much to worry about*. While isolated statements such as these are not abnormal and even if everything else—grades, friends, openness, sleep/eating habits, cheerfulness—is normal, I'd still keep eyes and ears open and if her words linger in your mind, trust your instinct and dig deeper. And when you dig, keep an eye out for sad-faced emojis on her tweets and texts keeping in mind that in our instantaneous communications world "dislikes" carry far more weight than "likes" regardless of our age or position in life. Further, should your digging make you feel uneasy or if you discover any evidence of self-mutilation by your daughter, seek help immediately. Contact the **National Suicide Prevention Lifeline at 800-273-TALK (800-273-8255)** for information or assistance.

DOMESTIC ABUSE

Whether incidents of domestic abuse are on the rise because of more incidents or better reporting is irrelevant. What is relevant, however, is that it happens all too often—even a single incident is one too many. In the event of physical or sexual abuse by your daughter's father, stepfather, other family member, friend or your boyfriend against you, your daughter or any of your other children, do not look for excuses for the perpetrator or blame yourself. Instead, as soon as it is safe for you to do so, **using the phone of a person not known to your abuser, call the National Domestic Abuse Hotline (1-800-799-7233)**. (Just ask to borrow a phone—you left yours at home, your phone is out of battery power, whatever...and then to assure privacy, delete the call after you're finished.) The Hotline will give you information and guidance as to how and when to report the matter to the police and how and where to obtain shelter and money to see you through this difficult time.

If your daughter is the abuser against you or any other family member, contact the above Hotline (**1-800-799-7233**) and/or United Way's website at **www.211.org** for guidance. You should also contact your local police department—not for the purpose of having your daughter arrested but for advice and guidance as to help available in your area since it's likely that you're not the only one in town that has this problem.

DRUGS, ALCOHOL & CIGARETTES

DRUGS. Misuse of prescription drugs and their derivatives are a major killer of teens in the United States. If you use pain pills or other drugs, even judiciously, make sure you take such medications discretely and keep them out of sight, even under lock and key if necessary. Remember too that if your daughter sees you popping a pill or taking a drink every time the going gets tough, you are teaching her to do the same. Teens have shown a propensity to turn even seemingly benign medications into dangerous drugs and given the Internet, such "how to" information is readily available to your daughter and her friends in a nanosecond. Moreover, "non-drowsy" over-the-counter allergy pills or cold remedies should also be kept out of sight since even one or two of these pills can give your daughter a high that she might want to repeat.

The physical pain suffered by severely injured athletes of all ages regardless of sex is very real but so is the Opioid-to-Heroin epidemic. Thus, unless and until our government gets a handle on controlling cross-the-border heroin traffic and cracks down on the distribution of opioids to bogus pharmacies, more and more of our children will continue to become addicted and die. In the meantime, if a doctor treating your daughter for pain from a serious injury prescribes an opioid ask for an alternative. It's true that alternatives to opioids may not work as well but they do subdue pain to a great degree without being a route to addiction. If, however, your daughter's pain is unbearably excruciating, ask the doc to write a non-refillable prescription for only a three-day supply and then, if possible, scale down to a less threatening pain-killer.

Current statistics show that young people who have become addicted to opioids or heroin or other drugs are routinely in and out of rehab or jail and all too often wind up overdosing. If you suspect your daughter is using an illegal drug, opioids, or the latest concoction of otherwise legal drugs, confront her for affirmation and go from there. Regardless of whether she admits or denies usage, seek outside counseling as to what your next step should be and follow through. Meth, opioids and heroin, particularly heroin laced with fentanyl (a synthetic opioid, one or two milligrams of which can be fatal), are particularly dangerous concoctions that are easily and cheaply obtainable but where withdrawal is difficult under the best of circumstances. If warranted, get your daughter into rehab—the sooner, the better.

Thereafter, if recommended by the rehab center, be prepared to pull out all the stops—to change your daughter's school or to move to a different neighborhood or even to a different town. I realize that there may not be a different school for your daughter to attend and that not everyone can just pull up roots and move elsewhere. Perhaps you have a friend or family member in a different town where your daughter can get a fresh start. A woman I know was able to do this and sent her high school drop-out user daughter to live with her sister in another state.

While in a totally different environment, the girl got a job and earned her GED and then went on to becoming a nurse. On the other hand, uprooting your family or your daughter in any way may just add to your daughter's negative feelings about herself or make her more prone to peer pressure, either of which can result in a relapse. Best to fully discuss your daughter's post-release treatment plan down to the grittiest detail with the rehab people making sure that it's not a one-size-fits-all plan but one specific to your daughter's psychological triggers and family situation.

Should circumstances be such that even though a fresh start in a new environment was recommended for your daughter but that such is not possible, don't despair. You can still help your daughter get a fresh start by helping her to change her daily routine so that she doesn't begin her day facing the same triggers that ultimately led her to drug usage. Humans are creatures of habit and, though this may sound lame given the seriousness of her addiction, you need to help your daughter get hooked on an easy-to-follow daily routine and safe substitutes. Morning coffee beckons; runners get high on endorphins; chicken soup is said to be a balm for the soul. Even a fixed healthy routine can become addictive.

Encourage your daughter that before she goes to sleep to make a plan of what she wishes to accomplish the next day starting with making her bed. (*See* "Make Your Bed" by Admiral William McRaven where he advocates that starting the day with the completion of a task sets the tone for a productive and satisfying day.) Her list should be short and simple but include a daily chore for her to do that benefits others such as taking a busy neighbor's dog out for a run or listening to a younger sibling read out loud. Your daughter needs to feel needed, not only loved. Though prayer won't solve your daughter's problem, her getting involved in a religious or social cause might help, particularly since it would be an opportunity to find new friends. Perhaps too having a puppy to care for might help give her a sense of purpose but if that's too much responsibility for her at this time, suggest that she volunteer at the local pet shelter or food bank after school or on weekends.

Most importantly, ensure as best as you can that your daughter follows the regimen recommended by her doctors and counselors. If she complains that you're checking up on her too much because you review her homework and go through her back-pack every day, don't argue. Instead, blame the rehab folks—explain that they gave you marching orders too.

Remember, we can only do what we can do. Ironically, the stepson of Dr. Jack Fishman, the developer of Naloxone (the injectable antidote to an opioid or a heroin overdose) died from overdosing on heroin. At the time, Naloxone was only available to first responders and health care providers but now it's often available to individuals by prescription or through certain pharmacies. Thus, check with the team treating your daughter about getting a prescription for Naloxone for you to use should you ever come home to an over-dosed daughter. Check with the rehab team too whether your daughter should even know about such purchase or where it'll be kept. You don't want your daughter to play Russian Roulette by overdosing on the living room sofa thinking you'll soon be home to rescue her.

In some situations, the prescription for Naloxone is given directly to the addict to keep on their person in the event he or she shoots up and has a change of heart. The pros and cons to this are obvious—will an immediately available antidote save the user's life or give him or her a false sense of safety by thinking that he or she will know when they've shot up too much? Again, discuss your daughter's treatment plan with the rehab staff down to the tiniest detail—no concern of yours is too small or too trite. For example, how much should you restrict your daughter's access to cash? Do you take away her piggy bank? Should you lock up your jewelry? Or will such actions cause her to prostitute herself for money?

Legalizing marijuana for medical reasons makes sense to me but only time will tell whether its legalization for recreational use by those older than twenty-one will cut down on the use of addictive drugs and the resultant crime and personal tragedies such use engenders. That being said, in Colorado, a state that permits recreational use of marijuana, opioid-related deaths have decreased. Whether the decrease is merely an anomaly or whether it's because marijuana users do not feel the need to try opioids or whether marijuana use is an antidote to opioid addiction is unknown as of this writing.

It's probably the rare teenager who will not try at least a puff of marijuana during the high school years. Note though that under Federal law it is illegal to sell, possess or use marijuana even in states that allow its usage. Thus, if you believe your daughter is an occasional pot smoker, instead of getting into an argument with her about the perceived or real dangers of marijuana use, remind her that you did not expend years of TLC to see her spend her teenage years in a jail cell.

You could also remind your daughter that any drug, legal ones included as well as stimulants like caffeine, affect everybody differently. Remind her that because her body is going through so many changes, a pill that might be harmless for one person could seriously harm her. Remind her too about the time Cousin Iris went into shock from penicillin and how even a child's dose of over-the-counter cough medicine makes your heart race. Tell her also that even super caffeinated drinks have caused the death of some teens. Somehow get your daughter to understand that since common drugs and stimulants can have serious and sometimes deadly side effects, she should be quite wary of smoking pot or experimenting with any other mind-bending drug whether because of peer pressure or idle curiosity. Remind your daughter too that no one eats just one potato chip and that using marijuana during her formative years can also lead to addiction.

If her reaction to your "talk" is more than the usual roll of the eyes or other expressions of extreme boredom whenever you say anything, trust your instincts and assume her marijuana use might be more than a Saturday night puff or two. Any changes in your daughter's grades or behavior or her having a new set of friends could also be indications of frequent usage. Seek professional advice how best to handle your suspicions.

Even if recreational pot is legal in your state, if you or anyone in your family or any of your visitors smoke pot, do not allow such usage in front of your children. Just as with cigarettes, your children are not immune to the effects of second-hand smoke. Further, marijuana-infused Brownies and the like should also be kept safely out of sight and out of reach by your children.

Fearing abduction, we caution our children not to take candy from strangers. Such admonishment is particularly important nowadays however since drug pushers can be anyone, anywhere—even senior citizens selling a few pills saved from a legally obtained opioid prescription. Thus, you must remind your children at every opportunity to not ingest any proffered pills or the like from anyone regardless of peer pressure. Ditto re unwrapped or suspicious looking Brownies, particularly in states where recreational marijuana is legal. Repeat Nancy Reagan's mantra of "**Just say *No***" over and over as often and as loud as necessary.

If you are addicted to opioids, any other pain medication, or any illegal drug, immediately make plans to conquer your addiction. *Your very life may depend upon your doing so.* Whatever the method, whatever the cost, you must rid yourself of such a scourge. To take care of your daughter, you must first take care of yourself. **Contact the National Substance Abuse Hotline 1-800-662-4357** for assistance.

ALCOHOL. While you daughter is unlikely to die from drinking alcohol though unfortunately every so often there are reports of teens who knowingly drank themselves to death, the possibility that your daughter might be killed by a drunk driver is far too real and far too often the drunk driver is one of her friends. You can give your daughter some leeway on the issues of dating and curfews but you should make her swear on her iPad that she will never ever go in a car with a driver who is even slightly drunk; that she will instead call to be picked up, no matter where she is, how late the hour, or what she may have been doing. Get your point across. Exercise your parental authority loudly and convincingly. And if you ever get such a call, respond immediately (even if you need to call a pricey car service) and ask no questions. None. No lectures either (at least, not then). If your daughter was smart enough to call, she's smart enough to know she was in a situation where she shouldn't have been. Discuss it with her when appropriate, of course, but remember to compliment her about calling you for a ride home instead of getting into a car with a drunkard. Just get your message across that her safety comes first.

Your daughter's drinking is a different matter. Some adolescents get drunk with their friends just to see what it feels like. Often it is the result of simple curiosity no different than the nine-year-old who throws tomatoes from a tenth-floor window just to see them go splat.

A nine-year-old does not realize that she could hurt someone with such a prank; a teen girl is probably oblivious to the fact that sampling alcohol could actually hurt her. If you believe that your daughter and her friends have been experimenting in your home and all else seems in order, lock the liquor cabinet and don't say a word. Your daughter will get the message next time she and her friends try to experiment. If you believe the experimentation may be going on elsewhere, discreetly contact her friends' parents so that they too can lock their cabinets and take other precautions as necessary.

If your daughter has a drinking problem, you must face the situation squarely and seek outside advice. Alcoholism is no different than drug addiction and is best handled by professionals. How your daughter handles alcohol may often depend on the situation at home and how she feels about herself in general. Clearly though, however you decide to handle the situation, if your daughter has time to get drunk, she has time for a part-time job, an extra-curricular school activity, or to volunteer somewhere. Help her get involved elsewhere so she'll have less free time and less time to spend with so-called friends who instigated or supported her alcohol problem. Since a picture is worth a thousand words, see if you can rent "Days of Wine and Roses," an award-winning film that portrays the downward spiral of a newly married couple going from a social drink or two to alcoholism without a happy ending. Watch it with your daughter—you need not say anything. The movie speaks volumes.

If the problem is teenage drinking at unsupervised parties or parties where the parents think serving a beer or two to older teens is harmless, your immediate reaction would be to tell your daughter loudly and clearly that she can't go. However, such a response might mean that the next time she's invited to a questionable party, she'll lie and say she's going to a movie or some such thing. Unfortunately, we can't always know where our children are, especially when they're in their late teens and have access to a car. Obviously, you want your daughter to be safe but before you put your foot all the way down and have her stay home, weigh your daughter's and her friends' emotional maturity and age. It's a tough call and one definitely worthy of you repeating your stock lecture that when at a party she should not only not drink any alcohol but drink only from bottles or cans opened in her presence and to never leave her drink unattended. Suggest too that she and a trusted girlfriend buddy-up at the party so as to look out for each other. For good measure, have her come home an hour earlier than her usual curfew. Additionally, extract a promise from her that she'll never get in a car with anyone who has been drinking and reiterate your mantra that you will pick her up anywhere, anytime, anyplace—no questions asked. I know the foregoing sounds scary but even at supervised parties, there's often some older teen wanting to show off and since we're not always there to protect our daughters, we can at least guide them as best we can as to how to protect themselves.

Whether or not you let your daughter have an occasional sip or drink at home is your business. Some people advocate that children should be taught to drink at home; others say parents who drink even socially set a bad example. Remember, however, you do not have the right to serve alcohol to your daughter's friends even if it is a family or holiday celebration. These days with everyone so litigation happy, I wouldn't even offer someone else's child a sip of champagne on New Year's Eve. (*See also* Chapter 11 at "Staying Safe" and Chapter 13 at "*Where Are You Going?*")

CIGARETTES. E-cigarettes (electronic smoking devices) contain a metal tube and a battery-operated heating element which when heated delivers vapors of nicotine and flavoring agents or other substances through an atomizer. Short-term side effects from the use of E-cigarettes such as dizziness, slurred speech, diarrhea and worse have been reported. The FDA has moved to restrict their sale to minors and to prevent their sale from vending machines as have most states. However, given all the other tasks of law enforcement, such laws are not always aggressively enforced. Besides, many high school seniors are over the age of 18 and therefore can legally purchase E-cigarettes. Warn your daughter about their dangers such as internal bodily harm from their noxious vapors and the all-to-real chance that an E-cigarette's heating element will burst into flames quite possibly causing considerable damage to her face and hands.

And if E-cigarettes aren't worrisome enough, you have just discovered that despite all the publicity about the dangers of cigarette smoking, your daughter's a smoker. Nicotine, whether inhaled via an E-cigarette or a traditional one, is addictive. Like any other addiction, nicotine addiction is difficult to conquer—just ask any smoker or former smoker. Don't waste your breath with threats of punishment if your daughter doesn't give up her smoking habit. You shouldn't expect your teen daughter to have will power superior to millions of adult smokers. You can of course remind her that smoking causes wrinkles and stained teeth and that the money she spends on cigarettes would help pay for that pricey acting camp that she would like to attend the following summer.

If your daughter smokes, whether or not she intends to stop, don't buy the cigarettes for her or allow her to smoke in the house. She has no right to pollute your air. You must however accept the fact that your daughter is a smoker and help her to stop if she expresses any desire to do so. Encourage her to go to a stop-smoking clinic or begin a stop-smoking program (along with you or any other family member who smokes). Your daughter, however, should be the one to pay for her attendance at the clinic or program. Smoking is her problem and she is the one that needs to resolve it. Besides, if you pay for the program and it doesn't work, she will blame you for her failure saying it was your idea.

HITCHING A RIDE

You cannot warn your daughter enough about the dangers of hitchhiking, particularly these days when human trafficking of teen girls for sexual exploitation is a world-wide menace. Set a good example by not picking up strangers. I know it is tempting to pick up a teen girl looking to hitch a ride because you are concerned about who else might pick her up. However, don't—instead, use your cell phone and call the police. If you pick up a hitchhiker who looks safe, your daughter may hitch a ride with someone she thinks looks safe. Your daughter should also know not to stop to help a motorist in distress since all too often it's become a ruse for robbery or worse.

Avoid temptation for your daughter to hitch a ride by letting her know you will pick her up anywhere, anytime. If, for example, you dropped her off at a party at Jenny's and she calls you from the town's Bar to pick her up, do so quickly and do so without any questions. Obviously, your daughter and her friends were out for some mischief and she should suffer some consequences. Tread carefully here though— your punishment or wrath for her deceit should not be so great that your daughter would rather risk a ride with a stranger than face you should a similar situation arise again.

Hitchhiking doesn't apply only to sticking one's thumb out along a country road. It also refers to taking a ride from strangers in a public place. While years ago, you may have met your hubby by accepting his offer to drive you home from a rock concert even though you'd just met him, the world is a far different place nowadays. And name recognition is no guaranty of safety nor is the fact that the person may come from a "good family" or is known to others present at the time. Be sure your daughter knows about Natalee Holloway—a high school senior with everything to look forward to who disappeared after accepting a ride from some boys (one of whom was the son a judge) she met at a bar. Natalee was never heard from again nor has her body been found as of this writing. More recently, Yingying Zhang, a grad student, while waiting for a bus accepted a ride from a stranger who happened to be a former grad student at the same school and likely identified himself as such. Ms. Zhang was never heard from again but is presumed dead. Make sure your daughter understands that an offer of a ride home by a boy coming from a "good" family" or by anyone who professes a mutual connection or even someone well known in the community is no assurance of safety. (*See also* Chapter 11 at "Staying Safe.")

SEXUAL PREDATORS *(see also this Chapter above at "Hitching a Ride" and Chapter 11 at "Assertiveness Training" and "Staying Safe")*

Sexual predators and perverts have various ways of preying on innocents and hacking into computers and cell phones so as to obtain your daughter's trust or garnering personal information about her and your family for illicit and criminal purposes. Thus, you must caution your daughter to never transmit over the wires or through the airwaves any personal information about her or her family to anyone. She need not broadcast to the world that she will be alone for the evening, that she now wears a B-cup, or that she has $500 saved in her piggy bank. You and your daughter should also know not to respond to any e-mail or other request for information that is from an unknown sender or caller. Messages that look suspicious (asks for too much information, contains misspellings of simple words, uses wrong tense, contains awkward idioms, uses nicknames for full names or *vice versa*, requests Social Security numbers, etc.) should not be responded to and the transmission should be reported via other means to any named individuals, banks, credit card companies, and state and local law enforcement as appropriate.

You must also warn your daughter that she is never ever to meet anyone in person that she met on the Internet or through any other media mode no matter how trusting or nice the person seems to be, particularly if the person attempting to meet her professes to be from a modeling agency or offers to set up a screen test. Your daughter should also know to let you know of any such attempted meetings.

Sometimes though current technology is useful for making connections. For example, it may be that through technology your daughter, the rock hound, learns that a known gemologist that she'd like to meet will be in town. You don't know this guy from Adam but if you forbid all personal meetings through such connections, your daughter may do so on the sly. Thus, instead of forbidding the meeting, let your daughter know that if she wants to meet an Internet or social media contact in person, she may do so only if you or another adult you know is present. Make sure any such meeting occurs in a very public place and only if you have checked the person out on the Internet or obtained references through other means.

Sexual Predators, however, are not always strangers. They can be anyone—family members, friends, neighbors, co-workers, employers, teachers, coaches, doctors, public officials, or even members of the clergy. As uncomfortable a conversation it may be, be sure that your daughter knows that if any adult says anything or acts in a way that makes her feel uncomfortable, she should report the incident to you. You should also tell her to put politeness aside and to say "No" loudly and clearly and to remove herself from the situation as soon as possible.

Be sure to tell her too not to succumb to any untoward advances out of
fear because of threats to her or her family made by the predator—such
threats are for you to deal with, not her. And if your daughter comes
to you with her concerns, believe her. Follow up with the police even
if the accused is well-regarded. (Larry Nassar, the doctor who treated
U.S. Olympic gymnasts, was finally outed and found guilty of sexually
molesting more than 200 girls.)

Let your daughter know also to come to you even if she acquiesced
to the predator's advances out of fear or feels that she precipitated them
because of her flirtatious behavior. In her autobiography, "I Know Why
the Caged Bird Sings," Maya Angelou wrote that she remained silent
about succumbing to her stepfather's advances because he threatened
to hurt her brother if she told anyone and also because she felt that
the warm and tender hugs she received afterwards made it all okay.
Ms. Angelou was only eight years old at the time and no matter how
much she liked those hugs or even looked forward to them, she was
in no way responsible for her stepfather's wanton acts. Similarly, your
daughter should not blame herself nor should you blame her for testing
out her attractiveness on someone that turns out to be a sexual predator.
Note though that even though a teenager is not considered responsible
enough to follow through on a contract until the age of 18 or see an
R-rated movie without an adult until the age of 17, many states consider
the age of consent to sexual activities to be sixteen.

STDs/AIDS

There is no such thing as safe sex when it comes to teenagers.
Condom use helps reduce the risk of HIV (the virus that causes AIDS)
transmission and other STDs but they are not 100% effective in the best
of circumstances. Condoms break. They fall off. They leak. They are at
best only 90% effective in preventing pregnancy and no more effective
in preventing HIV or other STDs. Further, even adult women are not
always successful in having their partners use condoms. Thus, you cannot
expect your young and inexperienced daughter to be assertive enough
to insist on condom use. And even if she is and her partner knows how

to use a condom, what about the missing 10% of prevention? Further, it's unrealistic to expect that a young and inexperienced girl will ask a potential partner about his prior drug use and sexual history when things are hot and heavy. Even if your daughter manages a feeble question or two, I would not trust a young man to answer with anything but his hormones. It is also unrealistic to expect a teenage girl to turn on an overhead light and examine her young man's body for telltale needle marks or sores while lying in the back of a car or on the living room sofa. Don't assume that just because you live in a small town where you and your daughter know the backgrounds of the boys she dates that she is "safe." You have no idea of the boy's sexual behavior or drug use when he's out-of-town or even when he's in town.

Further, don't let the recent medical advances in the treatment of AIDS and HIV and the seemingly robust health of AIDS and HIV-infected persons depicted in the media lull you or your daughter into complacency. Current statistics reveal that AIDS and HIV infections among teenagers and young adults are rising faster than those of the general population. Believe me—the physical devastation wrought by AIDS is ghoulish and the pain endured pathetic.

Unfortunately, AIDS is not the only serious sexually transmitted disease out there. HPV (human papillomavirus) causes cervical cancer; untreated Chlamydia can leave your daughter sterile; herpes-2 can lie dormant until pregnancy and then cause serious harm to a fetus; Gonorrhea is on the rise and has become resistant to current antibiotics. Best to preach abstinence until marriage or at least until adulthood—not that your daughter will necessarily follow your advice but that should be your position since at a minimum it will buy her some time and the older your daughter is when she starts having intercourse, the more likely she will be able to protect herself. It is incumbent on you to talk out of both sides of your mouth as your daughter moves through puberty—preaching abstinence on one side, and on the other, ensuring that your daughter knows not only the "The Facts" but how to protect herself as she moves forward to adulthood. (*See also generally* Chapter 14 at "*It's Time We Had a Talk.*")

You should also encourage your daughter's school health office to provide condoms to high school students upon request—90% protection is better than 0%. Also, age-appropriate sex and hygiene classes should be part of every school's curriculum. Such programs should be taught in conjunction with advocating abstinence. Barring condom distribution in public high schools and teaching "abstinence only" sex education programs puts all children at a greater risk of contracting AIDS or other STDs. No one has the right to put another person's child at risk because of their personal or religious beliefs and whether your child is male or female, your child must be made to understand the possible consequences of his or her sexual actions.

A vaccination against HPV is currently available. Don't decide against vaccination simply because you fear that having your daughter vaccinated against an STD will cause her to be promiscuous despite all of your admonitions. You have a duty to protect your daughter from disease and decisions about vaccinations should be made on the then-current best medical advice not unsubstantiated fears or rumors. Most importantly, keep the channels open between you and your daughter that should she ever have even the slightest suspicion that she has an STD or is pregnant, that she can come to you and not fear judgment or your wrath. Assure her that her health and safety come first with you. If you are uncomfortable about discussing such things with your daughter (or she will run when you try), pick up the pertinent pamphlets from your doctor's office or local health clinic and leave them on her dresser with a note that she can always come to you for help. No questions asked.

4. HER ATTITUDE

Absentmindedness — Being Fourteen
Disrespectfulness
Insolence — Miss Know-It-All
Pronouncements — Rebelliousness
She Doesn't Like You Anymore
Sweetness & Light — *Techitis*
TV Reality & Talk Shows

ABSENTMINDEDNESS

If your daughter is not tripping over her Crocks, it is only because she cannot find them. Nowadays, she cannot find anything. Bus passes and keys get lost. School assignments mysteriously disappear. Lunches and schoolbooks get left at home. I know a teenage girl who reached her first-period class before she realized that she had left her backpack at home. One forgotten book I could understand but I still cannot fathom how someone who usually walks almost a mile with a huge pack on her back would not miss it—but then again, I'm not a teenager.

During this phase, your daughter also has a complete block with respect to anything you asked her to do. Actually, the only thing she can remember your saying is that you would increase her allowance. As with much of your daughter's adolescent behavior, the only remedy to this phase is time.

BEING FOURTEEN

Regardless of your daughter's personality or rate of development, at some point she will be "Fourteen." Being Fourteen is not a chronological age but a unique phase in your daughter's development. At Fourteen, the typical teen girl, no matter how petite, resembles a giant blob and shows no indication that she will ever become anything else.

You feel as if your home has been invaded by a new species. Everything your daughter does nowadays is exaggerated. If she tends toward messiness, you can't walk in the kitchen without your feet sticking to the floor. If she tends toward laziness, she now never rises before noon on weekends. She's grotesque—she stuffs whole packs of chewing gum in her mouth at once. She plops so hard on the couch that the mantle denizens shake with fear; even the goldfish dive for cover. And of course, her cell phone has become a permanent appendage.

Your daughter will be around even when she isn't. She forgets to turn off her light or stereo. Pieces of gum wrappers mark her trail. Smells of spilled nail polish and heavily scented body wash permeate the house. Don't fret—she will soon be fifteen. In the meantime, just open the windows (but don't jump!).

DISRESPECTFULNESS

Personal. We tell our children to respect their elders, their teachers, the police, people of the cloth, and a host of others but we seldom take the time to explain what respect is nor do we generally think about our children's need for self-respect. At its most basic level, I think "respect" is a two-way street that can best be described as treating others as we would like to be treated whatever the age, color, sex, ethnicity, or background of the people involved. No one likes to be made fun of or have their ideas mocked, be invited somewhere as an after-thought, or be the target of someone else's bad day. Thus, when someone has fallen from grace, even temporarily such as when an overworked parent lets off steam over a child's failure to follow through on a chore or when a teen blatantly disrespects her parents, the wrongdoer should still be treated with respect.

That's not to say the wrongdoer should be excused for the poor behavior and that apologies shouldn't be made but I would not add to a teen's wrongdoing by insisting on an apology. While you might get one, an insisted-upon apology is unlikely to be from the heart and consequently will be a lie by your daughter that is sanctioned by you. Thus, instead of demanding an apology or shouting back at a child, a parent should clearly and firmly state that's an inappropriate way to talk to anybody. Of course, none of us are perfect and most of us will shout back all too often but every time we act disrespectfully, we are teaching our children to do likewise. Even worse, tantrums by parents whether instigated by them or in response to a child's outburst, is setting the child up to disrespect him- or herself as well.

I know it's really hard to keep cool against a verbal teen onslaught but keep stock responses at the ready...*I'm sure you're really disappointed about not getting the lead in the school play.* Or, *I'm sorry I forgot to pick up your tennis racquet and that your team lost the match because you had to play with an unfamiliar one. Forgive me?* Thus, rather than take the bait and shout back with demands for apology and reprimands, validate your daughter's feelings as calmly as you can, apologize where appropriate, and then remind her not to speak to you or anyone else in a disrespectful way. Children learn by example and if we want our children to respect us and themselves, we must act as if we respect not only them but ourselves as well. Nobody ever said parenting was easy!

Possessions. Whether you are for or against global trade it has, among other things good and bad, resulted in a plethora of cheap material goods available for purchase. I wouldn't be surprised if today's girls reach their teen years with enough Legos and stuffed animals to replicate the National Zoo being visited by Barbie and Ken and all their relatives. And it's not only toys and frivolous goods that have come inexpensively to market. Even some of the poor among us have smart phones and HD TVs.

The availability of so many goods across a broad spectrum of wants and needs coupled with the fact that today's parents are so pressed for time—they work outside the home, they coach their children's teams, they chauffeur their children to school and elsewhere, they have meals to cook and homes to clean and elderly parents to care for—it's understandable that they often show their love, care and concern for their children with goods instead of time. Consequently, children have little incentive to take care of their things since replacements are so easy to come by. You've tried to get some order...e.g., a*ny [whatever] found on the floor will be thrown away* but that doesn't happen. You don't follow thru because you didn't really mean what you said or the look of devastation on your child is too heart wrenching. Basically, you're a softy.

However, economic volatility is ever present so you do have a responsibility to instill some respect in your daughter for material goods. First, take good care of your own things since children learn best by example. Next, wean yourself from feeling guilty for not being around more and compensating for your absence with goods. Instead, be brave— say "No" to an unnecessary purchase since these days all you'll be facing is a pouting adolescent, not a shrieking six-year-old. Next, insist that your daughter start taking care of her big ticket and favorite items—she should be picking up the Legos not you; her smart phone shouldn't be left on the couch for someone to sit on; the silver necklace from Grandpa shouldn't be left out to be a plaything for the cat. By not insisting on at least the foregoing, you are allowing your daughter to disrespect the giver who spent not only money but time and love when thinking of her.

INSOLENCE

You don't know which is worse—your daughter's whining when she was four or her contemptuous attitude of today. *You just can't do anything right!* Accept it. Your daughter is not rejecting your values and teachings. She is just testing them out so that when she adopts them, she will feel they are her own ideas and values and not yours. In the process, she alternates among being rude, obnoxious, condescending and contemptuous toward you. You may even be told that you "disgust" her. You are also accused of being dishonest (once you sampled a cherry from the supermarket fruit bin), ignorant (you don't remember the name of the first female astronaut [Sally K. Ride, *Challenger*, June 18-24, 1984]), selfish (you get a weekly manicure but she doesn't have a smart phone), lazy (you have someone come in to wash the windows), unfeeling (you still buy white tuna fish) and a phony (you had dinner with a woman you dislike). React to your daughter's actions, however, not to her words. Most of the time she does what she has been brought up to do, not what she says she will do. She may answer your every comment, your every request, no matter how innocuous, with an impudent remark or smirk—but remember, despite her "not again" roll of the eyes, she does help out with her siblings when you need to work at home.

Generally, it is best to ignore your daughter's insolence unless she does or says something that is particularly offensive to you. If, for example, she uses foul language in your presence, explain that you don't like to hear such talk. You could point out once or twice what a bad habit it could become and that in some places use of foul language in public is a misdemeanor. Since such words will probably fall on deaf ears though, just tell her that if she feels she must speak that way, to please do so where you cannot hear her.

Count to ten (more than once, if necessary) when you ask your daughter *How did your day go, dear?* and she responds with a look that would cower the country's No. 1 hunk. Even though you feel like ringing her neck, don't. And you cannot respond to her glaring look with concern and say *I guess it wasn't so good* because she will accuse you of prying. You can't completely ignore her either because she will use that against you later and claim you don't care about her. The best response to her glare is to let it pass and chat about your day instead. After the tension of the moment wanes and she realizes you are not going to keep after her, she may come around when she feels she is in charge of the conversation.

Don't take your daughter's insolent looks or remarks as a personal rebuff. If you do, you will set up a no-win situation between the two of you that will persist throughout your relationship. Neither of you will ever get beyond her insolence nor will you ever find out about her day. Even if your daughter's response to your first question was *Why the hell [or worse] do you care?* simply say that you do care because you love her and then move on and talk about something else. If you respond in a positive manner (as long as your patience holds up), she will get the right message. If, instead, you react as she acts, you are in effect sanctioning her rude and disrespectful behavior.

Remember, too, that your daughter probably behaves much nicer to others than she does to you. Of course, it's more pleasant for you if your daughter is well-behaved at home, but it is far more important in terms of her personal safety and future success that she not be a smart aleck in the street or a wise guy at school. Allow your daughter some mini-rebellions. Otherwise, you run the risk of crushing her spirit or forcing her to separate herself from you too soon—and when it is more dangerous for her to do so.

MISS KNOW-IT-ALL

Once you accept the fact that you don't know anything about anything, life will run a lot more smoothly. What this means is that you need to be adult enough to let your daughter have the last word. Your daughter is embarrassed when she's wrong. She views the correction of her comments as a criticism of her entire self. However, you, being the adult, should be able to be contradicted without your ego being involved.

As your daughter gains more confidence in herself, she will contradict you less often. But for now, if you tell a story in her presence about when she was a toddler and wouldn't wear anything that wasn't blue because that was her favorite color and she indignantly interrupts to say that she'd only wear something purple, let it be. Don't get into an argument with her about interrupting or the color. Remember, she is not correcting you to be obstinate or rude—she really believes that she is right. You can correct her manners later and in private by reminding her that it is embarrassing to you to have her contradict you. This way, you are not taking issue with what she believes, only with how or where she expresses her beliefs.

PRONOUNCEMENTS

Your daughter doesn't mean to be disrespectful. She is just very frightened about crossing the bridge between childhood and adulthood and you are the most likely person upon whom she can test what she perceives to be adult rights and privileges. Therefore, she "announces" that she is going to the midnight movie; she is getting her nose pierced; she is quitting high school and hitchhiking to Alaska.

Most of the time, it is best to ignore such pronouncements. The outlandish ones will likely never come to pass and the others are relatively harmless. For example, my daughter at age fourteen "announced" a planned evening bus excursion with three of her friends to a tawdry amusement park. *Over my dead body,* I thought. However, rather than react to something that was highly unlikely to occur since the four of them had pledged to go together but had never yet been able to get together for anything, I held my tongue. Besides, they probably didn't really want to go. Otherwise, they would not have been so insistent about needing to go as a foursome. The girls knew the area was seedy and unsafe. All they really wanted to do was to assert themselves. As long as they were allowed to assert their capability to do so (e.g., having the money for the bus and rides, etc.) through a verbal effort, there was no need for me to engage in a confrontation about something that was 99% unlikely to occur. Of course, however, if there's even a 1% chance that a seemingly unsafe adventure was going full steam ahead, you need to take action. Start with contacting the parents of the other children involved. Perhaps your worries are overblown or that the excursion could be made safer. Again though—it's *your* daughter—trust your instincts.

The following year the same girls "announced" they were going to get summer jobs as waitresses in a swank resort town and share an apartment. This time, since there was no "joint pact," I decided some early intervention on my part was necessary. Rather than point out all the dangers that could befall high-schoolers living on their own, I suggested they fully research the idea by comparing wages to the cost of apartment rentals. I also suggested in a very friendly manner that my daughter and her friends each take over all of the family housework, cooking, laundry, shopping, gardening, child-care, etc. over the next several weekends in preparation for their intended ten-hour a day, six-day a week, waitressing jobs. Somehow, their plan was never mentioned again. However, my daughter did not lose face and we did not need to exchange harsh words about something that had little chance of taking place.

If you pick your battles carefully and allow your daughter to freely express her thoughts and ideas, she is unlikely to feel pressured to act them out physically just to prove she is "grown-up." Your daughter needs to know she is her own person. So, if you react with patience and tact, and cross the bridges as they come, it will be less likely that your daughter will do something foolish just to prove herself to herself.

REBELLIOUSNESS *(see also generally Chapter 11 at "Assertiveness Training")*

A certain amount of rebellious behavior has always been accepted of boys but not of girls. Teenage boys are encouraged to learn from experience, yet society often denies such opportunities to girls. Parents get less excited about their teenage son getting caught skinny-dipping in the local reservoir or being discovered drunk in the family den than they would if their teenage daughter behaved the same way. Some parents may even brag about the mischief their sons get into or about their son's sexual prowess yet would be shocked by anything similar that their daughter may have done.

Your daughter has as much right to make her own mistakes as does your son. Sometimes she may seem overzealous in her efforts but, remember, the tighter you hold the reins, the more she will struggle to be free. Don't force her to break the reins completely in order to be able to assert herself. Loosen up gradually but steadily. Give her the opportunity to learn to control herself.

Also, don't think you are not a controlling parent just because you are not strict. You may let your daughter do and try a lot of things, but you may still be controlling her by doing too much for her. Let her learn to take care of herself. If her button falls off, let her sew it on. Don't always say, *You look very nice dear but wouldn't lower heels be more appropriate?* Let her suffer the discomfort of sore feet—she'll dress more appropriately the next time. If she has a problem with one of her teachers, let her try to work it out. Don't always run interference for her. If she drove into a neighbor's flower bed, don't make the restitution for her—let her do it. In short, don't smother her.

Allow your daughter the opportunity to be wrong sometimes or to fail or worry—to be in charge of her life. Encourage her to participate in decisions that affect not only her but the whole family. Let her learn to stand up for her beliefs and act on them even when her beliefs or ways of doing things are contrary to yours. It is important not to quash your daughter's individuality. It is almost a certainty that teen girls growing up today will work outside their homes whether or not they marry or have children. Your daughter needs to learn to stand up for herself and discover who she is. Many women are underachievers because they were never allowed or encouraged to "go for it." Let your daughter know she has rights. If you always need to win or be in control, she will either break away completely so her self can survive or bend to your will and never learn to be her own person.

SHE DOESN'T LIKE YOU ANYMORE

While it is not pleasant to have your daughter not like you, she does have that right. She should, of course, be respectful and considerate but you cannot force her to think you're terrific. And it does not matter whether you are or not. Look at it from her point of view. She is entering a world where people look, feel, think and act differently than in her home and she finds you lacking.

It hurts. For several years, she depended on you for her existence and happiness. You were her best friend. You took her places and baked cookies together. You took care of her when she was sick and gave her money for ice cream. Now, almost overnight, it seems you have become a cross between a dullard and a dithering fool and are a constant source of embarrassment to her. She takes your every flaw and magnifies it. You are no longer her beautiful, well-dressed "Mommy" but a wrinkled and hopelessly old-fashioned has-been. You are no longer a good neighbor but a busybody. You're revolting—you snort and snore. You're a failure—you have yet to sell a painting or become financially successful. You're a bore and your friends are even worse. She doesn't even like your cooking any more. Before, all you had to be was her mother. Now, even if you were Superwoman, you still wouldn't be good enough. You may be a perfect person or have just made your first million—you may still be inadequate in your daughter's eyes.

Recognize that it is not abnormal for her to feel this way. Her disapproval of you is just another one of her ways of putting space between the two of you. However, let her know loudly and clearly that you still deserve to be treated with respect simply because you are a human being whether or not she approves of you. Don't try to make her like you or feel guilty for not doing so. Don't defend yourself either—you don't have to. Just ride it through—but you must make sure your daughter understands that while she has the right to not like you, she should not turn her dissatisfaction with you inward. For example, explain that she shouldn't smoke to spite you—she will only hurt herself. Ditto for using drugs or dropping out of high school or not attending college. Make it clear to her that if she has problems with you, it is better to put the relationship on the shelf for a while rather than for her to take out her disappointment in you (justified or not) on herself. Make sure she realizes that your primary concern is how she views herself, not how she views you.

SWEETNESS & LIGHT

This phase usually occurs twice. The first phase usually manifests itself when your daughter is around 12-years-old. She is content to talk to you, read, or daydream. Between periods of lazing on the couch and petting the puppy, she offers to help with dinner and the dishes. She's thoughtful, considerate and kind. She brings you coffee; she folds the laundry; she converses politely with your friends. Don't congratulate yourself just yet! You're not going to miss the teenage turmoil. This is merely the calm before the storm.

The second angelic phase usually occurs sometime during your daughter's senior high school year. She is sooo polite to you—she even speaks civilly to her brothers and sisters. She is constantly offering to help you. She calls to let you know she'll be ten minutes late. She asks you about your day. She's so sweet you may have to watch your sugar intake! Don't worry—she's not trying to hide anything except her fear about soon being on her own. So, enjoy the moment.

TECHITIS

Techitis afflicts almost all adolescents. Your daughter is addicted to Instagram, texting, e-mails, blogs, Facebook, U-tube, chat-rooms, snap-chat, tweeting, twittering, whatever. Typically, your daughter and her friends will text each other constantly to discuss who said what and when, their homework, whether to polish their fingernails all one color or each nail a different one. Your daughter does not do anything without first checking it out with her friends. In the meantime, your home is a cacophony of ringtones, beeps, whirrs and sound blips from every electronic gizmo known to man. You have tried reason, logic, threats and punishment to convince your daughter to spend her time more productively. Nothing works. Nothing will. That doesn't mean you should cease trying. As a parent, you are supposed to nag. Otherwise your daughter will feel neglected and your not nagging will justify umpteen hours of texting and tweeting about how you don't care about her.

Obviously, the hours that your daughter spends on social media and texting, etc. are a waste of time. She should be doing something productive like practicing the piano or cleaning her room. However, since the advent of the telephone, perhaps even since the advent of smoke signals, parents have attempted various ways to limit teenage chit-chat—locks, passwords, restricting hours of use, charging for use, etc.—none of which work in the long run since as soon as the ban on whatever is lifted, the time-wasting habit returns.

Generally, there is no cure for *Techitis* but you can help your daughter to control it somewhat. You can, for example, insist that your daughter not bring her cell phone to the dinner table or to bed or that her cell phone and other tech gizmos are off limits during certain hours. However, such limits can only work if a parent is around to enforce them. Keep in mind too that the earlier in life *Techitis* strikes, the more severe it will be. However, if your daughter's *Techitis* is so severe that it interferes with her sleep, school work, or her other usual activities, you need to step in and redirect her energies. Give her an ultimatum—either she gets a part-time job or does some volunteer work. If part-time jobs are not available in your area, consider paying your daughter to do some of the work that you normally do as long as she agrees to do it on a consistent basis and takes responsibility for the chore. For example, you might "hire" her to weekly mow the lawn or do the daily vacuuming making it clear to her that she is not only to do the task but also to remember to do it and to treat it and you with the same respect she would treat any other job or boss. Another way to help subdue *Techitis* is for her to spend time volunteering, perhaps at a food bank or pet shelter or for a not-for-profit where her computer skills will probably be greatly appreciated. Remind her that these types of activities will look good on her college applications.

A teen I know who was a mediocre student and addicted to more tech items than I can even name was re-directed to helping out at the local pool. She developed a special rapport with a child who had a mild disability and because of her patience and persistence, was able to teach the child to swim. The girl's experience was the subject of her college application essay and I'm sure it was one of the reasons she had a choice of colleges despite her average grades and mediocre SAT scores.

What you don't want to do is hound your daughter about how she is wasting her life without providing feasible alternatives. Like most teens, she's compulsive/obsessive—now she tweets constantly; another time she will obsess about her hair, washing it over and over again; next she might glue herself to the computer screen gossiping about the latest Facebook entries. However, don't allow *Techitis* to steal your daughter's life and if it appears to do so, take some constructive action to divert her to other activities. Also, get your daughter to recognize her disease and get her input as to the best way to treat it. She may need to go cold turkey!

***Special Note: Techitis* can indeed steal your daughter's life.** Constantly checking one's cellphone for texts, tweets, e-mails and the like, particularly when she's supposed to be sleeping, causes the body to release chemicals such as dopamine resulting in highs and lows similar to that felt by an alcoholic or drug user. Further, such constant use of social media, especially with its ability to monitor and report the number of likes and dislikes, only increases the roller coaster effect of these chemicals with the result that there is a marked increase in depression and suicide among teen girls who spend inordinate amounts of time on social media. (*See* Chapter 3 at "Depression/Suicide.")

TV REALITY & TALK SHOWS

Nowadays, your daughter's interest is directed at just about anything that wastes time. She is totally engrossed in her favorite television reality show or is busy exchanging text messages about the latest tell-all. As with most things your teenage daughter does, her involvement is total. Your daughter will rush home and turn on the TV as soon as she walks in the door to watch a show featuring someone's bare-all relationship miseries. She will even TiVo the show if band practice gets in the way. And forget about studying.

I remember sitting for hours with my friends playing Canasta (a card game) while our mothers badgered us about the beautiful weather outside. We, however, never altered our daily routine of rushing home, dropping off our books, and running to Shari's house for three solid hours of Canasta before dinner. I remember Shari's mom hounding us to go outside and screeching that we'd all wind up being old maids since the boys would never find us.

Teens don't change, only the focus of their obsession does. One month it may be the latest Reality show; another month, American Idol may be viewed over and over. As a parent, you have a role to play. You must tell her that she will need trifocals by the time she is twenty if she continues to tweet and text while watching TV. You must constantly remind her that there are such things as fresh air and blue sky. You must repeat such admonitions the requisite number of times so that she cannot accuse you at some later time of not caring.

In the meantime, rather than fight the inevitable, join it. Use the subjects of the reality/talk shows to get your own message across. These programs often deal with the tough issues of the day such as drug and alcohol addiction, date rape, unwanted pregnancy, sexual abuse, divorce, pedophiles, homosexuality, domestic violence, suicide, bullying, sexual harassment and so on. Listen to your daughter's comments. She may surprise you with her own sensible solutions and pragmatic views or you may discover she is on the wrong track about a particular subject. It will be easier to set her straight by discussing what's happening on a reality show or soap opera than by lecturing her about what she should or should not do. Also, the myriad problems presented on these shows give you an opportunity to discuss topics that you may have felt uncomfortable about bringing up or which had not occurred to you.

5. HER FEARS & ANXIETIES

Generally
Appearing Foolish — Crime/Terrorism
Miss Doom & Gloom
Of School — Timidity

GENERALLY

Fears usually have a reasonable and logical basis whether it is fear of radiation poisoning, terrorists, strange situations, elevators or nuclear war. Most people are afraid of something and your daughter's fears should not be made light of or classified as foolish. Instead, help her to come to grips with her fears and not let them intrude in her daily life. For example, if she is fearful of global warming, she can do two things: she can do something constructive such as becoming involved in environmental concerns or she can live under a cloud. Don't be too surprised if your daughter decides the latter though as pessimism is often a preferred teenage state. What she cannot do, however, is let her fear dictate her life or use it as an excuse for not doing things.

Young teens especially are full of fears—fear of being unpopular or being bullied, of crowds, of high places, of snakes, of their parents dying. These fears will come and go in varying intensity depending on your daughter's personality and the "in" fear of the day be it a world-wide threat such as the possibility of a pandemic or nuclear war or something closer to home, such as a fear of bugs. Thus, don't be alarmed if your daughter goes through a phase where she refuses to enter the kitchen unless a family member checks it out for bugs first. She is as extreme about her fears as she is about anything else she likes or dislikes.

Not all fear is bad though; some fear is healthy. Fear protects us by heightening our senses and making us more aware of our surroundings. If it weren't for fear, we wouldn't drive slower on icy roads, we wouldn't be alert for strange sights and sounds when hiking in the wilderness or walking through a strange city at night.

If your daughter changes her fears as often as she changes her clothes, you need not be concerned. However, a fear that interferes with how she lives is cause for concern. For example, I know a teen who was so smart that she entered college at 16 but dropped out because she was afraid to give a speech in front of her class. If your daughter is fearful of doing something because she cares too much about what others think, do what you can to boost her confidence. Try roll-playing or discussing in depth the reason for her fears. Perhaps she feels embarrassed about her weight or her looks. (*See generally* Chapter 11—Health, Hygiene & Safety.)

If your daughter seems overly fearful about almost everything, it might stem from your coming home with too many horror stories about street crime and are at the same time overprotective by not letting her walk home the two blocks from her friend's house even though it may only be 7:00pm. True, there are some neighborhoods where your daughter should always be escorted home and there is always the risk of a random act of violence or kidnapping by a pervert. Thus, while it is best to err on the side of caution, tell your daughter that it is your penchant for being over-cautious that prompts your protectiveness not that you doubt her capabilities. The point is that you should make your daughter aware of real dangers but explain them objectively. If you are honest with her and differentiate between the times that you are acting on your own paranoia on her behalf rather than because of real dangers, there will be less chance of passing your fears on to her.

If your daughter is fearful of going out for a first job interview, perhaps you, her father or a friend could go along and wait in the car (or in a near-by coffee shop) until the interview is over. That way, she'll be free to concentrate on the interview and won't have to worry about what to do if the car breaks down or the bus is late. And someone will be there waiting to offer moral support when she's finished. Or, your daughter may not choose to apply to a certain college because it has an essay requirement and she is so fearful of putting something down on paper that will be "judged." Reminding her that she's never at a loss for words because she's able to yakity-yak forever on the phone or send out zillions of tweets in a nanosecond doesn't help. You can help her though by reminding her that she's not applying for a Pulitzer Prize and that she doesn't need to be a pro the first time she does something. Take some of the pressure off by suggesting that she apply to a third or fourth choice school that has an essay requirement. Upon completion and a few tweaks, she may decide the essay is good enough for her first choice. Regardless, her putting pen to paper and completing an essay to send out will get your daughter started on a path that will enable her to overcome her fears.

There are, of course, some fears which all teens have at one time or another. *Will my parents die soon and leave me all alone? Will I pass my exams? Will I make a good impression? Will I ever have a boyfriend? Will I get into a good college? Will I be able to get a job? And, if I do, will I be able to do it?* If your daughter seems concerned about these things, explain that everyone worries about them too. No one is totally free from concern about the future or what others think; no one never doubts their own ability or never wonders whether they will be able to cope with difficult situations no matter how brazen or bullish they may sound. Explain that if she allows herself to recognize her fears she will be more likely to overcome them and meet them head-on as the situation arises.

Your Fears. Anxieties about money, work, marriage, health, death, etc. are part of life. How you handle your own anxieties and fears will influence how your daughter copes with hers. Show her that you are in control of a difficult situation. If, for example, you are in a new neighborhood and miss having friends nearby, instead of staying home and complaining about being lonely, join a community group. If you are concerned about losing your job, show positive action by getting your resume ready or signing up for a retraining course. If you are concerned about losing your looks, start exercising regularly and paying particular attention to eating right. Admitting your worries to your daughter and letting her know of your plans to allay your own anxieties will set an example for her to follow. You want to show your daughter that she can control her own worries and fears and not let them control her.

APPEARING FOOLISH

If, for example, your daughter is worried about doing a somersault in gym class because she is clumsy and/or overweight and fearful that the other students will laugh, explain that her weight is no secret. She probably will look funny, but so what. Tell her about the time a date took you to a popular new Japanese restaurant and you dipped the shrimp in the tea instead of the sauce and then remarked loudly that the sauce had no taste. Or when a new acquaintance arranged a tennis game with you, you couldn't even connect with the ball, let alone get it over the net—and it was the center court too—right in front of the club's grandstand. Or what about the time you froze at your class picnic because there was a very large insect on your knee? You refused to move for fear it was poisonous. The bug turned out to be a praying mantis (a benevolent, but large, grasshopper) and the whole class had a good laugh at your expense.

Your daughter needs to know that everyone gets laughed at sometimes. Sure, you feel embarrassed at first but soon you realize how funny you must have looked to everyone else and it becomes just as funny to you. Let your daughter know it is normal to be afraid of making a fool of one's self. However, she needs to understand that no matter how hard she tries not to have that happen, some time in her life, she will be the butt of a joke. Doing a somersault in gym class may be the first time she gets laughed at but it's almost a certainty that it won't be the last. So she may as well be a good sport and join in the laughter.

If, however, after all your talk, your daughter is still overly fearful of participating in a required school function, don't force her to. Let her stay home this one time. Write the required excuse note. Your daughter may still need your protection in some seemingly innocuous areas and it is important for her to know that you are in her corner. As she grows more confident in herself, it will become easier for her to attempt things that she cannot do well or at all. In the meantime, give her as much moral support as you can. Let her know you love her. Encourage her to like herself well enough to overcome her fears and be understanding about her feelings regarding her real or perceived shortcomings. Also, you can help your daughter gain confidence by having her expand her horizons. Introduce her to new experiences and new places. Encourage her to participate in activities outside of school—perhaps assist in a political campaign or volunteer at the library or pet shelter. Feeling good about herself overall should help her suffer through a few embarrassments here and there. If your daughter's fears keep her from doing too many ordinary things, seek professional help. And, in the example above, consider a few sessions with a "gym tutor" for your daughter.

CRIME/TERRORISM *(see also Chapter 11 at "Staying Safe")*

Vulnerability. Sadly, the world is such that the minute we step outside our door, we all become vulnerable to human madness be it domestic or foreign terrorism, racism, road rage, or a sickie with a personal grudge. As dreadful as these incidents are, particularly mass shootings, there is little we can do to fully protect ourselves or our families from them but we can be somewhat over-cautious.

Ensure that your daughter knows her neighborhood and gets a feel for it so that when she needs to walk home from school or a friend's alone she'll be able to sense if something is amiss and where and how to seek safety. In this regard, it is my view that one should never second guess their instinct when it comes to safety about a place or a person. Thus, despite mass vulnerability, rather than shut your daughter off from the world, she should learn to be out and about on her own so that she can develop her own instinctive sense of things. Also, it should become second nature to her that whenever she's in a public place such as a movie theatre, outdoor concert, widely attended sporting event, etc. she knows where the exits and bathrooms are and has made a mental plan of the best way to get to them in an emergency. She should also always let you know when, where, how and with whom she's going and when she'll be home. Again, act like a Secret Service agent, but especially with an older teen, by only needing to know such things for safety reasons. Thus, for example, if she's going to a café to play the latest tech game, your only concern should be about safety—say nothing about the arrangements even if you think the activity a total waste of time.

Basically, I view terrorism and the wackos out there as just other dangers that one needs to prepare for so rather than not go out and about and let fear control my life, I walk purposefully and confidently with car or home keys at the ready. Also, I don't park in indoor parking garages.

And I follow my own advice as stated herein and more particularly in Chapter 11 at "Staying Safe." Your daughter should do likewise. When it comes to new experiences for your daughter, discuss areas of possible danger and what precautions she could take to protect herself. Basically, I believe in the Boy Scout motto—Be Prepared. For example, she should know what to do if Aunt Bella's not at the airport to meet her and what to do in the event of a fire or an earthquake or if a stranger keeps knocking on the door when she's home alone. Just as you teach your daughter to slather on sun screen when she's to be out in the sun you shouldn't fear to go over what she should do in onerous circumstances. I don't mean to trivialize today's dangers but your daughter should not live in fear. Yes, she is vulnerable, as we all are, but such vulnerability can be mitigated somewhat with common-sense precautions and awareness.

Invincibility. Don't be surprised if your daughter is not as fearful as you of city or suburban crime or terrorism. She takes news of random muggings and murders in stride—unless, of course, it happened to someone she knew. An adolescent often enjoys a certain status among her peers from having observed a mugging or by knowing someone who unfortunately mysteriously disappeared.

Your daughter is not hardhearted or unfeeling. She has just learned to adjust to today's horrors just as the women of yore had to accept the very real possibility of dying in childbirth or the frequent loss of an infant. In other words, your daughter has learned to adapt to her environment and shrugs off concerns of crime or terror attacks. Of course, you don't want her to be careless. You want her to always be aware of her surroundings and take extra precautions as discussed above and in Chapter 11 at "Staying Safe." Be happy though that she feels secure enough to feel invincible.

MISS DOOM & GLOOM

Pandemics are just a plane flight away; the threat of terrorism lurks in every parking lot or at every public event; global warming is destroying forests and melting icebergs; flotsam and jetsam are turning oceans into cesspools, and nuclear weaponry is increasing world-wide.

You can't remember the last time you saw your daughter smile. Instead, she lurks about the house with the dourest of looks. The obvious disdain she feels for her elders for messing up the world clouds even the most joyful of events. She's just a pill to have around.

Your daughter has a point though—it's true that much of the world is in a sad state these days. However, if your daughter claims that her elders have screwed up the world irrevocably and thus she need not listen to you, do her homework, clean her room, whatever, because nothing matters anymore since we'll all die of radiation poisoning or be blown away by a tornado or some such thing, tell her to get a life. Remind her that the earth's been around for zillions of years and even the dinosaurs didn't go extinct in a nanosecond. Thus, even if the end is coming, it'll take a while and she can either mope around for the next fifty years or so waiting for Armageddon or she can prepare herself so that when she's an adult, or even starting now, she can do her bit to make the world a better place. After all, little bits of betterment add up and she owes it to her friends and family, but mostly to herself, to do her part and not just complain and mope about.

OF SCHOOL

Aside from school bullying (*see* Chapter 3 at "Bullying") your daughter may be afraid to go to school on a particular day out of embarrassment. Perhaps she's such a terrible runner that she fears she will cause her team to lose the school's relay race or fears being laughed at after she reads her book report in front of the entire class. Try roll-playing re the book report even if it's only for a few minutes by having her read it to you and *vice versa* but don't go heavy on the suggestions or corrections—reading or hearing the report aloud should enable her to smooth it out herself. Practice may not make perfect in this case but it will go a long way in ameliorating anxiety.

Further, the old joke about how one gets to Carnegie Hall is by *practice, practice, practice* holds true even for physical activities. Thus, if it's a gym thing that's creating an immediate crisis for your daughter, you might consider letting her skip school that day but as soon as you have time, have her practice the activity that she's afraid of so she'll be ready the next time. For example, if it's a relay race, run a few laps with her if you're able; if not, you can still practice her picking up and handing off the relay Baton while she's running.

If it's an exam she's worried about, instead of just telling her to study more, take the time to find out why she is having difficulty with the subject. Is the teacher just not getting through to your daughter? Is the material too complex for her? Is she spending too much time on social media or at a part-time job? In other words, rather than harp or make her feel worse than she already does, find out the cause of her anxiety and take appropriate action to improve the situation in the future even if it means letting her skip school so as to skip an exam. Just once won't hurt especially if the two of you can work together to solve the problem. I remember a time when my middle school daughter received a 20% on a physics exam. Obviously, physics was not her thing and the teacher wasn't reaching her. Telling my daughter to study harder was not going to do the trick. Instead, I set aside a Saturday and the two of us did the examples in the book. We turned bicycle pedals forward and back watching the chain move over the gears, we swirled cups filled with water round-about in the air, we blew air into bottles, we pierced tin cans with holes large and small. My daughter never received an A in the course but she did pass it. More importantly, my daughter learned that problems have solutions. Even if you can't help your daughter directly, the same result can be reached regardless of the subject matter via hiring a tutor or directing your daughter to a free on-line tutorial. Also, your local library should be able to help you out re available tutorials.

TIMIDITY *(see also Chapter 11 at "Assertiveness Training")*

You want your daughter to feel confident and assertive enough to withstand peer pressure, politely debate a teacher, ask for a job. Accepting your daughter for who she is and recognizing her as her own person is one part of building self-esteem. Another is allowing her to have the experience of exercising some control over her life. Give your daughter the opportunity to know that she is a responsible person. Let her learn from experience even if the experience sometimes results in failure.

Perhaps you can arrange for your daughter to travel alone by air to visit a friend or relative in another state. True, she may worry about getting lost or losing her ticket but your daughter must have the opportunity to face a problem or to be afraid and be able to resolve the situation herself. I know there are a lot of weirdoes out there these days but there always will be. Thus, it is incumbent on you to help her learn to assess situations for herself. You cannot shelter her completely and then, when she's sixteen and driving or eighteen and with strangers for the first time, expect her to be able to protect herself against potentially dangerous situations. Let go gradually—it won't be as scary for you that way either.

As an example, before the time of cell phones, an eleven-year-old girl I knew was invited to spend a day at an elite private school located in the outskirts of a large city. She was to get there and back via the school's bus. While at work, though, the mother received the following voice mail message: *I missed the bus. Don't worry.* The mother wasn't worried—she was frantic! It was the middle of January, it was 5:00pm and already dark and snowy, and her daughter was on empty school grounds in the middle of nowhere! Fortunately, the girl arrived home before the mother called out the National Guard. The mother thought her daughter would be upset. Instead, the girl was exhilarated. She told her mother she was afraid but that she'd *whistled a happy tune.* She found an open office and called a car service and had waited almost an hour for the car to show up before realizing that she had given the service the wrong street intersection. She then went back to the empty school building and called the car service again, explaining the mix-up.

The school's behavior in not making sure the girl was safely *en route* home was unconscionable and thankfully no harm came to the girl as a result of the school's negligence; however, the girl's handling of the situation was exemplary. She'd thought to call her mother (cryptic message notwithstanding) and let her know she'd be home late. She had the presence of mind to call the car service again and explain what had happened. Perhaps another child would not have waited so long.

However, knowing first-hand that she was able to handle a frightening situation gave the girl more confidence than could any laudatory words.

Encourage your daughter to experience being in a position of authority (other than bossing around her younger siblings) or in a situation where she stands on her own merits. Suggest babysitting, working as a camp counselor, volunteer work, teaching Sunday school, a part-time job. Remember, you probably boss her around at home, her teachers are always telling her what to do, and her older siblings tease her. All that can make your daughter's self-confidence pretty thin. Give her some responsibility at home. Let her do the laundry, not just help you. Take the chance of her not sorting the clothes properly and having a red shirt run all over the white socks. (If she did this to spite you or to get out of doing the laundry again, read this book twice.) Also, don't make your daughter feel she is incapable of doing a job from beginning to end. Don't intervene in the middle or redo what she has done because you can do it quicker or better.

Also, encourage your daughter to try new things and expose her to as many positive experiences as possible. Set an example by letting her know that at times you lack confidence too but you don't let your uncertainty prevent you from trying. For example, perhaps you are running for the local school board and your daughter asks if you think you will be elected. You respond *probably not* and she wants to know why then are you spending all your free time putting up posters and giving speeches. You explain that even though you have many doubts about your chances of winning and tremble when speaking in front of a group, one thing you know for certain—if you didn't run, you would never be elected. Tell your daughter that if she wants something, she should not be afraid to go for it. If she received a B on her history paper but thinks she deserved an A, she has nothing to lose by asking her teacher to reread her paper. Even if her voice squeaks when asking, the important thing is that she asks. At worst, the teacher will say no; at best, she will receive her A.

6. HER STRANGENESS

Clothing (Style, Appropriateness & Packing)
Life on a Small Bed — Makeup
Manners — The Recluse

CLOTHING

Style. Your daughter appears in the middle of the living room and asks, *How do I look?* How she actually looks is irrelevant unless she's nude except for body tattoos or is wearing pierced earrings weighing at least five pounds each. The problem is how to answer. Your best response is *hmmm* because she may be showing you the awful way her best friend wears her hair and you would be in a lot of trouble if you answered *Great!*

Your daughter will possibly go through a time where she has absolutely no taste when it comes to her appearance. Some teens have a natural flair for choosing and wearing clothing and completely miss an awkward phase but not your daughter. Instead, she selects clothing that is not only abhorrent to you but also totally unbecoming to her. For example, at some point in puberty, pink is "in" and ruffles or other frau-frau appear everywhere even if the girl wearing them is short and chunky. Ribbons, barrettes and beads adorn the hair, often with a headband added. Sunflower yellow also becomes popular, even on especially tall girls. At the other extreme are girls who think maroon is too bright and the mere suggestion that they wear something "burgundy" is enough to keep them behind closed doors for days.

As awkwardness phases out, kinkiness phases in—barrettes lose ground to "punk" haircuts, "grunge" jeans lose out to the vampire look, ruffles give way to multi-feathered earrings. Patience, humor and a little tongue-biting are the only remedies. At some point, your daughter will learn to wear colors that flatter her or that ghoulish nail polish is not for her. The important thing is not to destroy her confidence. Right now, it's how she thinks she looks that's important. Thus, unless there is something terribly wrong with how she is dressed—she's wearing a skimpy T-shirt the day of her class trip to a Mosque—let her discover her best style in her own way.

Appropriateness. You may think summer begins on the twenty-first of June. Actually, however, if you have a teenage daughter, it begins the day after summer clothes are purchased. It may be only March 10th and the wind's howl warns of a blizzard, but your daughter appears at the breakfast table in a gauze blouse and lemon-yellow cotton coveralls. You explain, *Sweetie, we're going to have a snowstorm—it's 20° outside right now—you'll freeze.* Her response, of course, is that she won't freeze because she will wear a sweater under her ski jacket. You next try playing on her vanity and mention how out of place she will look compared to all her friends who will still be dressed in angora and fleece. She will promptly remind you how often you have told her not to do something just because her friends do. She has you trapped in your own argument. You could make a scene and get her to change clothes. But why? There really is no harm in her looking like a misplaced daffodil. Besides, this is your opportunity not to walk on the same side of the street with her. Short of waiting until June to buy summer clothes, there's really no solution to these types of winter blooms.

Sometimes inappropriate dress is not a superficial concern. For example, my daughter announced one icy January morning that she was going to wear her new clogs to school to show them off. School was a 16-block walk away. Rather than confront her with the idiocy of her plan, I let money talk. Casually, I told her she could wear what she wanted but she would have to pay the medical costs of a broken ankle out of her allowance. She silently left the room and went to school; the clogs stayed home.

You should certainly voice your opinion when you believe your daughter is dressed inappropriately. However, how adamant and strict you are in your actions should be based on real dangers, not merely differences of opinion between you and your daughter. For example, one extremely hot summer evening, my daughter was leaving the house wearing shorts and a T-shirt. She said she was meeting her friend on a downtown corner to go to a movie. I screeched, *On a corner? You can't wait for anyone standing on a corner dressed like that!* She very patiently reminded me that she was old enough to stand on a corner. I explained, *Yes...*

that's exactly why you can't stand on a corner dressed like that...because you are old enough. She got the message but rather than change, she called her friend and made arrangements to meet inside the theater. My concern about someone mistaking my daughter for a teenage prostitute was worth a scene; however, notwithstanding personal religious orthodoxy, the possibility that she might be ogled on a public bus, was not. If you are selective about when to assert your authority you will find you need to do so less often. Also, you will be listened to more quickly and more often than if you constantly veto your daughter's actions.

Sometimes, too, the way your daughter and her friends decide to dress can have amusing results. Several eighth-grade girls I knew decided to dress for a costume party as glamorous movie stars. Out came hoop earrings, faux feather boas and nightgowns doubling as Lady Gaga outfits. On went gobs of eye shadow, false eyelashes and bright red nail polish. They left looking far too slinky and sexy for their years. It must have been an unusual party though. The eighth-grade boys dressed as alien creatures or robots and spent a good part of the time blowing pretzel bits through straws aimed at the girls. Also, don't be surprised if your daughter goes to the beach in the heat of summer wearing jeans and a sweatshirt and heavy knee socks with her sandals. She's covering up her budding breasts and hairy legs. In another summer or two, she will have learned to deal with her emerging sexuality and will appear on the beach in the skimpiest of bikinis. However, you are not supposed to know she has "emerged." She and her friends may brazenly parade bikini-clad on a boardwalk or around the local lake or pool but you will not be permitted to see how she looks in her new swimsuit.

Packing. Today, our daughters go off to camp, to out-of-town relatives, to summer-study abroad, to grandma in Florida, to college. By the time your daughter is an adolescent, she will likely have her own philosophy about packing. She will want to go to summer camp with either a small overnight bag or a U-Haul. Letting her pack exactly what she wants results in either pneumonia for her (rain slicker not taken to camp) or backache for you (squeezing oodles of luggage and stuff into your car and then carrying all to a cabin tucked in the woods.

I had not been able to participate in the actual packing since my daughter was seven. You can, however, maintain a supervisory role through perseverance and ingenuity. You can make piles of camp-labeled clothes and hope they make it into the trunk. You can pack the rain slicker during the middle of the night. If, however, your daughter is one of those who must take everything everywhere, just grin and bear it. However, the fees for transporting clothing and possessions beyond what is necessary should be borne by your daughter directly or come out of her allowance. In any event, even if you have succeeded in keeping her luggage physically manageable, you will be barraged via text and tweet the entire time she is away that she has nothing to wear and that everyone else packed twice as much.

Your success with the toothbrush-only type will not be much greater. Most likely, even if you manage to convince your daughter to pack all the necessities plus some, she will never look beyond the first layer of the trunk and will accuse *you* of not packing her shorts or a single towel. Your only reward will be very little laundry to do when she returns home.

LIFE ON A SMALL BED

Whether your family lives in three rooms or ten, chances are that your daughter lives on her bed. She sits on her bed to listen to music, to do her homework, to tweet and text, to play video games, to polish her nails. What makes the situation even worse is that the air pollution level in her room rivals big city smog because the window never gets opened and the door to her room is always closed.

I was never able to displace my daughter from her private throne but I was able to convince her to open the window when using nail polish remover. I was also able to secure her solemn oath that she would never, ever, under any circumstances, strike a match in her room. Of course, she insisted she never struck a match anywhere because she never smoked anything nor would she. I saw no point in getting sidetracked into a discussion about cigarettes or marijuana since my concern at the moment was the horror that a spark could cause in a room filled with stuffed animals and enough electrical gizmos to give Thomas Edison pause. My hope was that, should the situation ever arise when she felt "compelled" to try smoking a cigarette or a joint in the house (despite my oft-time beseeching), at least she would try it in a less flammable area.

MAKEUP

Lately when you come home from work, or when your daughter arrives home, your hand automatically touches her forehead to check for fever. She has dark circles under her eyes and her cheeks are always flushed. Finally, it dawns on you—the circles are from smudged eyeliner and the flush is from too much blush.

You tell your daughter about the inadequacies of cheap makeup and launch into a discussion about waterproof mascara and blendable blush. You even offer to take her shopping so she can buy what's best for her. Surprisingly, she eagerly agrees to go with you. It is only when you're swiping your charge card to the tune of eighty some odd dollars that you realize you've been had.

Notwithstanding the above, it seems that these days the natural look is out and heavily made-up eyes and eyebrows are in. The women do look quite nice so heavily made-up but the fact is that they *are* made-up. Whatever happened to women's lib and the natural look? However, most of us do look better with some makeup but seeing heavily made-up women everywhere regardless of the occasion does not send the right message to today's teenage girls. Moreover, I wonder how a woman's skin will look after twenty years or so of being subjected to so much goo. Thus, I think it wise not to encourage, or even allow, a young teen to use makeup except on special occasions. If she insists and it's somewhat of a peer thing, give in a little so as to keep the makeup as minimal as possible and make sure she knows how to remove the stuff, particularly the eye makeup, and does so before she goes to sleep.

MANNERS

Nowadays, the only time you hear the word "please" from your daughter is when she wants something from you. "Thanks" and "thank you" have also been dropped from her vocabulary except in rare instances when you might get a *merci* or a *gracias*. Reminding her about her lack of manners usually results in her responding that she said *thank you* but that you didn't hear her. Don't bother defending yourself by pointing out that your hearing is just fine. It's not worth an argument particularly since teenage girls always need the last word. Best to continue with your good manners and trust that she acts politely when away from home.

I know the latter is difficult, particularly when she also seems to have forgotten how to use a knife and fork and to chew with her mouth closed. It is often difficult for her to partake in even the most rudimentary elements of conversation. She grunts a "hello" to your guests and slams the door when she leaves. A short while ago she was ever so polite. She knew the difference between a salad fork and a dinner fork. She offered to make you coffee when she went to the kitchen for a snack. Now, she picks up each French Fry with her fingers and places it in a mouth as wide open as baby bird's, uses napkins to wipe ketchup off her knife, and lifts her plate to lick it clean of gravy.

You're horrified. The last time her tables manners were this bad, she was in diapers. You berate her, asking where she learned to eat like that. All you get from her is that she knows what to do—but she's in her own home and she should be "comfortable." You order her to leave the table, never to return. The scene is oft repeated over different offenses—elbows sprawled across the table, legs propped on the opposite chair, earphone still attached and so on. Obviously, this is not the same daughter you raised with such patience and care. *How are you ever going to be seen with her in public? You're all invited to your boss's house for dinner next week!* Be prepared. One of two things will happen. Either she will behave beautifully and you will be astonished or she will tilt the chair backwards after finishing dinner and emit a loud belch. Just hope that your boss has teenagers too.

THE RECLUSE

Your heretofore active and joyful daughter has become a recluse. She is content to stay home and daydream and speak to her one friend occasionally. She is also so very sweet to you, though secretive and uncommunicative. If you ask her what she is doing in her room behind closed doors, she will respond *"Nothing."* Most likely she is right. She is doing nothing.

As long as your daughter's reclusiveness resembles down-time and not depression (*see* Chapter 3 at "Depression/Suicide") don't worry if she behaves this way from time to time. She is probably getting ready for a major change in her life—a growth spurt (physical or emotional) or a different school or realizing that someday she will be leaving home. She's just gathering her reserves to meet the upcoming challenge. There is not much you can do except understand that she's not behaving abnormally. I know it is annoying to see her just sitting there doing nothing (or more likely checking and rechecking her messages while lazing on the couch), wasting her life. If it really irritates you and she's already done her homework and chores, go to a movie.

Your daughter, "The Recluse," might even suggest playing Scrabble with you or ask that you teach her to knit. Don't think she's peculiar if she does spend time with you when your friends' teenage daughters won't even sit in the same room with them. Every teen has her own developmental schedule. If your daughter will still do things with you, enjoy the time because she won't for long. Don't worry either that you will become such good friends that she won't ever again want to be with friends her own age. You might well be a terrific person—but not terrific enough to permanently displace her peers. Also, don't make her feel guilty about dropping you like a hot potato when she emerges like a butterfly from her cocoon a short time later. If your daughter's reclusiveness lasts for more than a few weeks though or if she seems depressed rather than merely reclusive, seek professional advice.

7. HER CHARACTER

Dishonesty (Cheating, Lying & Stealing)
Prejudice/Discrimination
Religion — Selfishness — Stinginess

DISHONESTY *(see also Chapter 9 at "Punishment")*

Cheating. Your daughter comes home and informs you that *everyone* cheated on the chemistry exam. Don't ask whether or not she cheated too. If she didn't, she will let you know; if she did, your asking would only cause her to lie. It's much better at first to listen to all she has to say about the incident. You will soon be able to discern whether or not she participated in any wrongdoing. When she has had her say, you should of course point out that children who cheat on exams really cheat themselves.

If you believe your daughter acted with integrity during the exam, your tone should be one of empathy. Explain that you understand how she feels, particularly since she studied so hard for the exam. This is not the time for a lecture about cheating. She didn't cheat—what she needs is positive affirmation of her hard work and honesty.

If you suspect your daughter of having cheated, do not act as if she committed treason. Cheating is certainly wrong but stay calm. Try to determine why your daughter cheated by first fishing around asking if any of her friends cheated and why. Perhaps it was to be part of the crowd or perhaps the exam was particularly difficult. Perhaps too the students were under pressure, either self-inflicted or from their families, to get an A because they are hoping to get into a prestigious college. You might also consider that students sometimes cheat because they are afraid of failing the exam and are too embarrassed or afraid to let their parents know for fear that a sibling or other family member might call them stupid or that they might be punished for poor grades.

Once you're fairly certain that your daughter cheated on a test or handed in a copied report as her own, reiterate without any outright accusation the wrongfulness of cheating, and discuss with her ways to ensure that she would never feel the need to cheat on an exam or hand in another's work as her own. Ignore your daughter's protests that she didn't cheat. Instead of getting into an argument about whether or not she cheated, focus on her doing better in the future.

So as to avoid future cheating, getting a tutor or using another educational aid for a poor student is the easy part. More difficult is lessening the pressure felt by a student to get A's whether the pressure to do so is self-inflicted or family-imposed. In either case, everyone needs to lighten up. Your daughter may not be Ivy League material if she feels she needs to cheat to get top grades unless she plans on cheating her entire way through college. Also, just because you or her siblings excelled in school doesn't mean she has similar ability or is less intelligent. Intelligence, competence and test-taking skills come in all forms. Helping your daughter find her unique strengths instead of concentrating on test marks should lead her away from cheating and into self and family appreciation of who she is and enable her to maximize her strengths. Consider also whether your daughter's cheating may be due to unpreparedness caused by despondency resulting from a break-up with a boyfriend or family issues such as divorce or illness. In this case, if you daughter doesn't perk up relatively soon, seek some counseling.

Also worrisome is your daughter having allowed someone to copy her test paper because of peer pressure. If you daughter seems to go along with the crowd most of the time against her better judgment, try to find out why she has so much need to be liked and accepted by others whose values are so different from hers. Perhaps she is unhappy with her looks and a few trendy clothing items or a visit to a dermatologist might give her a needed security boost. If you cannot determine what's causing her insecurity and cannot help her to become more confident and self-reliant, seek professional assistance before her vulnerability to peer pressure involves her in something more serious than helping another student cheat on an exam. (*See also* Chapter 15 at "Peer Pressure.")

Also, a big no-no for your daughter is to allow other students to copy her exams or do reports for them for money. Some whiz-kid test-takers think that's an easy way to earn money. However, your super smart-daughter will eventually be found out and possibly face suspension. And if that's not bad enough, such actions could go on your daughter's record and may prevent her from being accepted by the college of her choice. The foregoing consequences would also apply to your daughter if she paid someone to take an exam or do a report for her.

Lying. Children lie all the time. They will never own up to having finished the last piece of pie or for texting in the middle of the night. You're not going to get a straight answer about these kinds of things and it's best to let this stuff just slide by rather than taking a Gestapo attitude and having your children dig in their heels. They will then feel worse about themselves for their lying but will still eat that last piece of pie and keep texting their friends in the middle of the night and *deny, deny, deny.*

Realistically, very few of us are 100 percent honest 100 percent of the time. Everyone lies a bit—we tell our friends they look good when they don't, we make excuses so as not to attend certain parties, we refuse to make cookies for the bake sale saying we're too busy when we're not, we call in sick so as to attend our daughter's music recital. Knowing when to tell a white lie is often a sign of maturity and your job is to guide your daughter through the social morass surrounding truth vs. lying.

The really tough part though is knowing how to answer your daughter when she asks you whether or not she should lie. For example, my twelve-year old daughter, who used her allowance money to pay for the movies, wanted to know if she should lie and say she was eleven so she could still pay the children's price for the ticket. She wasn't asking what the "right" thing to do was. She already knew that she's not supposed to lie and should pay full price. What she was really asking was for permission to lie. I told her that as a parent I couldn't tell her to lie but said that I also understood that she didn't want to pay $10 for a movie instead of $7.50. I sympathized with her argument that children shouldn't have to pay adult prices unless they received adult privileges. However, I also told her that I believed she was mature enough to make her own decision about the matter. My solution may seem like a cop-out since I didn't tell her outright not to lie. However, my daughter already knew not to lie—otherwise she wouldn't have asked my permission to do otherwise. Mostly though I took the position that I did because I wanted my daughter to learn when to "walk" when the sign says "don't walk." Discerning when, and when not, to stretch the truth or obey a rule is an important lesson.

It's true that society cannot exist with everyone making his or her own rules, but neither can it exist with everybody following blindly. The former will result in anarchy and the latter in stagnation at best, Nazism at worst. If and when you tell a lie or bend any rules in your daughter's presence or with her knowledge, make sure she knows your reasons. You want her to know that at certain times she might feel the need to circumvent the truth or break a rule but that such action should not be done lightly. Sometimes the right thing to do is to "walk" when the sign says "don't walk." You should not want your daughter to grow up blindly following every rule. You want her to feel free to question, to challenge, to innovate. However, make sure your daughter knows that if and when she fudges the truth or breaks a rule, she should have good reason to do so and be ready to suffer the consequences.

If your daughter is a habitual liar (whose "stories" have nothing to do with imagination but with "cover-ups"), she likely does not view herself in a positive light and any time she gets away with a lie, it only enforces negative feelings about herself. The best thing to do in such circumstances is to adopt a two-prong approach. First, appeal to her positive aspects by joining her in activities that she's best at or directing her towards opportunities where she can use or show them off more. The other thing to do is to eliminate her opportunities to lie. If it's about texting in the middle of the night, don't let her take her cell phone to bed even if you have to hide it. If she lies about doing her homework when she hasn't, ask to see her homework every day. If it's pilfering from your purse, put your purse in a dresser draw instead of leaving it on the kitchen counter. If it's about smoking marijuana while you're at work, insist that she get involved in an after-school program or two or find a part-time job or volunteer somewhere. Be sure to tell her that you're doing these things not as a punishment but because it's your job to help her control her negative impulses until she has learned to do so on her own. Remind her that everyone develops at a different pace and just because she's lagging in controlling her impulses, doesn't mean she's a bad person. However, seek outside help if the foregoing measures are not available or don't seem to have made a difference in your daughter's behavior.

Stealing. Teenagers often steal either because they are pressured into it by their peers or because they enjoy the thrill of it. If your daughter is caught stealing, don't make a federal case out of it and treat her as if she committed murder but do try to get at the root of the problem.

If your daughter claims that this was her first theft and she will never do it again, give her the benefit of the doubt. She may just have wanted to see what it was like to do something wrong. Of course, you should express your disappointment and see that the money or item is returned. Hopefully, her fear following her crime and embarrassment at being caught will be sufficient to prevent her from stealing again simply because the experience was unpleasant. Most people tend not to repeat embarrassing behavior that had distasteful consequences.

If your daughter claims to have stolen because that's what her friends do, try to determine why she needs the acceptance of others who behave so differently from the way she was taught to behave. She may have too much pressure in her life and need some assistance coping with it. Perhaps she is being picked on too much at home or at school or her sibling completely outshines her. Be firm, but loving. Explain that she made a mistake which you do not expect her to repeat. Generally, she should be the one that returns the items, but that might be a close call if doing so might subject her to ridicule or a vengeful peer group. In such a case, you should return the goods on her behalf. In any event, your daughter should pay for the stolen goods and for any damage caused by her theft either directly using her savings or by doing special chores at home for money. Also, find out what *she* thinks would help her not be so vulnerable to peer pressure in the future. Obviously new friends would help but that's not always so easy, especially in a small town. Your daughter may also need some professional counseling if she's easily swayed by peers.

A sense of civic duty might tempt you to report, if not already known, the other wrongdoers to the authorities. *After all, somebody has to take a stand against local hoodlums.* On the other hand, Scriptures state that we are not our brother's keeper. Basically, this is a tough call that only you and your daughter can make considering primarily the safety of your neighborhood and the school and the mental toughness of your family. Regardless of your decision, be aware that a vengeful peer group might disallow any "defectors" and a barrage of bullying might follow (*see* Chapter 3 at "Bullying").

It's a different problem if your daughter steals for excitement. That's a high, like a drug, and her stealing should be treated as if it were an addiction. There will need to be a major change in your daughter's life-style so she will be able to channel her need for adventure into a more productive activity—or at least one that is not illegal. Looking at stealing objectively, it requires creative planning and generates a high level of excitement. Your daughter will either have to be directed toward not needing this excitement on a physical level similar to drug withdrawal or her need for a "high" will have to be rechanneled.

As an example of re-directing illegal activities, before cell phones, a NYC neighborhood community was concerned about teens being paid by bookies and drug dealers to run messages for them. Discussed was using the grant money, not for after-school carpentry programs and the like, but to teach the teens about the stock market by giving them each $5000 of "monopoly" money to invest. Playing the market involves risk and excitement—things that the teen runners were hooked on. You get the picture—you need to find something legal and productive for your shoplifting daughter that will involve and excite her passions. Finding a worthwhile cause for her to champion whole-heartedly should work. Check out the not-for-profits in your area where your daughter can make an immediate difference such as helping to ensure that poor children have warm coats for the winter. If you are unable to redirect your daughter's energies or if after time the stealing returns, seek outside help.

Also, don't expect your daughter to be a saint. If you constantly leave your purse open or change for the parking meter lying around, expect to lose some money. Either she or a friend will pilfer a few quarters from time to time. If you allow this to occur over and over again, your daughter might think you a fool and might lose respect for you. Mostly though, she'll likely resent you for putting her in the uncomfortable position of condoning something that she knows is wrong whether it's she that does the stealing or a friend that instigates or indulges in the petty theft. If you find that your pile of change is getting smaller and smaller despite your additions to it, don't waste your breath by confronting your daughter about it. She will merely deny it so no need to make a liar of her too. Just keep your purse out of the way and don't leave loose change around. Your daughter will get the message and will probably feel relieved. (It's similar to not leaving knickknacks within easy reach of a two-year-old.) The money jar can discreetly reappear at a later time, in a different locale and perhaps in a different container, when your daughter's compulsion is directed toward something else—like never-ending tweeting.

PREJUDICE/DISCRIMINATION

I'm not into today's mantra that we "love" everyone. Instead, I believe that every individual deserves to be treated as we would like to be treated—with respect and fairness—regardless of gender, age, race, religion, ethnicity, whatever. I also believe that Martin Luther King, Jr. had it right when he said, *We should be judged by the content of our character and not by the color of our skin.*

Your daughter should understand that "being different" is not better or worse, just different. Moreover, we should all be glad for the differences among us. Think pizza, bagels, chili, salsa, Chow Mein, humus, spanakopita, curry, teriyaki sauce, tacos, etc., etc., etc. and all the other wonderful choices, particularly in music and art, we're able to experience in this country. Think too of all the immigrants who have made our lives better through technology and innumerable medical advances.

Today's divisiveness is in part the result of fear emanating from the *9/11* attack on The World Trade Center and exacerbated by terrorists inflicting random attacks not only in this country and abroad but by also inflicting horrific barbarian acts against their own people. Foreign trade, though resulting in more jobs and a better quality of life for most Americans, have left many bereft. Moreover, at the same time, this country has become not only more racially diverse but more and more women are in the work force doing jobs formerly only held by men. Thus, while this is an ideal time for women and minorities to be able to follow their dreams, their success often comes at the expense of the white male. While there's absolutely no excuse for the KKK and other groups espousing racial and religious hatred, I get it that for centuries all a guy had to be was white and a Protestant to enjoy a privileged status. Nowadays, he has to compete with everybody else and he's angry. We must all, however, take special care that we do not, nor allow our children, to disparage an entire racial, religious or ethnic group because those formerly at the top of the pile solely by chance have lost their privileged status.

If your daughter vehemently or frequently mouths hatred of a particular religious, racial, ethnic or political group or verbally supports violence against any such group, listen closely and contact appropriate resources (minister, police, guidance professional) for advice before she gets into some kind of trouble. Ditto if you find bizarre drawings depicting death to others or other indicia of a predilection toward violence by her or any of her friends on her media sites, in her desk, or among her things.

RELIGION

Sometime during her teens, your daughter will go through a religious or spiritual phase. She will be very intense about her feelings and beliefs, pro or con. She may speak of joining a religious order. Other teens may embrace philosophy with the fervor of the most devout. They become apostles of Thoreau ("Walden Pond") or Kahlil Gibran ("The Prophet"). Some may decide the Eastern religions are their path to enlightenment. Others become cultish about being a vegetarian or believing in reincarnation. At the other extreme are those who become devout atheists believing that humans are solely responsible for their own actions. As with most things your daughter espouses when a teen, it's best to pay as little attention to her extreme pronouncements as possible. Don't tell her she's foolish or doesn't know what she's talking about. She knows how you feel and what you believe. She's just exploring new ideas. Let her find her own way.

Even if you are a religious church-going person, do not force your teen daughter to attend religious services if she doesn't want to. (Most likely her attendance will depend on how cute the attending boys are anyway.) Conversely, you should honor your daughter's desire to participate in religious activities even if you're a non-believer. You want your daughter to develop inner strength. She can develop that by finding her own way whether it's through religious orthodoxy or atheism. She takes her beliefs seriously and you should let your daughter feel she is her own person and has control over her life. She's the one who has to make decisions about drugs and sex when she's with her peers. If you make her feel that her beliefs are silly or wrong (assuming they're not evil but just different than yours), she may not have the inner security to do what she knows is right. Anyway, her religious fervor or lack of any is likely temporary and if you are supportive of her explorations, don't be surprised if she ends up having values similar to yours regardless of whatever tag she puts on her beliefs.

SELFISHNESS

Everyone in the household should have an opportunity to come first. However, if you have a teenage daughter she will feel that she never comes first. *Everyone else gets what they want except her!* Your explanation that life evens out in the long run will fall on deaf ears because as a teen, she lives in the moment. Realize that during her period of intense selfishness what to you is a simple *want* is a *need* to her. This isn't an easy time for you. You may find it hard to even like her, let alone favor her, because of her selfishness. Further, during this phase, a variation of Murphy's Law (i.e., *if anything can go wrong, it will*) is probably at work too and everything is wrong or out of kilter in the household. There may be illness, unemployment or whatever, but your daughter's only concern will be herself. She simply has no capacity for reason or empathy during this phase.

You have a choice. You can either harangue her for her selfishness and get nowhere or help her through it by recognizing that her selfishness is simply the symptom of tremendous insecurity and fear. Right now, your daughter is not much different from the toddler who misbehaves most when the mother says she has a headache. The toddler is insecure because she knows she is dependent on the mother and recognizes that her mother's illness is a threat to her own well-being. Your teen daughter

63

is insecure because she realizes that soon she will have to depend on herself. Extra effort is required to bolster your daughter even if you feel her need to be first is trivial in relation to other family needs. You may disagree and think that catering to her quest for attention and concern for self in a time of someone else's real need is ridiculous. However, your daughter's need for extra attention at this time is just as real a need to her as is an ill person's need for special care.

For example, a young teen I know was in the midst of her self-centered phase while her brother was seriously ill. The mother, a working mom and night-school student, was also studying for finals at the same time. Objectively, the brother's need for care and the mother's need for time were greater than the daughter's concern about whether or not she would have the right shorts for camp. Wisely, though, the mother took time to take a good long look at her daughter. She realized she was a pretty pathetic creature at the time. The "right" shorts were just a cover for her fears and insecurities. The young girl was going on a backpacking trip and she was worried. *Would she be able to keep up? Would her pimples go away in time? Would the boys notice that she didn't swim on "certain" days? Would she get what her brother had? What if her brother died? Would it be her fault? Would her mother blame her?* No wonder the girl had to focus on little things like the right shorts. The other worries were just too much for her to cope with at the time.

Look beyond your daughter's seemingly selfish behavior and try to understand what's triggering it. Find the time and energy to pay attention to her so she will feel like a worthy person and have the confidence to work out her own fears little by little. You can give her the little "extra" she needs in simple ways—by bringing home her favorite frozen yogurt or magazine or, if time and money permit, by seeing a movie or getting a manicure together.

STINGINESS

Your daughter is exceeding cheap. She thinks spending $5 on a gift is extravagant. She's not any more generous to herself. She shops only in secondhand stores and tells you she'll make do with one bathing suit even though she's to be a lifeguard for the summer. Even her pencils are used until they are no more than stubs.

You don't need to worry about this child spending a week's allowance on one eyeliner pencil or finishing a quart of milk and a box of cookies at one time. You are worried, though, because all your friend's daughters are buying six different bottles of nail polish at once and are eating quarts of ice cream or a whole pint of strawberries at one sitting.

Relax. Nothing is wrong with your daughter. If you look closely, you will see she is really as excessive as are her friends. The only difference is that her compulsive excessiveness is stinginess while theirs is extravagance. If, however, the stinginess lingers after she has outgrown excessiveness in other areas, it may be just her nature to be a tightwad or it could be rooted in a lack of self-esteem. If she is only tight about spending money on others or always looks for bargains, she is entitled to be that way. (There is definitely some virtue in being frugal.)

However, if your daughter refuses to spend her money on things that she likes or interest her and the family does not need her money, she might need assistance in building up her feelings of self-worth. For example, if she loves to go to the movies with her friends but stays home instead because she "can't afford it" (and is not saving her money for something special), try to determine why she feels the need to deny herself pleasure. Perhaps she blames herself for your divorce or feels guilty about all the money her recent illness cost. Perhaps she is harboring a secret guilt, thought or deed and is afraid to tell you about it. Try a few stabs in the dark to open her up. Mention that everyone does things they wish they hadn't. Everyone has thoughts they are not proud of. Everyone feels guilty about something from time to time even if they had no control over the underlying situation. Tell her she doesn't need to punish herself regardless of the cause of her anguish. Explain that adolescence is a time to learn from experience and most likely she has learned not to do whatever it was that's causing her present pain again.

Be gentle, especially if you suspect her guilt is based on some form of sexual behavior. A thirteen-year-old who has engaged in petting may think she has done the worst thing in the world. She hasn't. Ditto for a teen who engaged in sexual intercourse—definitely an unwise and potentially harmful act but not indicative that the girl is a "bad" person. What you want to convey is your love and acceptance of your daughter even when she's done something she shouldn't have and guide her toward learning from her mistake rather than punish herself. A lack of self-love or feeling unloved by family members is what often leads to undesirable behavior. It's not necessary for you to always know the cause of your daughter's angst; however, if you suspect she is engaged in activities that are truly harmful to her such as deliberate unprotected intercourse, drug use, shoplifting, vandalism, cheating and the like, seek professional assistance.

8. YOUR ROLE

Acceptance — Communication
Giving Advice — Nagging — Spying
Togetherness

ACCEPTANCE

One day you decide you don't really like your daughter. Of course, you love her but whenever you look at her, she's sprawled all over the couch amidst cookie crumbs and gum wrappers with her mouth always on the move, either talking on the phone or chewing wads of gum, or both. Nothing else moves. She has more rolls of fat on her body than you; or if she is thin, you are convinced that her bones will snap from disuse. What has happened is that you have just realized that your daughter is not the superstar you once thought she was. The A's stopped in middle school; she did not make the varsity team; she will never have the chin to become a model. Don't despair. Your daughter is not any different than before but you have just discovered that she is who she is, not your idealized image of her. Don't fault her for not being a superstar.

Of course, you're disappointed that she'll never get a soccer scholarship or have the grades to go to your college alma mater. Hiding disappointment is never easy but it's best to go with one's winners and you and your daughter should appreciate her winners regardless of the subject, hobby or sport. If she has none at the moment, be ready to nurture one when the time comes. In the meantime, introduce her to as much as possible but don't force anything—let her find her uniqueness in her own time. Something will click in sooner or later and be ready to support it but again, go at her pace.

You also need to help your daughter accept her own limitations. If, for example, there is objectively no hope that she will ever be a prima ballerina because she's more the size and shape of a football player, don't behave as if you still expect her to be. In such a situation, encourage her to continue with her dancing lessons if she enjoys them but help her look at what she enjoys most about ballet. Is it the grace, the choreography, the music, the costumes that attract her? Perhaps she can expand her ballet experience by trying her hand at choreography or costume design or even apply her love of dance to some form of folk dancing since that also combines grace, athleticism, and beautiful music and costumes. You need to step carefully here though. She may know she's not a super-star but thoroughly enjoys the activity anyway. Don't spoil it for her by calling it a waste of time because she does not excel at it. The important thing is that she needs to know that she need not always win or be the best to merit your approval. She has a right to be ordinary. Love her, and help her to love herself in spite of any of her failings or shortcomings, imagined or otherwise. At the same time, point out that she will always be a winner if she gives whatever she does her best shot regardless of who takes first prize in any competition and especially when she's the only competitor.

COMMUNICATION

Communication need not always be a "meaningful" conversation. Communication is respect and understanding and sensing where your daughter "is at." Don't force discussions just because you know parents are supposed to communicate with their children. The best way for you to communicate is by listening, observing and setting a good example. Keep in mind, too, that communication includes disagreements but be sure that after the smoke settles, your daughter is left with feelings of self-respect and self-worth.

If your daughter comes into the kitchen and sniffs the pots while you're cooking, chances are she has something to say. Don't pounce or she will clam up. Wait for her to begin. She'll probably start off with either a cheery *Hi* or a grumpy *Ugh!* about what you're preparing. Keep your ears open, mouth closed, and continue with what you are doing, taking your cue from her. For example, if she then next complains that her teacher is unfair, listen and agree—at least at first. You can always defend the teacher later if necessary. Right now though your best response would be an *Oh* and a few *hmmms* here and there until she has had her say. Try to see it from her point of view and agree with her position as much as you can. If your daughter's view is right but it is about a relatively trivial or inconsequential matter, you can simply dismiss the situation by agreeing with her and pointing out that the teacher was probably just having a bad day. If, however, something does seem seriously amiss with the teacher's actions, follow up on the situation with the teacher or the school.

Conversely, if you disagree with your daughter's take on a situation, feel free to voice your opinion but take care to emphasize and acknowledge that she has a right to her opinion regardless of the subject matter. For example, you probably would totally disagree with your daughter if she said there was absolutely no harm in smoking marijuana whatsoever. In such an instance, voice your opinion but don't start haranguing her about smoking the stuff. Assume she's speaking hypothetically. If you think she's feeling you out because of some experimentation she has or is planning to engage in, add some general comments about the illegality of its use, special danger to teens, etc. (*see* Chapter 3 at "Drugs"). If you suspect heavy use, keep the discussion short and seek professional advice before you pursue the topic further with your daughter. If she's already a user, she probably already feels somewhat alienated so step lightly so as not to widen the breach without a plan and some professional guidance.

But suppose your daughter never talks to you! That's probably not true—she just never talks to you when you want to talk to her. Maybe, too, that when she wants to talk to you, you're unavailable or unaware of her signals that she's ready to talk. Or your daughter may be the broadcaster type who delivers bulletins the minute you walk in the door: *she got a 90 on her math test...her physics teacher is sooo unfair....Andrea's in the hospital...she's decided to become a vegetarian...you have to go to Parents' Night on Tuesday...*all delivered in ten seconds or less. But you really don't want to talk to her right now. You need to unwind and relax a bit but by the time you've changed your clothes and sat down ready to talk, it's too late to find out which Tuesday, which hospital and why. By this time, your daughter is busy with her homework or engrossed in social media. And she doesn't want to talk to you after dinner either. By then it's all old news to her and the most you will get in response to your inquiries will be monosyllabic utterances decipherable only by another teen.

Some teens have strange ways of communicating. Listen and look for your daughter's signals. For example, my daughter and I hadn't "communicated" for what seemed like ages. It wasn't until she started going to parties with her friends that we had "meaningful" conversations. I waited up for her the first time she went out and rather than incurring her displeasure for "treating her like a baby," I discovered she loved to talk at night. Thereafter, I'd always be up when she came home and we'd have a snack and talk for an hour or so about all kinds of things—her life, the world, my problems. Another girl I know communicates with her mother indirectly. Though the girl has her own phone, she makes some of her calls within easy hearing distance of her mother. She appears oblivious to her mother's eavesdropping. What she is really doing though is letting her mother in on her life and trusting her mother to interfere if something doesn't seem right. Be alert for your daughter's signals.

If you and your daughter do not seem to be communicating at all though take a step back and view the situation objectively. Perhaps your daughter is a very private person and likes to keep things to herself. That's not a bad trait to have. Or, it may be your interests and those of your daughter's are so different that you really have very little to talk about expect perhaps your respective daily caloric intakes. However, the fact that you may not be speaking "meaningfully" to each other does not mean that there's no communication between the two of you. You are communicating love and respect each time you remind her to eat broccoli or bring home her favorite shampoo. She, too, is communicating love and respect each time she offers to turn the music down when you're on the phone or empty the dishwasher when you have a headache. It's OK to keep in touch through everyday living. You need not feel that you must always discuss "Life" with your daughter. Besides, conversations about "Life" often wind up being monologues given by a parent and devoid of any two-sided dialogue.

GIVING ADVICE

The purpose of your advice is not to order your daughter to do your bidding but to guide her toward making a wise decision on her own. If you give advice, give it as advice, not as an order. If you want to tell your daughter what to do and what not to do, by all means do so but when you give advice allow her the right to reject it. If she does not follow your advice and even if it was a mistake for her not to do so, do not accuse her of disobeying you. Remember, advice is for those instances when your daughter will need to make her own decisions. You give it to make her aware of problems or dangers that, because of her youth and inexperience, she may not be aware of.

It doesn't matter whether your words are pearls of wisdom or that you are permitted to utter them only between biology chapters or during blogging breaks. However, if you repeat your usual "tried and true," your words will go unheeded. Therefore, it is better to say the unexpected. For example, if your daughter is going away to camp, don't just give her a list of do's and don'ts. She has heard them all before (or something similar) and nothing you say will register unless you say something different and unexpected. A remark such as *If you're going to do something wrong, do so because you really want to do it, not because someone else wants you to* is far more likely to get her attention. Furthermore, a remark like that will make her focus on the fact that she is the person responsible for her actions and it lets her know you have confidence in her judgment. What you want to do is to remind your daughter to be guided by the values you have already taught her and not for her to succumb to peer pressure.

Even if your advice appears to fall on deaf ears, it may still be effective. Something of what you say will sink in sooner or later. Your daughter hears what you say even if she claims otherwise or walks out on you before you've delivered the punch line. Don't let her rude behavior sidetrack you into a lecture about slamming doors. Ignore her bad manners for the moment and continue with your discussion about hitchhiking or drugs or whatever. But be careful not to give advice about every single facet of your daughter's life or you will run the risk of being shut off completely.

My daughter let me know I was too heavy into my advisor role by ordering me not to give her any more advice about anything. I told her it was my job as a parent to give advice and that nobody was insisting that she follow it. She said, *I'm not stupid! Don't you think that if what you say makes sense, I'm going to follow it?* I asked, *Then what's the problem?* In her usual tone of annoyance, she explained that she did not want any advice because she wanted to figure things out for herself and make her own mistakes. It seemed we had come to an impasse. She had a need to be able to err and I a need to guide her. Anyway, we solved the advice-giving problem by agreeing that when I felt a need to advise, I could do so, but she was free to leave the room. Thereafter, my advice was spoken to a wall—hopefully with her listening on the other side. Don't be tempted though to give more than cursory advice to your daughter via a tweet or text. It's likely that she'll just scroll past them. Best to save those modes of communication for messages about family schedule changes and information that would be important for her to know ASAP.

NAGGING

Your daughter always accuses you of nagging. *Pick, pick, pick. That's all you do*. She's probably at least half right, but best to ignore her comments. You're entitled to nag, but you don't need to overdo it by picking on her about picking on you. Or you may be a "screamer." If your screaming is merely an occasional and brief temper tantrum and is not giving you high blood pressure, don't worry about it but do try to control yourself a bit more. Remember, every time you scream at your daughter, you're teaching her to scream back at you.

Most teens will take their parents' ill-delivered expressions of care and anger in stride provided that what is said is constructive and not merely derogatory. For example, if you want your daughter to get more exercise, don't keep telling her she looks like a lump of lard; instead, remark about how beautiful her arms are and how exercise will keep them that way or something along those lines. If your daughter never calls when she's going to be late, don't scream that she is a thoughtless and inconsiderate wretch; instead, remind her how good a simple text will make you feel. If your daughter's grades are poor, don't call her an idiot; instead query her as to the reasons and suggest private tutoring or an on-line tutorial.

If your daughter tunes you out, change your style of delivery. Perhaps you should whisper or update your vocabulary. I agree that adults who speak like teens do sound ridiculous but doing so may get your daughter's attention.

SPYING

When written messages were only sent the old-fashioned way via mail, fax or telegram and your daughter's private thoughts were only in her personal diary and not texted or e-mailed anywhere, absent any definitive cause for concern, your daughter's privacy should have been respected—whether she was eight or eighteen. Today, however, it's an entirely different matter. Cyberbullies lurk everywhere as do malfeasants preying on the young and gullible. Thus, you must draw a fine line between what's spying and protection. I think the fairest way to do this is before you buy her a cell phone or other device or allow her to buy such things for herself, is to let her know that you must have all appropriate passwords and/or will be using pertinent monitoring programs. When discussing this, assure her that the foregoing is solely for her safety and explain that you will be as discreet and tolerant as are the Secret Service agents who watch over a President's children. (*See also* Chapter 3 at "Cyberbullying.")

It's also wise to have applicable protections on your computer and other tech items. Any tech store can keep you apprised of the latest gizmos to ensure that your daughter doesn't inadvertently come upon pornography or other purveyors of inappropriate goods and services. Next, just like you tell her 1,000 times over about the dangers of smoking or drug use, don't neglect to go on *ad infinitum* about cyberbullies. Yes, she will roll her eyes and appear to tune you out but your message will be heard. Basically, though, trust your instincts--if something doesn't seem right, it often isn't. Thus, it's best to err on the side of caution but be discrete and if you find something that's truly major, talk to your daughter about it. Be careful however not to over-react. As a guide, has your spying uncovered possible physical or emotional harm to your daughter or others? Your daughter and her friends discussing among themselves that so and so's hair is just awful is different than a scheme to emotionally taunt a disliked girl because her father is in prison or because her brother is gay.

If you found nothing worrisome but your daughter catches you snooping around, explain that you acted not out of distrust for her but because you believe it your parental duty to check things out every once in a while. Assure her that it's not something you do every day—just something you did because of some news report or something a friend said or that she'd been out of sorts lately. Explain you understand her feelings of violation. Remind her that you are uncomfortable about today's times making you a sometime spy. Remind her too that you understand how she feels because she knows how you hate having your packages checked before entering a store or going through a metal detector at the local library as if you were a thief. Explain that until the world changes, one must take the world as it is, not as one would like it to be. We do indeed live in difficult times requiring unpleasant accommodations.

In the meantime, you can mitigate the uncomfortable effects of snooping by respecting your daughter's privacy and remaining silent about things she is doing that you disapprove of but are not harmful to her or another. As an example, I once accidentally came across some notes passed around in class between my daughter and some of her friends making tasteless comments about a teacher's physical appearance. While I think there is never an excuse for vulgar language and that the comments were totally inappropriate, they did not contain even a hint of danger so I saw no reason to mention them. I would have fessed up to snooping though had I discovered a scheme to cheat on exams. At least then, had she railed at me for spying on her, I could have countered that I saved her from a blotch on her record. Like many things these days, to snoop or not is a balancing act because a child mistrusting a parent is a danger in itself.

TOGETHERNESS

Togetherness can't be forced. It may be that you and your daughter appear to have nothing in common and therefore she sees no reason to spend any time with you. However, with a little thought, you probably can find something your daughter will agree to do with you. For example, my daughter was interested in interior decorating so we'd sometimes attend the Sunday real estate "open houses." Together we'd comment on the furnishings and plan how we would furnish the place. We'd also compare sales prices and decide the best values considering taxes and upkeep. While real estate agents seldom approve of non-serious buyers, it was a way for my daughter and I to bond and also for her to learn how to assess price versus value and, since we were apartment dwellers, the costs and benefits of home ownership.

Perhaps your daughter loves to read. You could visit bookstores together and though you might browse separately, you could meet at the bookstore's café for a latte and discuss your "finds." Discussing which books to buy could lead to a friendly chit-chat about everything from popular novels to finances to classics to science fiction.

Your daughter might not want to "share a moment" with you under any circumstances—not even a movie. After all, her friends might be there and if they see her there with you, they might think she had no one else to go with. That's also why she won't go shopping with you—unless, of course, you offer to take her to the most expensive store in town. Though your daughter may not want to go anywhere with you, she'll willingly go everywhere with her father. It's hard not to feel hurt by her refusals but keep in mind that teen girls often need to emotionally separate themselves from their mothers in order to stand on their own. And when they do, they're often just like their mothers though they'll seldom admit or even recognize that. If you really want or need your daughter to accompany you somewhere, don't ask *Why won't you go anywhere with me? Are you ashamed of me?* etc., etc. Instead, simply say you need her presence at a certain time, at a certain place, for a specific reason. She may surprise you and not only concede to have lunch with you and your second cousin Lucy but may actually do so ungrudgingly.

Naturally, you would like your daughter to go bike riding or attend an art opening with you—both of which she finds equally distasteful. (The art opening you can understand, but what's wrong with a bike ride?) After all, you would like to do something with your daughter that's fun other than shopping at a pricey boutique. Following are some suggestions about how to be "together" with your daughter when she refuses to go anywhere with you. They may seem trivial but they epitomize what home and family are all about. Coupon clipping, pantry checking and meal planning can be shared activities. It's amazing how simple things can become a family ritual. For example, every Thursday night after dinner, my daughter and I would check the newspaper for coupons, plan the week's meals and prepare the shopping list. My daughter so looked forward to this activity since I gave her a lot of say in the menu planning. She even bought a coupon box for the house with her allowance and, years later when she had her own home, we'd still send each other food coupons.

Also, all that advice to the working mother about cooking ahead can spoil a lot of togetherness. However, if you want to do the week's cooking ahead of time, pick a time when your daughter is available. Don't just use her to peel the carrots and take out the trash—let her try her hand at the cooking too. Also, setting the table, making the salad, fixing coffee, etc. if done in the right atmosphere, can be shared activities, not chores. When there is time for the family to have a leisurely dinner together, even if it is only a family of two, light some candles, use cloth napkins, do something to make it special, especially if your daughter helped with the meal. Also, her reading the newspaper to you—even stock market listings or the weather where friends and relatives live—while you fix dinner can foster non-threatening communication between the two of you.

What's important is the sharing, not the subject of the experience. Seize the moments as they come. Planned fun is seldom as good as when it is spontaneous. Be flexible enough to be aware of the potential of the moment and don't squash a good time by thinking now that you are "close," it's a good opportunity to deliver a lecture. If the two of you are having a great time while she's teaching you to roller-blade, don't bring up the subject of her being too young to date. It's unlikely anything you say at that time will change her feelings. All you will do is spoil the fun that you are having and wind up angry with her and yourself. A memory of a good time with you is more likely to get your daughter thinking about what you have said in the past than is a repeated lecture at an inopportune moment. So if you and she are having fun together, enjoy the moment. Perhaps, she might even invite you to share her "Cinnamon Sin" lip gloss—do so even if it stings.

9. DISCIPLINE

Punishment—Spoiling Her
Using Clout—When to Say No

PUNISHMENT

For many parents, punishment is used as a means of showing that they "care." Punishment is also a tool that parents use in order to feel they are doing something. However, punishment usually doesn't get the room clean or the homework done on a regular basis.

You may feel the need to punish your daughter if she stayed out too late by making her stay in the following weekend. However, if it becomes a pattern of one weekend out late and one weekend home, it's obvious that the punishment is not effective. You need to work with your daughter so that she understands that you want her home on time for her own safety and out of consideration for you. Review your behavior and that of your daughter's when you find yourself meting out punishment for the same wrong over and over again. Are the limits reasonable? Does the punishment fit the crime? Is the punishment wanted because it is her way of getting your attention? Or does the misdeed arise because she cannot handle the situation for which she is repeatedly being punished? Are your expectations unrealistic?

If you find yourself punishing your daughter often for a variety of offenses, you are wasting your time. Punishment used sparingly and with a light touch will remind your daughter of what is expected of her but will only work as a sanction if she is controllable—either by you or by herself. Try to determine the cause of the problem that triggers repeated punishment. For example, your daughter might truly be the forgetful type and you may need to text her a reminder it's 5:00pm and time for her to start her homework or a reminder that curfew time is approaching. In other words, determine the root of your daughter's disobedience and together try to come up with a solution to the problem other than punishment. If your daughter continually invites punishment by engaging in activities harmful to herself or others or deviates from socially acceptable behavior, get professional help.

SPOILING HER

If you take the time and energy to discipline your daughter fairly, and if the limits you set have a reasonable basis, you will not spoil her. Giving your daughter extra attention is not spoiling her; giving in to her because it is easier to say yes than no, is. Take the time to set limits and standards which are for your daughter's benefit or if the limits are for your benefit or for others, say so. Don't lamely disguise one of your actions as being good for your daughter when in fact the action is merely convenient for you or good for her sibling. Just be honest with your daughter.

Also, you shouldn't deny your daughter something simply because you feel it's for her own good to be denied something. It's fine not to buy something for her because the family cannot afford it. However, there is no reason not to buy her special shampoo if such "luxury" item is well within the family budget. Your daughter thinks she is special and you should too. If your daughter feels valued at home, she will value herself and, if she values herself, she will be able to resist the girl friend that asks her to shoplift or a boyfriend's request for sex.

You need not worry about your daughter becoming spoiled just because you treat her as a special person. For example, a family I know recently inherited some money. This family had gone through unusually difficult financial times and the parents decided to let each family member buy or do something from the inheritance that they felt they had been deprived of or that the family hadn't been able to afford. The parents chose eating out in a nice restaurant once a week; one son chose to resume his trumpet lessons; another child chose to visit a friend from camp who lived in another city. Everyone thought that Anna, a 15-year old typical teenager, would want the latest smart phone or expensive leather boots because she was very materialistic and always concerned about being up-to-date. Her choice? A label maker! It seems that through all the hard times, she had never felt deprived. She always got what she felt she needed. Her family had respected her expensive taste and she had respected the family budget by "needing" fewer things.

At this stage of your daughter's life what may seem like "wants" to you are "needs" to her. For example, you may think she needs two more pair of jeans. Your daughter, however, pleads for a pair of designer jeans that are beyond the reach of your budget. Give her a choice—one pair of the expensive jeans or the two pair that you think she needs. My guess is she'll choose the designer brand. Respect your daughter's choice—don't try to wheedle her down claiming that since she's said she can manage with one pair, she can manage with one pair of the cheaper brand. Your daughter doesn't want one pair—she "needs" the designer brand. (She should keep up her part of the bargain too—don't let her wheedle you into buying her a second pair of either type.) Fitting in fashion-wise is one of the most innocuous ways for a teen to "fit in" the middle and high school milieu. If your daughter's fitting-in in this regard puts a real strain on the family budget, sit down and talk to her about it. Be as flexible as possible though and see if there is some way that some of her needs can be accommodated.

Wealth or lack of it is often subjective. Some folks would consider anyone above the poverty line to be wealthy; others reserve that term only for the likes of Oprah and Bill Gates. However, knowing how much to spend on or to give a teenager is a universal problem regardless of one's position on the financial scale. For example, today prices for a pair of sneakers range from $20 to well over $100. Most families can afford a $20 pair but few can afford the expensive brands. But just because you can afford $100+ for a pair of sneakers for your daughter, should you spend that much? Do you buy your daughter a pricey 21-speed bicycle? Or a car? Or, when she's older, a home? We all want our children to have their own resources and successes and to do for themselves but at the same time we want them to have the best. The most reasonable approach is that if you can afford it and the object of the request is reasonable, enjoy your good fortune. If your daughter is a dedicated runner, why not buy her the best running shoes you can afford (provided that her obvious family affluence does not set her apart from her peers or expose her to danger). For example, a wealthy friend of mine lives in an area where most high school students have their own cars. The family can easily afford a new car for their teen daughter so they need not worry about the temperament of a used car. However, it doesn't mean that the new car need be a BMW. Also, as my friend said, she will buy her daughter a car and pay for the insurance and maintenance because she can afford to, but that doesn't mean she will pay for the gas or her daughter's parking tickets. Because of my friend's wealth and the community norm, withholding a car from her daughter or making the girl pay for it so she could learn "responsibility" would seem artificial.

Conversely, if times are difficult for you financially, don't hide that fact from your daughter. She has a right to know what the situation is and participate in it as well. If a family breadwinner has lost his or her job, rather than just eliminating your daughter's allowance, ask her how much it could be cut. Get her input on exactly how important it is to her to continue her music lessons—perhaps they could be changed to once a week instead of twice or perhaps you will learn that she will give up something else just to keep on with the lessons. Perhaps too she can earn some money by baby-sitting, dog-walking or weeding someone's garden.

Basically, you can give your daughter many opportunities to be responsible regardless of your economic status even if you "spoil" her. (*See generally* Chapter 10—Instilling Responsibility.) Just because you worked hard and scrimped and saved, doesn't mean she has to—not all the time anyway. Isn't one of the reasons we parents work so hard is so that our children will have it easier? That being said, let your daughter know that while hard work is no guarantee of success, goofing off is a sure route to failure. Also, I'm mindful that many families think children should work for what they want. That's a fine plan too provided that it is fairly administered among all children in the family and does not result in your daughter being the only one of her social group that does not have sneakers that light up or whatever the current fad is. It's one thing to draw a line in the sand over a moral issue but think hard before you subject your daughter to possible mockery because of her lack of a common material item when buying the item for her would not cause familial hardship. More simply said, if there's a need for material deprivation, your daughter will have to learn to deal with that but when there is none, your daughter should have what is customary in her group whether you buy it for her outright or advance her the money and have her work it off via doing extra chores.

USING CLOUT

It is easier to have clout if you are a major family breadwinner. However, you can have clout even if your job is that of a homemaker only. Clout is what you carry with you when you say no or lay down the law. If you work outside the home, make the most of any "perks" you get. Do you receive any special discounts or tickets as a result of your job? Are you so important that your company sends you on a business trip even if it is only to the next town? Do you have an expense account or get taken out to lunch often? Have you won any awards or special kudos for your work? Do you work in a prestigious building or office park? Is your boss someone famous? If you don't work outside the home, there are other ways to achieve clout. Are you a troop or club leader or officer of the local parents' association? Have you won any awards for your artwork, sewing, or cooking? Do your photos appear in the local paper? Do you sing in the church choir or deliver meals to the homebound? Are you a member of the auxiliary police or fire department? Do you mentor the disadvantaged?

The point here is that whatever you do or receive that is "extra," flaunt it. Don't trivialize your rewards or accomplishments. Be proud of yourself and let your daughter know that you are. You are proud of her achievements; let her be proud of yours. You shouldn't "lord" what you do over her but if you are proud of what you do and who you are and believe in yourself, you will find that your daughter is not only respectful and mindful of you, but will also be proud to be your daughter (but don't be surprised if she doesn't let you know that she is!).

WHEN TO SAY NO

One day you realize with a shock that you no longer make the decisions for your daughter; the decisions that affect her are made by her. For example, your daughter announces in a rather defiant tone that she could go wherever she wants. Your mind tells you, yes, she could. She has enough money for a ticket. However, instead of reacting as if she were leaving on the next bus, ask her where and why she plans on going. *Ahh...*you learn that there's to be a political march half-way across the country. You think that she mustn't go—it's too far away and far too dangerous an event. The answer is to do nothing for the moment except listen. Your daughter never said that she was going to go to the march or even that she wanted to go. All she said was that she *could* go. So, for the moment, agree with her that she's capable of making such a trip and see what happens next. Often, when teens come up with seemingly outlandish ideas, they just want recognition and affirmation of their capabilities. You need not respond to what may occur in the future. You only need to respond to your daughter's initial remarks. Often the best response initially is a short *Oh* or *hmmm*, no matter how off-base the pronouncement.

If she asks to do something truly dangerous or outlandish, or announces that she is going to, before you automatically say "No," ask yourself why you do not want her to do it. If it's a political type march, do you not want her to go because it might be dangerous or because you disagree with the purpose of the march? Or do you want to say "No" because you are concerned about what your friends or neighbors would think if you allowed her to go? Remember that your daughter has some sense. Look objectively at all aspects of the contemplated trip. How far is it? How will she get there? Who is she going with? Your goal in these instances is to get her to make decisions wisely—to consider all that is involved.

As an example of parental assessment of their child's maturity and ability, some years ago parents of a 16-year-old girl allowed the girl to attempt to sail solo around the world. (Her trip was aborted due to storm damage and she needed to be rescued.) While I am not advocating allowing such extreme journeys, I am mindful of the fact that in this country boys and girls may enter the Armed Services at the age of seventeen and a half and may shortly thereafter kill or be killed.

Ask your daughter the questions you asked yourself. Ask her how much the trip would cost and remind her that she's saving her money for the latest Notebook or a car. After all, you don't want her to agree to do something without appropriate forethought; thus, you shouldn't say no without thought either. Remember too you can forbid your daughter from doing something but if your grounds for doing so are unreasonable or dishonest, she may not ask the next time.

Perhaps too the dangers of a contemplated trip might be negated. For example, some older teens I knew wanted to travel to a large city and participate in the Occupy Wall Street movement. They planned to drive, leaving at the crack of dawn and returning at midnight. The parents thought the trip dangerous but didn't want to quell their children's desire to be part of history by standing up for something they believed in. After analyzing the situation, the parents realized that they were not worried about anything their daughters or their friends would do. They were all good drivers and didn't drink nor were they wild—just full of life and energy and anxious to express their views and participate in their world. The parents' fear was that a riot might break out and that the children might be hurt or arrested. They lectured the girls about the importance of keeping an eye out for what was going on around them and for them to use their instinct if things didn't feel right. They were also told to stay away from anyone who smelled of marijuana and to obey the police without any argument or back-talk.

The teens certainly didn't want to be mixed up in a riot or roughhoused by the police. And they certainly didn't want to be hauled off to jail. They were not looking to be heroines. They took the warnings seriously—so seriously that they stayed at the fringes of the demonstration. They were happy though to have had the opportunity to stand up and be counted for something they believed in. The sit-ins leading to the Civil Rights Act of 1964, the anti-Vietnam War demonstrations, the Occupy Movement or other acts of civil disobedience are all fraught with danger but older teens should not be deprived of participating in something they believe strongly about. These days, your daughter and her friends might want to attend protests against racism or marches about women's rights or environmental issues. If your daughter is an older teen and she and her friends are generally sensible, consider allowing your daughter to go. I know it's particularly scary these days to let your daughter have wings but she has a right to try and shape the kind of world that she will live her adult life in. You should though point out all the possible dangers and discuss ways of avoiding them.

If, however, you refuse to allow your daughter to go somewhere because of a personal need of yours, even a selfish one, be honest and tell your daughter the reason. Don't attempt to disguise something as dangerous when her marching off to demonstrate would upset your plans. You too have a right to come first sometimes. If you tell your daughter the truth behind your nay-saying, she will respect you for your integrity and will be less likely to argue with you. Conversely, your daughter also has a right to say no. For example, one mother I know was very proud of her daughter's charm and maturity and she wanted to show her off at her office. However, the girl refused to go—it was a free afternoon off from school and she wanted to spend it her way. The mother was very annoyed at first but later realized that her daughter had a right to decide to either please her mom or spend the afternoon with her friends. The daughter's refusal was indeed selfish but so was the mother's request. Thus, unless there is an important reason for your daughter to go to your office or it is really important to you that she go, your personal requests and preferences are not the type of things for you to bring out the parental guns. So swallow your disappointment and save your ammunition for the real battles.

Consider too that your daughter may sometimes want you to say no. My 17-year-old daughter announced one Saturday night that she was going to a party in a seedy part of the city. I asked her how she planned on getting there since it was snowing heavily and it would be impossible to get a taxi. And how would she get home? She said that she and a friend were going to go by subway. *Travel there at night by subway? How are you going to get from the station to the party? Walk around in an unknown neighborhood on a cold snowy night? No way…you can't go!* I braced myself for a stiff argument. However, all she said was *OK* and called her friend to say her mother wouldn't let her go. My daughter wasn't stupid—she didn't want to do anything as crazy as traipse around a strange and likely unsafe neighborhood on a dark wintry night. How much nicer, though, it is to blame one's mother for something you don't want to do yourself.

You will not be in on many of the decisions that your older teen daughter will need to make. This is especially true if your daughter has "wheels" (either her own or access to the family car). In any case, some of her decisions you will disapprove of and some will be harmful to her. However, you must always be honest and reasonable with your daughter if you want the communication channels to stay open. Otherwise, if you say "No" too often and without reason, she will no longer come to you for permission or advice but will start covering up some of her activities. As long as she asks permission or tells you of her plans, you have the opportunity to point out the dangers and pitfalls regarding her planned actions. Regardless of whether she furtively disobeyed you or seemed to pay no heed to your warnings, she did hear you and will remember what you said. Thus, whether she's aware of it or not, your advice should guide her (at least most of the time!).

10. INSTILLING RESPONSIBILITY

Allowances & Her Money — Babysitting
Chores — Curfews — Driving — Home Alone
Part-Time Jobs & Volunteering
Technology — Voting

ALLOWANCES & HER MONEY

A **weekly allowance** is a great way for children to learn self-discipline as well as the value of money. If your daughter doesn't have the opportunity to practice self-discipline about buying more movie popcorn or makeup, she is going to find it more difficult to learn self-discipline with respect to drugs, alcohol and sex. Moreover, your daughter should not have to go to you for money on a daily basis nor should her weekend plans be contingent on *your* finances at that time. Control by the purse is no control—when the purse is gone, so is the control. Also, in my view, allowances shouldn't be tied to the doing of routine chores (*see generally* this Chapter below at "Chores") because I believe the very fact of an allowance not only teaches a child how to handle money but also enhances a feeling of self-worth and of being a valued and integral part of the family. In any case, your teen daughter should not have to go to you for money every time she wants to buy another hairband or barrette.

If your daughter is not yet receiving a weekly allowance, start now and endeavor to ensure that the allowance is given freely and on time. It should be given with instructions as to what you expect the money to cover. Your daughter's allowance could cover school lunches, carfare, school supplies and expenses, entertainment, personal items such as makeup, etc. and, if you can afford it, should also be of a sufficient amount to allow your daughter to treat a friend to a slice of pizza once in a while. Obviously, this adds up to a tidy sum and the items to be covered by an allowance should be expanded or reduced in accord with the current level of your finances and your daughter's fiscal maturity.

Consider also whether her allowance will be supplemented through babysitting, other part-time work, and/or from completion of special chores. However, you and she should be in clear agreement as to what expenses "her money" (i.e., her allowance, babysitting money, etc.) is to cover and how much should be saved toward college, a car, or other special something.

Allowances can also give your daughter the opportunity to learn how to maximize her money. My daughter had eagerly looked forward to junior high when she'd be allowed off the school grounds for lunch. All summer, she and her friends saved their money so they could buy lunch out. However, after spending more than $20 on lunch the first three days of school, she announced that eating out was a waste of money. She went back to brown-bagging it (no charge for food from home) and bought lunch out only once a week. Actually, it was a lesson for her friends as well. They worked out a system where they would each buy lunch on a different day. The buyer *du jour* was their ticket to a table at a deli or pizzeria while the others opened up their brown bags. Of course, this system didn't go over very well with the local eateries but my daughter and her friends managed to eat off the school grounds once or twice a week.

Take care not to give your daughter extra money if she overspends during the week and has no money left to go to the movies with her friends on the weekend. Doing so would defeat the purpose of the allowance. You could, however, give her an extra few dollars to spend if she has a friend visiting from out of town or if she plans to go somewhere with a friend whose family has very little. In the latter situation, especially if there is a big income gap between your family and her friend's family, don't front an "extra" so big that it would be embarrassing to the friend. It could be something as simple as treating them both to pizza at the Mall or extra popcorn.

Your daughter should also have a **clothing allowance** (exclusive of special occasion clothing and sport/school uniforms) perhaps three times a year—for school clothes, to take advantage of Black Friday/Christmas sales, and for summer clothes. Discuss your daughter's needs with her and estimate the cost. Add about 10% to cover fads. Be realistic when deciding your daughter's needs. Consider local styles, your budget and how easy a fit she is. For example, a slim, flat-chested teen can easily wear an inexpensive swimsuit but it might be necessary to spend big bucks on a bathing suit if your daughter wears a D-cup. If your daughter's a newbie shopper, go with her the first few times serving as a guide not as critic. Even though mother/daughter shopping trips can be fun your daughter should have the experience of shopping on her own so as to better learn budgeting skills.

How you handle the logistics of her shopping depends on where the stores are, how fiscally mature your daughter is, and how payment will be made. For example, if your daughter is reasonably careful and responsible, you could buy her a prepaid store card with the proviso that if she loses the card, she's out the money—not you. However, if she's a newbie when it comes to shopping for anything on her own, you could drop her off at the Mall and let her pick out what she wants to buy leaving the items at the register awaiting your arrival. In this case, pay for whatever she's bought (providing everything is returnable) and save your comments until you are home. Another alternative would be for your daughter to shop on-line with you reviewing the "shopping cart" for accuracy before entering your charge card info. In this regard, suggest that your daughter shop only on sites that don't charge for returns reminding her that any such charges (as well as any initial shipping charges) will come out of her clothing allowance.

Remember to keep the conflicts between you and your daughter about how she spends "her" money or her clothing allotment to those that concern your daughter's well-being and to skip the small stuff. Give her the freedom to make mistakes as she will learn from them. Your daughter's shopping on her own, using her own or allotted money, will not only improve her monetary skills but give her additional opportunities to enhance her decision-making ability.

Her Money. Sometimes **loans** for major items or fads are appropriate even if you disagree with the intended purchase. For example, maybe all your daughter's peers have pricey western-style leather boots and your daughter is pining away for a pair too. You, of course, either don't have money to spend on such luxuries or think they're just a passing fad and don't want your daughter to waste such a large amount of her money. However, let the decision be hers. If she really wants the boots, loan her the money if you are able to and set up a repayment schedule. She may change her mind completely if she discovers that it will take her more than six months to repay the loan at $5 a week. If she's still adamant about the purchase though, advance the money (if you can afford to) but be firm in collecting the agreed-to weekly payment at the agreed-to time. If she balks, remind her that you're not charging her any interest. Don't waive any loan balance to be a "good guy"—doing so, would void your efforts at teaching her fiscal responsibility. It's best for her to learn how to manage loans and credit charges at home rather than be off at college running up a big charge card bill.

Generally, your daughter should be allowed to purchase what she wants with her money. Sometimes though it is very difficult not to say anything about your daughter's purchases when your family is worried about making the next mortgage payment and your daughter comes home with a pricey tech gizmo or designer jeans that she just purchased with her paycheck from her part-time job. However, unless you had arranged with your daughter that some of her paycheck was to go toward the household or that you expected to borrow money from her, don't get into an argument about her purchase. Agreed that under the circumstances, her purchase was inconsiderate and ill-timed. However, as long as it is her money, she should be allowed to do what she wants with it (excluding illegal purchases such as drugs, cigarettes, booze and the like). Of course, you could express your opinion that the item was a bad buy (if true) or ask why she needed another pair of jeans (also, if true). Further, there's nothing wrong with asking your daughter to contribute money to the household if she has a steady part-time job even if the amount is only $5 a week if your family is having some hard times financially or if you feel in principle that's what she should do.

Notwithstanding the above, we do not live in easy times and you should keep in mind the amount of, and limit as necessary, your daughter's cash on hand particularly if drugs of any sort are easily available at your daughter's school or in your neighborhood. This is especially important if your daughter is not used to handling money or has not yet learned to be discreet about her (or the family's) finances. Your daughter should know not to walk around with too much cash or brag to her friends about how much money she may have on her person or tucked away in her piggy bank. Should your daughter have accumulated more cash than she needs or you believe advisable, have her put her money in a CD (Certificate of Deposit) where the money will earn some interest (minimal though it might be). CDs with their various term lengths are a good place for your daughter to park her savings to be used for special things like a class trip to Washington DC or to go toward college expenses. If you hold your daughter's money for her, either directly as her banker or indirectly (banks usually require parental consent for children under 18 to have bank accounts or CDs in their own name) remember it is her money and return it to her as long as she wants the money for something that is not illegal or dangerous.

BABYSITTING

Babysitting has historically been a good way for adolescent girls to learn responsibility and to earn some money but nowadays it has its headaches. First, of course, you must be sure your daughter is ready for the responsibility. Further, several years ago, it was not uncommon for eleven-year-olds to baby-sit. Today, however, given the current social mores and our litigious society, you should check with a lawyer about your family's liability in the event of an unfortunate mishap while someone else's child is in your daughter's care. Many communities offer classes in baby-sitting for free or at nominal cost and your babysitter-to-be should avail herself of such opportunities with her paying the tab. (If she has no savings, perhaps you can advance her the money as a "small-business loan.")

Assuming your daughter is of lawful babysitting age and that your daughter has not misrepresented her experience or qualifications, do not presume that the family she will sit for will tell her everything she needs to know and do. Thus, before your daughter leaves for any baby-sitting job, she should let you know the name and address of the family and when and how she will be getting home. Establish a checklist of items that the family is to tell her—where and how they can be reached, emergency phone numbers, names and phone numbers of doctors, relatives and neighbors, the child's bedtime and bedtime routines, whether any pet needs special care, etc. Remind your daughter about not opening the door to anyone or to give out the family name and address to anyone and to not even tell her friends where she will be babysitting—you never know who among them (or a friend of theirs) might be up to some mischief. You should also assure yourself that if there are any guns in the house that they are locked safely away. Keep you cell phone handy in case your daughter needs some advice.

Regardless of the parents' instructions, you should also caution your daughter not to walk the dog if it means leaving the child alone, not to bathe an infant or a toddler, and not to use the stove. It's better to clean up after the dog than to risk an accident to the child and the baby will not develop a rash from missing a bath nor will the child suffer malnutrition from eating a cheese sandwich for dinner. Tell your daughter that you don't doubt her capabilities but there is no reason to take unnecessary risks.

How your daughter will get home is a major concern these days because so many mothers are single. While you can check out the people who ask your daughter to sit personally and via the Internet, social media and neighborhood acquaintances (and this is something that you absolutely must do before your daughter ever goes to a new family's home), you cannot check out the boyfriends of the single mom who hired your daughter. Unless you personally know the boyfriend and his character is acceptable to you, insist that the woman, not her date, take your daughter home. If the woman cannot or will not, pick up your daughter yourself and, if you cannot, your daughter should decline the sitting job.

The foregoing may sound overcautious but remember it may be the woman's first date with the man and she may not know him very well either. If she doesn't want to leave the man alone with her children, your daughter should certainly not be alone with him. If your daughter objects to your checking out the people who ask her to sit, or to your picking her up, explain that you don't run the world and you have absolutely no idea, for example, of the man's drinking habits. I do not want to scare you nor should you scare your daughter but you must convey to your daughter that it is not appropriate for her, or for you to allow her, to put herself in a vulnerable position—alone in an automobile with someone unknown to you and perhaps barely known by the mother. Unfortunately, married men too can be sexual perverts. If after meeting the parents, you feel any uneasiness about their character, trust your instincts and have your daughter decline the job. Remind your daughter that you are not preventing her from babysitting. All you are doing is your job—looking out for her safety. Plenty of other sitting jobs will come along her way.

Other questions arise concerning babysitting such as whether your daughter should sit on school nights or how late she should be allowed to sit. Unless you are involved in chauffeuring her to and from her sitting jobs, let her set her own schedule and curfew. She needs to discover her own limits. She is not going to want to be too tired to see her friends or slog half-asleep through the school day. After two or three late-night jobs which interfere with her life, she will turn down future late ones but if she can manage to stay out late and get up without being tired, terrific. Remember that she is the one who needs to get up in the morning and function well during the day.

Your daughter's babysitting can be a big nuisance for you. It can interfere with dinner plans and family activities. But it is worth it. Babysitting will help your daughter to learn to stand up for herself. She will learn to tell parents that she was hired to sit, not to be a maid. She will learn to collect promised money. She will learn to say no to adults who are always late. She will also learn more about how other people live and that differences in lifestyles are not necessarily better or worse but merely different.

CHORES

Household chores generally fall into two groups: those that need to be done inside the home and those that need to be done outside. Often a child who is vehemently opposed to doing one type of chore will not mind doing the other. Everyone who lives in a household should be responsible for its upkeep. Participating in family chores reinforces a sense of responsibility to, and a place in, the family. However, don't *ask* your daughter to do something. If you ask and she says *No*, you have the beginnings of a confrontation. It is better to tell her (nicely, of course) to do something. For example, *please take out the garbage* is better than asking *Do you want to take out the garbage?* You can't expect a "yes" from anyone to that question, least of all a teenager.

Some children rebel at doing any chores. Don't respond with a tirade about the ills of sloth and laziness. You needn't preach to your daughter that Life will beat her down—Life itself will do that from time to time without any help from you. Few people have a trust fund and most of us will need to work to get by but that doesn't mean that one's work need be unpleasant. So, if chores need to be done, it doesn't follow that your daughter must do the ones she finds most distasteful. Use a little imagination. For example, your daughter may not like to do anything that involves stepping out of the house once she is home. A whole afternoon of sulking may result if all she'd had to do was wheel the garbage bin down the driveway. She will however with only a dramatic sigh or two, fold laundry or empty the dishwasher—anything as long as she doesn't need to walk out the door. Conversely, your daughter might be the type that will go out anywhere, anytime—as long as she can wash and blow-dry her hair first!

The point is for you to convey to your daughter that she is a member of various communities—her school, her home, a camp bunkhouse, her volleyball team—and every community member has a responsibility to share in its burdens so as to share in its benefits. As much as you can, enable your daughter to participate in her various communities, including the home, in a way that is fulfilling and enjoyable to her, or at the least, not unduly unpleasant. Every community has tasks that no one wants to do. In my home, cleaning the blinds was considered the worst chore as it took a lot of persistent effort to remove all the soot they attracted. When something unpleasant or difficult needs to be done, first affirm the unpleasantness or difficulty of the task and then see if it could be shared or if taking turns would be appropriate. Also, for the really hard stuff, you might tell your daughter you owe her one. In any event, don't interfere if that when it's your daughter's turn to do something distasteful, she pays a sibling to do the chore for her. Absent a gross misuse of power by your teen, unless the sibling, not you, feels an unfair bargain was struck, stay out of the negotiations.

If your daughter procrastinates about doing her chores, try putting a time frame around the job to be done. Instead of badgering her about her promise to clean out the fish tank, ask what time she's planning to clean it out so you'll know when to be ready to take her shopping for her soccer uniform. This way, you've let her know what's expected of her but that the chore is under her control. Perhaps a fish or two might suffer the consequences of her procrastination if she fails to do the chore but she's the one that will have to show up at soccer without a uniform. Don't make her fish tank your problem. If you're the one who winds up cleaning the fish tank more than a few times and it's her fish tank, ditch the tank and return the fish for adoption. The trick here is to keep consequences appropriate to the task and to stick to what you say.

Sometimes your daughter will be under extra pressure due to participation in a school play, final exams, or a special research project. At such times, ask the other family members to pitch in and take over some of her chores. It's right for her to want to concentrate so as to do the best she can. Also, young women have a right to learn that sometimes they too deserve a right to come first or to special attention (and not because of how they look). Don't worry about her becoming spoiled—there will be plenty of opportunities for her to take over for you when your life is pressured and hers is not.

CURFEWS *(see also Chapter 13 at "Dating")*

Why set curfews? Why do you want your daughter home at a special hour? Are you worried about her getting enough sleep? Are you worried about safety? About sex? Does requiring her to be home at a certain time really guarantee her safety or virginity? I know you don't like to worry. You would love it if your daughter never ventured out at night, never rode around in a car with her friends, never did anything risky.

Treat a curfew as a safety measure—not as a test of who's boss. If your daughter is old enough to be out at night, she is old enough to start taking responsibility for herself. Thus, allow your daughter to suggest an appropriate curfew hour. This does not mean that she should be allowed to come home any time she wants, but as long as she has *a safe way to return home and the time she sets is reasonable in relation to the activity,* there is no reason to disallow the time she chooses. If, for example, your daughter calls from the Mall on a Saturday night and asks if she can see the 10:00pm show because the 8:00pm one is sold out and she still has a way of getting home safely, why not say yes. Even if it's a school night— if she can go to sleep at 1:00am and still function, more power to her. After all, if she can't make such a basic decision as to how much sleep she needs, she's going to find it very difficult to make other decisions affecting her well-being. (If you're still waking up your daughter in the morning, buy her an alarm clock. It's her job to get herself to school or work on time, not yours. Remember too that when it comes to teens using cell phone alarms, it's amazing how often the phone disappears or runs out of battery power.)

The curfew time should be based on safety—not the hour. What's the planned activity? How comfortable are you about her date? How old is your daughter? How old are the party-goers? How well do you know the hosting parents? How is your daughter to get home? Will she be alone or with others? And if others, exactly who with? If, however, you are a real worrywart and don't think anyone should ever stay out after 11:00pm except for special occasions, try a little persuasion. Explain how much *you worry* about unsafe streets or unsafe drivers. Point out that many people who are out late at night probably have had too much to drink and are likely to be rowdy on the street or dangerous on the road. Your daughter is no fool, and as long as you assure her that is not her you doubt, but others, she might surprise you and readily agree to an earlier curfew.

My daughter learned from experience not to stay out very late. She and three of her friends decided they couldn't go on living unless they saw "The Rocky Horror Picture Show," a cult-like movie with only a midnight showing. I offered to meet them after the show (the girls were to sleep over at our house) but they wouldn't hear of it. Since the bus stopped in front of the theater and also in front of our apartment building and thinking that there's safety in numbers and that lots of people would be leaving the theater at the same time, I acquiesced. I expected the girls to be home about 2:30am but it was almost 3:00am when they finally arrived. *You must have had a long wait for the bus,* I ventured. Silence. Then a squeak—*We stopped for a slice of pizza first. At this time of night?* I exclaimed and chastised them for not coming straight home. Well, it seemed they weren't too thrilled about being out so late either. They discovered for themselves that the world can be a seedy place in the wee hours of the morning. The streets smelled of garbage and urine, the bums were out in full force (as were the police), and sirens blasted from all directions. Thereafter, my daughter never came home later than 1:00am even when she lived at home after college.

I realize that few cities go twenty-four hours a day—that your community may shut down at 10:00pm and that many drunk drivers have started their dangerous treks home well before that time. Thus, as aforesaid, the curfew hour should be set for safety and be reasonable in relation to your comfort level with the hosts, your daughter's friends, the planned activity and its location and community mores, and not set arbitrarily.

That being said, you certainly have a right to act for your convenience and peace of mind—just don't pass off these reasons as something else. If you want your daughter home early, say so. Simply ask her to be home by such and such time because you have an important meeting the next day or are worried about something and don't want any additional stress. If you are reasonable in your request, it is likely that she will agree to come home earlier than she originally wished.

It's also completely understandable that you don't want your daughter out late because of worry about sex, alcohol or drugs. Teenage wrongdoing is much more likely to start after the party's over than before. Your job is to know what's going on in your community and what's a reasonable time for a party or basketball-plus-pizza to end. If for example, your daughter suggests a 1:00am curfew but somehow lets you know that the party is to end before midnight, she is sending signals to you that her boyfriend is pressuring her for sex and that she wants you to be a scapegoat. In that case, tell her in no uncertain terms that she is to be home by the time that you consider appropriate. Give her the excuse she needs to come home early. (*See also* Chapter 13 at "Dating" and Chapter 14—SEX.)

If your daughter refuses to set a reasonable curfew and balks if you set one, explain that you need to know when to start worrying. Point out that it is your job to make sure she's in a safe environment and that you need to know where she'll be and when she's expected home so if she hasn't returned by the selected hour, you'll know exactly when to call the police and what to tell them. You may also be the type of person who needs your sleep but feels you must wait up until your daughter comes home. If so, try a friend's solution. Instead of waiting up for her daughter's safe return, she would go to sleep and set the alarm for the time her daughter was expected home. That way, she got some sleep and also knew exactly when to start worrying.

DRIVING

Whether or not you own a car, your daughter should learn to drive and have the opportunity to drive often. Unless a person lives in big city with mass transit like New York or San Francisco, driving is a necessary skill in our society and is likely to be so for the next ten years. Unfortunately, many women who know how to drive are fearful of driving in the snow, at night, or for long distances because of having deferred such activities to their fathers, husbands or boyfriends so often. Even aside from the possibility of divorce, most women will live on their own and/or work outside their home at some time during their lives. Limited driving skills can seriously interfere with a woman's career or social life and also restrict where she may wish to live.

Once your daughter has her license, the family car should be shared in the same way other family possessions are shared provided your daughter is a careful driver. If she isn't, use of the car should be restricted until your daughter exhibits careful driving habits such as paying attention, not texting or using the phone while driving, never getting behind the wheel if she's been drinking (even if only a half-glass of beer) or doing drugs (even if only a puff of a marijuana joint), or can barely stay awake for having crammed for an exam the night before. If your daughter is a careless or know-it-all driver, she should not be permitted to drive, licensed or not. There is no reason for her to endanger her life or the lives of others. Have her take another Driver's Ed course--perhaps one geared toward adults rather than teens if she's embarrassed to repeat the local high school course. Then ride with her until you are satisfied that she fully appreciates the fact that an automobile can be a lethal weapon.

It is said that a person has to drive 10,000 miles over varied roads in all kinds of weather to become a good driver. Thus, even though it is unlikely that your daughter will reach the 10,000-mile mark while she's still living at home, let her take the wheel as much as possible. Let her drive you to Yoga, pick up Grandma from the airport, navigate Mall parking lots, and slosh through rain and sleet in the dark of night. Spend some time driving around unknown neighborhoods and negotiating dangerous intersections. You need not be the only person to ride shotgun—enlist other family members to assist. She needs to know how to handle a car whether the front seat passenger is tall or short, fat or thin. Your daughter should also know what all the dials on the steering wheel and dashboard mean and of course religiously obey any restrictions on her teen license. And most of all, she should never talk or text on her cell phone while driving.

I don't think it's a good idea to make your daughter's use of the car contingent on her completing her homework or doing certain chores. The homework or chores might get done, but you don't want to take the risk that your daughter would drive too fast just to get back at you for some perceived injustice. You don't want to win the battle of the painted porch and lose the war by a death or accident resulting from an angrily driven car. When she's able to drive solo, whether it's her own car or yours, she should pay for the gas she uses and contribute at least some money to the cost of the car's upkeep and insurance even if you can afford to pay for everything and even if her contribution is as little as $5 now and then.

Under no circumstances should you indulge any child who is a careless driver by buying a car for such child in return for promises to be careful if it was his or her own car, a new car, etc. Your daughter must prove to you that she is not reckless *before* she has use of the family car or gets her own. If she insists on buying her own car and she has the money to do so, don't put your reckless driver on your insurance policy. Hopefully, she'll think twice about her poor driving skills when she finds out what insurance and other costs are.

HOME ALONE

There might come a time when you need to be out of town and your daughter will insist on staying home alone. In the past, you have been able to convince her to sleep over at a friend's house or have a relative stay with her. This time, though, before you put your foot down and call Great Aunt Mable or cancel your trip, consider her desires. Your daughter is so anxious to prove to herself and you how grown up she is. Also, staying alone and being responsible for oneself, even if only for short periods of time, is an important aspect to becoming an adult. It won't be long before your daughter goes off to be a camp counselor or a college coed. She will have to make decisions and choices at such times not only with respect to her own behavior but also in assessing the behavior and motives of strangers. Like with everything else, experience helps.

Perhaps your daughter is ready to stay home alone assuming, of course, she is of legal age to do so. (If not, you might find yourself afoul of child welfare laws so check the laws in your state.) Consider how long you will be away and whether or not your daughter is generally trustworthy. Before acquiescing consider too the safety of your neighborhood and home, whether any neighbors will be around, and if younger siblings are involved.

For example, I allowed my teen daughters to stay alone for a few days. In reaching my decision, I considered that though my daughters' relationship with each other usually consisted of grunts and grimaces, a strong bond of sisterhood existed between them so I knew they would look out for each other. Also, our home was relatively safe as we lived in a good neighborhood in an apartment building guarded by doormen. Further, there were always plenty of neighbors around. However, before I gave the OK, I discussed the situation with a woman who had children the same age as mine and whose opinion I respected. She agreed that she too would leave her daughters alone even though her building had no doorman but only under the *proviso* that her children would not use the stove. I told her my stove worked fine—it was the toaster whose performance was erratic. (I put the toaster in the pantry and declared it off limits before I left.)

If you leave your daughter alone, whether it is for a few days or a few hours, make sure that she knows what to do in an emergency beyond calling 911. Leave phone numbers of neighbors, doctors, family friends and relatives handy. (They should be permanently and prominently listed someplace anyway.) Leave a number where you can be reached in the event your cell phone battery dies or cell service is unavailable. Make sure she knows never to open the door to anyone or to give out the family name and address to unknown callers or in response to random e-mail/social media inquiries. Tell her she is not to let anyone (including her friends) know she is staying alone. Don't arrange for any repair persons to call while you are away. Cancel the gardener. Put away the sharp knives and disconnect any temperamental appliances. Lock the liquor cabinet. Make sure all guns are left unloaded and under lock and key and that any ammunition is stored elsewhere, also under lock and key. Tell a trusted friend or neighbor where you will be going, how you can be reached, and when you're expected to return. Leave enough cash for a taxi to the hospital, a good friend, a relative, or the police station.

If you decide your daughter may not stay alone, take care to explain to her that it is not her ability or maturity you doubt (if true) but other circumstances. If these circumstances can be alleviated and you will not let her stay by herself even if it's just for an overnight, your fears may be somewhat irrational. However, you are entitled to be irrational at times. Parenthood does not require you to turn gray so your daughter can prove herself but it does require you to be honest with your daughter. However, if you really are holding on too tightly, it may do *you* some good to let go.

PART-TIME JOBS & VOLUNTEERING

Generally, depending on the state, teens between 14- and 18-years-old need working papers before they can legally work. However, that doesn't mean they can get jobs. Employers seem loathe to hire anyone younger than sixteen or even eighteen. Moreover, many of the jobs formerly available to young teens such as working as a file clerk at a small law or insurance office or pulling pin feathers from chickens at a local deli no longer exist due to modernization. Further, because of liability issues, some homeowners have become wary of hiring the kid next door to mow the lawn or shovel snow. Not-for-profits have become equally cautious when it comes to teen volunteers. These days, it's not unusual for the local food bank or pet shelter to require volunteers to be at least sixteen years old.

Finding a job for your daughter whether to earn money, increase her self-esteem, and/or provide her with alternatives to unsavory behavior, can be a real challenge. First, have your daughter explore the age-old neighborhood standbys such as babysitting and dog-walking. Next, suggest she check your local library—it may have volunteer programs for teens as young as fourteen. Political offices will often accept anyone willing to help with mailings. Assisted living and nursing homes might appreciate your daughter coming by one or two times a week to read to its residents. Your place of worship might need some clerical help or an extra helper at Sunday School.

Finding a paying job for your young teen daughter is more difficult. Check with your friends, neighbors and relatives to see if they could provide some work for pay for your daughter. Perhaps you have a neighbor who mentioned that she wanted to scan all her photographs onto a thumb drive but doesn't have the time or patience to do so. She might be willing to pay your daughter to do that. Or you might have a friend who needs a proof-reader or another who needs help cleaning her Airbnb rental or giving her dog a bath. Also, my guess is that some folks will gladly pay a nimble teen to wash the insides of their car windows, particularly the windshield and back window.

TECHNOLOGY

Your family should stay as up-to-date with technology as your budget will allow. Computers are obsolete the day you buy them but an every-few-years update should keep your system reasonably current. You don't need to buy the latest tech gizmo each and every time but you do need to give your daughter the tools to compete in the 21st Century.

Computer use and jargon should be second nature to her just as should be the multiplication tables. Every job in the future will need computer know-how. This is true whether your daughter plans on becoming a welder or a lawyer. Don't rely on the schools to give your daughter enough hands-on experience. You want your daughter to fully understand computers and the latest technological gadgets and their capabilities, not just be able to push a button or two to get an answer to a question. She should know how to do a power point presentation, make videos for U-Tube, transfer data from one media source to another, prepare charts, etc.—all of which will be useful for her in high school and college. Make sure she knows too that just because something is stated as fact on any electronic gizmo doesn't make it true and that she should always check more than one source for information.

You too should stay reasonably aware of current upgrades and advancements in computer and related media technology as that will allow you to better guide your daughter through the dangers and limitations of the Internet and social media use. It might also be a good bonding opportunity for you and your daughter to check out the latest technology at a store that specializes in various computer wizardry.

VOTING

Many eighteen-year-olds don't bother to vote or to even register. Voting is an area where nagging is not only appropriate but insufficient. As with so much else, your daughter needs you to be a role model. Thus, if you only vote in presidential elections or don't vote at all, take the time to set a good example by becoming aware of local and national issues and cast your ballot. Voting need not be time consuming as in the past. Many states allow voting by mail even if you will not be "absent" from the polling place on Election Day.

If you remind your daughter that now that she is eighteen (or will be by Election Day), she should register to vote and she responds that she will *"when I get around to it"* or that *"one vote doesn't matter,"* say no more. *Act* instead. Get the registration form for her. Even fill it out for her if necessary. Follow her around the house with a pen until she signs it. Mail it for her. If need be, when Election Day comes, go with her to the polls.

If she's away at college, help her arrange for an absentee ballot. Voting is so important that the goal is not who gets the registration form or fills it out but that your daughter assume some of the responsibilities of citizenship by being informed and casting her ballot.

It is important to impress upon your daughter that the only way to maintain freedom is to exercise the most basic right inherent therein—that is, the right to vote. If you haven't already done so, next time you vote take your daughter into the voting booth with you so she will realize the process is not mysterious or intimidating. Society cannot afford an apathetic generation. You need to impress upon your daughter that she has a stake in her future and in our complex society. Voting is one way she can be heard by the people who make the decisions that will have a major impact on her life.

If your daughter has an interest or concern about a particular public issue, suggest that she volunteer on behalf of the interest group or candidate—she doesn't need to be of voting age to do either. Even if she only volunteers because she has nothing else to do on Friday nights—or because she thinks the candidate is cute (or a certain other volunteer is)—she may be impressed enough to become committed to the workings of our political process. The charismatic candidate has brought many a young person from complete apathy to political activism. Depending on your daughter's interests, use issues that are (or should be) of particular concern to her such as cutbacks in education or environmental concerns or even Social Security and Medicare if you point out to her that unless the systems are appropriately stabilized, your old-age may hamper her ability to send *her* children to college. Even if your daughter's efforts do not result in a win for the cause or candidate at hand, she will have had the satisfaction that comes with being part of a team effort, win or lose. And think how proud she'll feel if her cause or candidate had won.

11. HEALTH, HYGIENE & SAFETY

Assertiveness Training — Bad Habits — Cleanliness
Cosmetic Surgery — Counseling — Exercise
Menstruation — Nutrition — Party Food & Drink
Physical Development — Staying Safe
Weight (Anorexia/Obesity)

ASSERTIVENESS TRAINING *(see also Chapter 5 at "Timidity")*

We still bring up girls differently than boys. Our sons are encouraged to speak out and to stand up for their beliefs and for themselves. However, we still encourage our daughters to always be polite and to not make waves. The effects of such ingrained politeness came to the fore in Taylor Swift's lawsuit against a groper during a photo shoot when Ms. Swift's mom reported that Ms. Swift agonized over the fact that she had thanked the groper for the photo instead of calling him out. And in promoting her book about her election loss, Hillary Clinton reported that she wanted to call then-candidate Trump a "creep" for moving in on "her space" during the second Presidential Debate but thought it would be too impolite to do so. Men in our society in similar circumstances would not have thought twice about verbally defending themselves. Further, physical aggression by males is often sanctioned while even verbal assertiveness by a female is all too often considered a big "no-no." Thus, at best, our daughters often grow up to be deferential and fearful of offending; at worst, they grow up accepting verbal and physical abuse. (*See also* Chapter 3 at "Sexual Predators.")

Books like "The Rules" and "Men are from Mars, Women are from Venus" encourage women to act in traditional submissive roles. In The Rules, women are advised to keep their thoughts to themselves if they want to catch their man while in Mars vs. Venus, women are advised not to speak to the men in their lives while they are in their caves of silence so as not to incur their wrath. The pages of Betty Friedan's "Feminine Mystique" must be curling in despair over such advice. Deborah Tannen, in her book, "Talking from 9 to 5," articulates the dilemma women confront in a society dominated by a male value system. Dr. Tannen's studies found that women in business who preface their ideas with "I *think* we should do such and such…" are perceived as tentative and unsure while women who say "We *should* do such and such…" are perceived as aggressive.

However, don't shy away from encouraging your daughter to be aggressive about things that she wants or believes in. She shouldn't be verbally abusive but it is true that *the squeaky wheel gets the most grease* and that *if you don't toot your own horn, nobody else will*. It's also true that aggressive women are not always liked but they are respected. And, they get things done.

At every opportunity, encourage your daughter to voice her opinion—at mealtime, while chauffeuring her to or from school, or scanning newspaper headlines, etc. Ask her what she thinks about the news, politics, the weather, whatever. Even if you're only answered with grunts, keep asking. And if she does volunteer a response that may be totally out of whack with your beliefs, don't belittle her ideas. You may challenge them, of course. A *bona fide* challenge will help her to reach inside herself for the answers. There is nothing wrong with a good argument based on intellectual thought. It will broaden both of you even if you agree to disagree. You will at least have heard another point of view and you will get to know your daughter better and she will learn that her beliefs have some validity.

Make sure your daughter is called upon in class. Studies have shown that commencing with the middle school years, boys volunteer answers more than girls and teachers tend to call on male students more often than on female students. Visit with your daughter's teachers and insist that they call on your daughter even if she doesn't raise her hand. Make sure though that the teacher knows to lay back when a child seems to cringe at the thought of speaking in class. If you perceive that your daughter has a problem in this area, perhaps you could arrange with the teacher for your daughter to be called upon for simple "answers" rather than for "explanations." This will give your daughter an opportunity to develop confidence in speaking out.

Other ways your daughter can develop more self-confidence is through participating in volunteer activities, sports, writing, art, etc. Help your daughter find a way to excel in a particular area and build on that. By excellence, I do not mean that she need be better than everybody else, but an area where she shines to herself. It may be that your daughter's particular expertise is understanding how power generates electricity or knowing every song sung by the teen pop star of the day. If so, maybe your daughter could enlighten you on the use of tidal action to produce energy or perhaps she could do a school paper describing how music trends reflect the socio-political climate of the day.

A positive, assertive mindset will enable your daughter to not only recognize opportunities, but to take advantage of them. The more ingrained your daughter's self-confidence becomes, the more likely it will carry over into her adult years whether it's going for a PhD, asking for a job promotion, or standing up to sexual harassment and she will not grow into a wallflower ready to wilt at the first sign of a breeze. Instead, she will stand sure and sturdy and bloom as bold and unabashedly as a sunflower.

BAD HABITS

Your daughter may have a bad habit such as biting her fingernails or twirling her hair. Nag, threaten, rant and rave as you will but the nail biting and hair twirling will continue. Bribery may work but usually only temporarily. The solution must be up to your daughter because it is her problem, not yours. Your problem is that you feel like climbing the walls every time you see her chewing her nails. Yes, it is irritating to watch but don't blow these types of things out of proportion or let them darken your relationship with your daughter. It's fine for you to offer suggestions how she may go about solving her problem but let her come up with the solution to it. Then, offer all the support and encouragement that you can.

You could, for example, encourage your daughter to set a goal such as not biting her nails for three months and, if she succeeds, to buy herself a present. Perhaps she would like a fancy lens for her camera but has been hesitant to spend so much of her savings on one because it seems so extravagant. Let her decide on her reward. After all, if she cures herself of nail biting, she will have learned that she has control over herself and she will have every reason to feel terrific. She need not share her accomplishment with anyone else or give anyone else credit for it. Every time she uses her self-reward, she will feel proud of herself. Most important though is that the self-reward and her nice nails will be a reminder that she had a problem that she alone solved. That self-knowledge will hold her in good stead for the rest of her life.

If your daughter fails in her efforts, be supportive and suggest that she try again a few months later or perhaps try for a lesser goal (and smaller self-reward) such as no nail biting for three weeks with a professional gel manicure as the prize. The important thing is for her to know that, ultimately, she is the person in charge of herself and her life.

CLEANLINESS

A short time ago you may have wondered if your adolescent daughter every really showered. Sure, the curtain was wet but the soap was dry and the washcloth untouched. Now she's always in the shower—the soap may still be dry but you know her hair is clean. She's also spending an inordinate number of hours in the bathroom examining her face. The medicine cabinet is stocked with every available acne cream known to man and she's only had one pimple so far. However, despite all your admonitions and threats to pick up after herself, dirty socks and undies rarely make it to the hamper but frilly blouses that need hand-washing do.

You finally realize that her habits so far have nothing to do with personal cleanliness. To her, cleanliness is still only a matter of how she looks. She doesn't yet think of her body as getting dirty unless she's been rolling in mud or has just returned from soccer practice. As she gets older, though, she discovers that bodies too need to be cleaned on a regular basis. She begins to notice teens who smell bad or who never seem to change their clothes. She becomes loath to share a pizza with a friend whose fingernails are always dirty. It dawns on her that showers are for more than washing one's hair. Now when you enter the bathroom after your daughter has showered, you are overcome by aromas of lemon shampoo and vanilla bath splash. The air is so thick with talc you can barely breathe. There are powdery footprints marking her trail through the house. And you now need as many towels as the local Hilton.

Also, sometime during your daughter's early teens, she might be "sneaky" clean. Despite the frequency with which personal products are advertised on television and via the Internet and social media, your daughter will put deodorant on in her closet because you are not supposed to know she has begun using it. As a matter of fact, she travels with a suitcase between her room and the bathroom. She is not to be seen even carrying a bra lest anyone know she's wearing one. She is so shy about her person she won't even admit to liking a special brand of shampoo. (Don't worry—enjoy it while you can since once she gets over this phase, the cost of her favored brands of soap, deodorant, shampoo and mousse can cause some real budget worries!)

Your daughter may also be so shy that disposing of sanitary napkins while in school will be a real problem for her. Be sensitive to her situation. Ignore her stained underwear. She knows she needs to change her pads more often but due to school budget cuts, school over-crowding, gangs and/or drug use, the restrooms in many middle and senior high schools cannot be used with any degree of privacy or expectation of cleanliness. Be tactful when she expresses embarrassment about carrying extra pads with her. Spend the extra dollar or two and buy the individually wrapped pads which she can squish down at the bottom of her backpack. After all, she might have to fish through the pack for a pencil and she'd die of embarrassment if somebody "*knew.*" (*See* this Chapter below at "Menstruation.")

As your daughter becomes more comfortable with her physical development, her shyness and self-consciousness will disappear. If, however, she should be using a deodorant and isn't, or is still wearing knee socks to the beach to cover her hairy legs, buy her the appropriate toiletries and leave them on her dresser. If she uses the items fine—but make no comment. If she doesn't or verbally balks at using them, let it go for a while. Try again in a month or so but if after a few attempts, she still hasn't started using a deodorant despite the fact that she needs to, tell her so. It may be that your daughter is truly the earthy type and will defy all conventions; however, more likely, your daughter's denial of her maturing body is her way of expressing normal fears of growing up. Acknowledge your daughter's concerns and remind her that there are some advantages to being an adult—no curfews, no pop quizzes, you get to meet lots of interesting people, become a mother, see whatever movie you want, travel the world—whatever works. You want your daughter to be excited about reaching maturity. Perhaps, unwittingly, she has gotten the impression that adulthood is all about paying bills and worries.

COSMETIC SURGERY

Much of your daughter's confidence depends on how she appears to herself not on how she actually looks. While the majority of girls develop into at least passably attractive young women, it might be difficult for your daughter to believe that she will grow into one. This is an area where a little bit of luck and some creativity are helpful. I know of twin (not identical) sisters, one of whom always appeared much more attractive than the other. One Halloween, the plain girl was made-up and dressed to look like a "lady of the evening." Reserving comment on her choice of costume, the result was that she looked absolutely gorgeous. Nobody (except maybe her mother) could believe the metamorphosis. That girl got so much confidence from knowing that she'd be pretty when she grew up that she was able to move out from under her sister's shadow and become her own person. She was so much more confident of herself that she started doing better in school and making her own friends.

Perhaps though no amount of make-up or style of dress can hide or camouflage a facial disfigurement or distortion. It's true that we all shouldn't have to be model pretty or storybook beautiful but, rightly or wrongly, so much of how we feel about ourselves depends on how others treat us. Accordingly, if your daughter has a feature that brings negative comments—perhaps an over-large nose, ears that stick straight out, grossly pockmarked skin—see a cosmetic surgeon as soon as your daughter reaches physical maturity so as to find if, how, and when her looks may be improved upon. Ditto re fixing buck or crooked teeth.

We live in a time where looks matter. Pictures of us are everywhere—they're on Facebook, in school year books, on resumes, on charge cards, on driver licenses and passports, in ads seeking work as a real estate or insurance agent, etc. Moreover, even jobs that used to be performed in front of small audiences are now performed on a worldwide stage. Remember Marcia Clark, the prosecuting attorney in the O.J. Simpson Murder Trial? I wonder how being judged on her appearance on a daily basis impacted her ability to function and perform as an attorney. I think of all the time that she must have spent on keeping herself fit for the camera—time that could have been spent preparing for the case. I'm not criticizing her but the truth is that the better we look, the more we're respected. Can you imagine how much more difficult it would have been for Ms. Clark had she looked like Eleanor Roosevelt? As it was, Mrs. Roosevelt, despite being admired world-wide for having gotten the United Nations to pass a Universal Declaration of Human Rights, was greatly caricatured because of her looks. Not only do personal disfigurements cause grief and humiliation to the person who bears them but I cannot help but wonder how much greater Mrs. Roosevelt's impact would have been had the reporters and cartoonists of the time not had such an easy target for ridicule and caricature. On the other hand, because of her looks, it was easy for Princess Di to quickly call attention to the human suffering caused by unexploded mines.

Both Princess Di and Mrs. Roosevelt were beautiful within and neither outer beauty nor the lack of it guaranteed either woman personal happiness. Beauty will not guarantee your daughter's happiness either. However, being bereft of any distracting or humiliating feature will free your daughter up to concentrate on things outside of herself. Most importantly, young women who are not self-conscious about their looks will feel a lot freer to speak out. Confidence gained from not having elephantine ears or some such thing will allow your daughter to assert herself in class, to stand up to a date or a boss, to voice her opinion in public.

Before you approach the subject with your daughter, get the facts. First make sure that it is not your ideal of beauty or need for perfection that is propelling the decision about cosmetic surgery. Seek the advice of your family doctor or your daughter's guidance counselor. Your family doctor can recommend board-certified plastic surgeons in your area. Generally, cosmetic surgery is not covered by insurance but there may be a medical reason for the procedure. You won't know unless you ask. Your daughter may balk at the suggestion. She may feel so self-conscious about her appearance that she's concerned what her friends would say or she may pooh-pooh the idea entirely as too bourgeois. Don't force the issue—if she's not ready while in high school, the summer before or right after her first year of college might be a better time.

The important thing is that your daughter be attractive regardless of any disfigurement. Wearing clothes that are right for her, being neat and clean, having a ready smile and a pleasant personality is the key. I do believe though that the more attractive a person is—and I don't mean beautiful or gorgeous—but pleasant to be with and decently groomed, the easier life is for such person. Thus, I believe that if your daughter has a huge mole at the tip of her nose or some other disfigurement, consider cosmetic surgery so that people focus on your daughter and not on any facial deformity.

You might think I'm making too much of how one looks, but on a personal note, I discovered for myself that the more beautiful I became *outside*, the more beautiful I became *inside*. I was never one much for makeup and tended toward dowdiness in dress. One day, when I was in my early 40s, a friend and former model told me I looked like a hag and she was going to make me over. Anyway, I went from gray-speckled mouse-brown to hair streaked with golden blonde, exchanged little pearl earrings for glamorous golden drops, glossed my lips, blushed my cheeks, darkened my stockings, heightened my heels and shortened my skirts. Lo and behold, extra slices of ham and turkey appeared in my Deli sandwiches; the coffee vender added a packet of cream cheese with my morning bagel for free; I was offered seats on the subway; and snooty sales clerks even stopped ignoring me. All this attention made me feel better and I actually became a nicer person. While you can't make your daughter talented or smart or beautiful, you can help her be attractive and nice to be around and that's a good start toward her success in whatever path she chooses.

COUNSELING

This book discusses fairly typical female adolescent behavior. It is not meant to be a substitute for professional counseling if there is an indication that your daughter is in need of it. Probably everyone could benefit from some outside help at one time or another but don't threaten your daughter with it. You demean her and yourself every time you say that she's crazy because she did such and such and that you're going to take her to a psychiatrist every time she does something foolish. You also demean her and yourself every time you offer to provide psychiatric assistance for a routine and ordinary failure.

Of course, if you believe your daughter has problems that she is unable to handle even with your help, don't hesitate to get professional assistance. In such case, simply explain to your daughter that it is not a punishment or a disgrace to seek outside counseling. Say that, as a parent, it is your job to help her and she has a problem that is beyond your ability to handle. Arranging for her to visit a psychiatrist or psychologist, for example, is no different than taking her to a doctor for a broken leg or paying for her allergy injections. If, however, you berate her by reminding her that no one else in the family needs counseling or make her feel guilty about the expense, she may refuse to go or be totally uncooperative during the visit. If you have a positive attitude about the matter, she is more likely to have one also and will, therefore, be able to receive the maximum benefit from the counseling.

A friend's twelve-year-old niece was having trouble dealing with her parents' divorce and the subsequent sale of the family home and move to another city. The girl became extremely difficult to manage. She was also verbally abusive to her mother and took to twirling her hair to the point that a bald spot had developed. Perhaps the parents could have managed their break-up better. Perhaps the girl was using the divorce as an excuse for her obnoxious behavior. Neither is the issue. The girl needed help. Wisely, the parents, instead of each trying to blame the other for their daughter's harmful behavior or denying the existence of it, sought counseling. Perhaps the parents should have acted sooner but at least they did act before the girl got into trouble. In any event, the parents' positive attitude concerning their daughter's problem reassured the girl as to their love for her and gave her the support she needed to be able to benefit from professional guidance.

Should you seek counseling for your daughter and, in doing so, the counselor advises that you too or another family member should either participate in the counseling or be counseled separately, listen to the counselor's advice. Don't take such advice as a put-down of your parenting skills or of your family. Often family members, though well-meaning, sometimes get into a pattern of behavior that is harmful to all. It takes an objective view of such behavior to identify it. Once identified, everyone can work on modifying his or her own behavior to everyone's benefit.

EXERCISE

If I had to do it over again, I would have incorporated exercise into my children's daily routine just as I did tooth-brushing and bed-making. Unfortunately, I didn't and one of my teen daughters considered it exercise to spend the afternoon yakking on the phone. Her friends were no different—the only other physical activity that I'd seen them engage in was yawning at my mere mention of anything involving movement. Suggestions about skating, tennis or cycling went unheeded. My daughter contended that she got sufficient exercise running up and down the stairs at school.

These days many teen girls are quite active but usually they are the girls who excel at a particular sport or physical activity. Many other girls though have no aptitude or interest in sports or they may just be self-conscious and inhibited when it comes to using their body. The latter is true particularly for girls who physically mature either early or late. A young girl's insecurity often prevents her from doing anything that she may not do well or that would require her to put her body on display.

Don't rush to blame your daughter's self-consciousness on your failing as a "modern parent" just because you may not be as open about discussing sex or feminine hygiene as you think you should be. Remember, your daughter may have developed earlier than her friends and may be experiencing hoots and whistles way before she is emotionally ready for them. She may be walking around looking for lost kittens to rescue with thoughts of boys still a few years away but her emotional immaturity does not prevent her from being ogled or whistled at.

It *is* a shame that so many young bodies turn to flab when they don't have to. Obesity has become an adolescent disease and it is, unfortunately, the by-product of modern-day technology and abundance. (American supermarkets carry foods to suit every taste and mood and at prices that are the envy of the world.) Teens, however, are particularly shortsighted and they see themselves lean and firm now and forever. Thus, cajoling your daughter into swimming or dancing class may work if she has an interest in such activity but your cajoling could just as easily turn out to be a waste of money even if she expressed an interest in the class. I know a young girl who cut her karate class. You'd think no one would take up karate unless they wanted to. While the girl likes karate, she's at the stage where she'd rather spend her time playing games on her smart phone. It turns out that she signed up for the class only to please her Mom.

Unfortunately, unless you can convince your daughter to get into the habit of a daily run around the block with the family dog, there is little you can do except continue your own exercise program (or starting one), nag as appropriate (but never in a disparaging way), keep lots of fruits and veggies around, and hope for the best. Maybe someday she will surprise you and suggest that the two of you enroll in an aerobics class—but don't hold your breath waiting for her to do so.

MENSTRUATION *(see also this Chapter below at "Physical Development")*

Despite the ads that depict menstruating young women and sanitary napkins with flowery grace and tact that appear on TV and in magazines, there is nothing dainty about that time of the month. Thus, in some ways, despite all the societal openness about the female body and its inner workings, your pubescent daughter has been exposed to myths about menstruation that, though different than the superstitions of yore, are just as misleading.

Some girls have no problem adjusting to becoming a woman and eagerly look forward to wearing their first bra. However, some girls regard menstruation as a personal affront and feel resentful about being female. If your daughter has these latter feelings, it will do no good to tell her about the wonders of love and motherhood. Those things are just too far away for her to conceptualize. Right now, she is embarrassed and confused. Protruding breasts and hair on her legs make her exceedingly self-conscious. She may refuse to wear a bra, or if she does, she doesn't want anyone to know. Treat her gently and don't buy short skimpy tops for her to wear, cute as she may look in them. Instead, army pants and fishing vests may be *de rigueur* for now.

She also may envy her male friends because they don't have her "problem." They don't have to worry about anyone "seeing something" through their clothes or bathing suits. If your daughter feels this way, explain to her that boys also go through embarrassing times during their adolescence. She probably knows a fourteen-year-old boy who looks ten and another who looks like a full-grown man. Tell her about boys' locker room games and ask her how she thinks the not yet fully developed fourteen-year-old boy feels in a "how high can you squirt" contest. Explain a boy's changing feelings toward females and mention how self-conscious he must be about someone noticing his erection whenever a girl passes close to him, or even worse, whenever the pretty new teacher calls on him.

Once your daughter understands that puberty happens to boys as well as to girls, she will not feel so particularly singled out. Even if she still regards menstruation as a gross intrusion on her life, she will not feel as negative about being female. She still, however, may feel embarrassed about buying or discussing her needs related to menstruation. Make sure there is a supply of the sanitary protection that she uses in the house. Little by little, she will feel more comfortable with her femaleness. She may even start mentioning the "unmentionable" by discussing the pros and cons of a particular brand or style of sanitary napkin. Later, she may ask your advice about tampons. Don't force or forbid their use. Instead, talk to your daughter and check with your doctor about them. Tampons are great for swimming, sports, parties and the like as long as they are comfortable. Because of the danger of Toxic Shock, teens should not use tampons overnight.

No matter how wonderful tampons are and the added freedom obtained by using them, a young girl may simply not be ready for their use. For example, a young and newly menstruating teen may want to use a tampon to go to a swim party. If she didn't wear a bathing suit and join in jumping the waves, everybody would *know*. However, every time she tried to insert the tampon, her muscles contracted and she wasn't able to. She just wasn't ready. If this is your daughter, reassure her that there is nothing wrong with her and she will figure it out soon enough. While your daughter may decide to skip the party rather than go in shorts, don't pooh-pooh her feelings. Instead be understanding and comfort your daughter by reminding her that there are lots of swim parties in her future and she will figure out tampon use pretty soon—maybe even the very next day! The important thing here is to respect your daughter's feelings.

NUTRITION

Nutrition is definitely an area where actions speak louder than words. In my view, soda, potato chips, cake, cookies, candy and the like have no business being in any home on a regular basis (though my own actions don't always support my "view" but I do try!). If you buy boxes of cookies, don't expect them to be eaten by your teenage daughter one cookie at a time—more likely she will go through the entire box in one afternoon. Teens eat compulsively, just as they do everything else. Thus, it's best not to keep non-nutritious foods stocked in the fridge or pantry. Such foods can be bought sparingly as the occasion calls for them. Instead, stock the refrigerator with nutritious snacks such as fresh fruit and veggies, cheese sticks, hard-boiled eggs, assorted nuts, low-sugar yogurt, a left-over drumstick, etc. Your daughter will be ravenous after school and will grab the easiest thing to eat. She may as well eat nourishing food instead of junk.

You can also satisfy your daughter's sweet tooth nutritionally by baking healthy breads and muffins. I know you're busy but try to set aside some time here and there—even only once a month—to do some baking. Bake up some banana bread, applesauce cake, muffins and/or oatmeal cookies using whole wheat flour (start with 2/3 as much white flour called for) and half as much sugar as called for by the recipe. Substitute like amounts of applesauce for oil or butter. Add an egg.

Raisins, nuts, chopped dates, grated carrots or zucchini, and/or mashed sweet potatoes, pumpkin or bananas can be added for extra nutrition and variety. If you can afford it, substitute walnut, almond or other specialty flour for some of the wheat flour. A few dark chocolate chips won't hurt either especially since dark chocolate (in moderation) has officially been declared to be good for us. Be creative…experiment… involve your daughter.

Shop carefully to make sure that the fruit and vegetables you buy are fresh and unbruised. No self-respecting teen will eat a piece of fruit that has even the slightest blemish. All fruit should be washed carefully before being eaten; however, since fruit that is washed tends to spoil quicker, just wash up a few pieces a day and arrange attractively in a bowl kept either in the fridge or on the table. (Fresh fruit that's seen better days can be washed and cut up, placed in the freezer, and then used for smoothies or added to cereal or yogurt.) If it isn't convenient or too expensive for you to stock a wide variety of fresh fruits and vegetables, stick with the basics such as baby carrots, celery, apples, grapes and bananas. Also, hard-boiled eggs and homemade potato salad and coleslaw (easy on the mayo) are also satisfying snacks. Bottom line is to keep nutritious snacks at the ready that need little attention in going from fridge to mouth.

Generally, extra calories should be kept to a minimum which can be done by not serving useless calories. For example, when serving potatoes, serve them baked or boiled with the skin on. They can be seasoned with garlic or topped with a dollop of sour cream or grated cheese. No need for butter. Serve more fish and poultry instead of red meat. If the only poultry your daughter will eat is a drumstick, that's okay; ditto if tuna is the only fish she will eat. She doesn't need to eat squab or sardines—better to avoid arguments and not be too adventurous with your daily meal planning.

Adolescent girls often have very limited food preferences and their tastes may be strange and unpredictable. One day, your daughter, who pretended to barf every time she saw a vegetable, declares herself a vegan. Another teen will declare romaine lettuce mundane and eat only arugula and baby kale. Still another girl whose taste buds never ventured beyond peanut butter and jelly sandwiches will order a burger made with bison or emu meat the next time you dine out. Also, don't be surprised however if your daughter's current idea of gourmet food is thick-crusted pizza or if the only thing she orders whenever you go out to eat are French fries and a grilled cheese sandwich.

When your daughter complains that *there's nothing to eat in the house ever!* (translation: no chips, soda, ice cream or cookies), let her do the family shopping. Hand over what you would normally spend for the week's groceries and challenge her to do better. Explain that she needs to choose so that the family will be well-nourished but that she can buy whatever she wants. And let her do it! You will likely find that, given the responsibility, your daughter will soon rise to the occasion. It's quite possible that your daughter's first foray as family food gatherer and interpretation of the protein, vegetable, dairy, carbohydrate and fruit requirements of the recommended food pyramid will result in the family's eating nothing but hamburgers drowned in ketchup and ice cream topped with cocoa puffs, all served with generous quantities of grape Kool-Aid. However, after two or three weeks of her listening to the family's complaints, she will become a good shopper and knowledgeable about nutrition. And, you will no longer hear from her that there's never anything to eat in the house.

What and when we eat plays a very important role in our culture. It's only natural to want to bring home a triple chocolate mousse cake laden with fresh whipped cream to celebrate a raise. However, when you are tempted to do something like that just to show your love, remind yourself that loving your family does not mean stopping off on your way home from work to bring home something that is not good for anybody. Instead, show your love with a goodie that's normally outside your budget--perhaps raspberries out-of-season— or something unusual for you to buy like a papaya or persimmons. Sometimes the treat might be a flop taste-wise but any strange or special food carried home will show your love and be appreciated as much as if you'd brought home double-dipped hand-made ice cream (well, maybe only *almost* as much!).

PARTY FOOD & DRINK

Teens just like to keep their mouths busy and are not particularly choosy about party food as long as the food is not too strange or "too mushy" (garlic mashed potatoes being the exception). Few teens will admit to liking hummus or Baba Ghanoush (a dip made with eggplant). However, such dips as well as salsa, guacamole, and any kale, spinach, garlic or onion dip (made with plain yogurt and/or sour cream) are at least minimally nutritious and go well with fresh vegetables, trans-fat free crackers and baked chips. Easy hors d'oeuvres can be cheese stuffed mushrooms or thin-crust pizza wedges topped with grilled vegetables. Substitute bowls of GORP (good old raisins and peanuts) for extra chips. If your daughter is adamant about serving junk food, serve some potato chips or pretzels but don't bother to refill any empty bowls unless asked. Drinks can consist of a variety of caffeine-free sports and juice drinks. Have some milk around too—athletic teen boys are known to drink gallons of it.

If your daughter says she won't have the party unless beer is served, don't have the party. It is illegal to serve alcohol to persons under the age of 21. It is also your responsibility to see that no teen goes outside to the street or hallway to guzzle up. Be careful to check the outside activity and confiscate any alcohol. If you find someone drinking who is supposed to drive home, call his or her parents to come pick him or her up. If they won't or can't do so, call a cab even if you have to pay for it. Alcohol and driving do not mix. Period. Explain to any who might be embarrassed by you (your daughter) or take offense at your actions (the drinker) that you care enough about them to risk their displeasure. Let them know that attending the drinker's funeral is not your idea of a fun way to spend your time.

If it is to be a large party and you are a single mom, ask a male person, preferably a large one, to act as host. Your daughter and her friends might be quite respectable and responsible; however, the situation may be different with a friend of a friend who appears the soul of perfection but has a stash of pot or booze in his car. If you have no male relative or friend to help you out, ask the parents of one of your daughter's friends or a married couple with whom you are friendly to do so. Having a bouncer or two at a teen party, particularly where all the guests may not be personally known to you, will go a long way toward preventing trouble.

PHYSICAL DEVELOPMENT *(see also this Chapter above at "Menstruation")*

Growth and development of the human body are extremely capricious during the adolescent years. The changes occurring in your daughter's body will affect her behavior and her feelings about herself. Such changes may make her feel unattractive and self-conscious. She will feel she is too tall, too short, too skinny, too fat, too flat-chested, too bosomy. She may even feel all of those things in the space of a nanosecond.

Breast development particularly will impact on an adolescent girl's social behavior. If your daughter develops unusually early, she may be cast off by her childhood friends. Her early development will scare them and they will find her freakish. She may become overly self-conscious and self-critical. Her present clothing will reveal too much of what she would like to hide. Bathing suits and leotards are definitely not made for her body. She may feel she will forever be left out by the "in" crowd, the popular people. She will look at today's media blitz and see only the too slim super models.

Your words to the effect that everyone has their own development schedule and that her friends will soon catch up to her will be of little consolation to her. Be patient and understanding. She may even be so embarrassed about her body that she won't even shop for a bra. If so, make the purchase without her and leave it on her dresser. Don't allow the family to tease her about being the next sex goddess. It's enough that she probably experiences teasing from the boys at school. Remember that though she may have an adult body, she is still a child.

Conversely, if your daughter is a late developer physically, it may follow that her social development and interest in boys lag behind those of her peers. And along with all of her other adolescent worries and problems, she may no longer have her best friend from first grade to rely on because that girl has already started dating. Your daughter may feel left out and lost. You know it's only temporary and offer solace and suggestions for her to make new friends. However, her reality may be that the only girls whose physical maturity is similar to hers are a year or two younger than she and it is, of course, *verboten* for her to even consider socializing with a girl still in middle school if she's already in high school. This young teen looks at the world around her and sees only cleavage.

As with the early developer, your words about individual development schedules, while they should be said, will offer little consolation. What you can do, though, is not criticize her for not keeping her old friends or make her feel silly about not wanting to make friends with girls a grade or two behind her. Instead, help her to expand her interests and horizons. Surely, she is not the only late developer in town. Soon she will meet others who are around her age and at a similar stage in physical development. Point out too that she could have boyfriends if she wanted. Many fifteen-year-old boys have not yet begun to grow tall, still squeak when they talk, and are still more interested in tossing a football than talking to a girl. Your daughter's lack of sexuality will make them feel very comfortable. For example, I know a fourteen-year-old physically immature girl who was going on a bike tour with a coed group of fourteen-seventeen-year-olds. Some of the girls in the group were real knockouts and a few of the boys were already six-footers. At orientation time, the young girl approached the group timidly. She was, however, eagerly greeted by a boy no taller than she. The two of them breathed deep sighs of relief.

STAYING SAFE

In keeping with my belief of "being prepared for the worst, but hoping for the best," if your daughter will be walking or driving in unfamiliar areas, suggest she do a test run (with or without you) in daylight hours. You might also want to enroll your daughter in a self-defense class if such is available in your area. In any case, whether your daughter is out and about on her own or with friends, she should always observe the following safety tips:

- walk or drive on a well-traveled and well-lit route;
- park on a well-lit street;

- have plenty of gas;
- avoid parking garages as much as possible but if no other choice, park on the main level in a well-lit area as close to the street as possible;
- always lock the car as soon as she gets in and when she leaves;
- walk with confidence and with car or house keys at the ready;
- have an easy to reach whistle on her person;
- be aware of her surroundings—know where the bathrooms and exits are and plan an escape route;
- not be the last one out of the movie theatre or of an indoor or outdoor event whether day or night;
- if being followed, seek help—cross the street and/or duck into a restaurant or store or even ring someone's doorbell;
- to trust her instincts and not second-guess herself and seek safety if she feels uneasy;
- to only drink from bottles opened in her presence and not to leave her drink unattended;
- to buddy-up with a friend at a party so as to look-out for each other; and
- if attacked or threateningly approached, to scream as loud as she can and to fight back as hard as she can.

While writing the above, I couldn't help wondering that if one of the two Indiana girls that were murdered in February 2017 while hiking on a local trail had picked up a rock and thrown it at their attacker that the outcome would have been different. But just what do you tell a 70 lb. ten-year-old or even a 90 lb. 13-year-old? I cannot imagine the anguish of the girls' parents going over all the possible "if only this," "if only that." My heart goes out to them but no words of condolence can ever heal their hurt. All we parents can do is our best and hope that the Fates are with us.

Special Note. Your daughter should learn to swim well enough to be comfortable in the water even if only for a short while and also know basic first-aid. Of course too she should know not to drink, smoke, text or even use her phone while driving.

WEIGHT

Anorexia is a disease that primarily affects teen girls that arises from psychological causes and far too often causes immediate health problems and in some instances death. **Obesity** has become an adolescent disease that will likely cause serious health problems in the future and while some cases of obesity are genetic or psychological, it is also largely the byproduct of modern-day technology and abundance.

Teen girls are seldom satisfied with what they weigh. They feel they are either too thin or too fat. However, it may be that your daughter really is under- or over-weight. If so, the first thing you should do is take her for a medical checkup, particularly if you think your daughter is obese or might be anorexic. Most likely there is no physical reason for your daughter's weight problem and the doctor will prescribe an appropriate diet and exercise regimen. Counseling for your daughter and the family may also be recommended.

Other things that you can do to help your daughter is to ensure that your pantry and fridge don't contain tempting goodies full of empty calories (*see* this Chapter above at "Nutrition"). However, in the main, it is up to your daughter to follow her doctor's advice and learn to eat properly. You should, of course, encourage her in her efforts and not act in a way to sabotage them. She is, after all, human and it is difficult for anyone to have just one potato chip. That being said, don't badger your daughter to gain or lose weight. Improper weight is often caused by psychological problems—even minor ones. Don't add to your daughter's discomfort by causing unnecessary friction between the two of you.

Whether your daughter is too thin or too fat, the goal is for her to learn to enhance or control her weight by modifying her eating habits regardless of whether she conquers all the causes of her under- or over-eating. While you should not nag your daughter about eating, you can help her to change her eating habits by creating a home environment that will assist her in solving her problem.

For example, **if your daughter is too thin**, make sure the mealtime atmosphere is pleasant and non-threatening. Perhaps it might be better if she ate by herself while reading a book or doing homework and nibbling on finger foods such as fresh fruit and veggies, cheese chunks, chicken fingers, fish sticks, deviled eggs, peanut butter stuffed celery—whatever works. There must be some food that she likes or will at least tolerate but keep in mind that when push comes to shove, empty calories are better than no calories. Picky eaters may also do better when food is served in small portions on divided plates. If it's a family meal, serve food family style and let her pick what and how much she will eat without comment, particularly if she goes for a second helping of anything. Also, don't criticize your daughter at mealtimes whether it's about her bad table manners, poor grades, tardiness, social media usage, etc. That can all wait for another time. The important thing for a finnicky eater is not that the food you serve be fattening or special but that she eats. Thus, try to ensure that mealtimes are non-threatening and that the food looks attractive but not overwhelming.

If your daughter is overweight, you should still try to make mealtime as pleasant as possible but serve meals restaurant-style so as to avoid the temptation of easily available second helpings. If your daughter does get up for more food, don't make a scene but next time put the leftovers in the freezer before everyone sits down to eat. Also, some people (especially me!) don't feel satisfied after dinner unless they have dessert. There are many low-calorie deserts that you can serve your family including your daughter such as fresh fruit topped with a dab of whipped cream, a dollop of fat-free yogurt atop a small slice of angel food cake, a small wedge of cheese, or a third of a cup of trail mix. The food you serve need not be diet food—just nutritious and devoid of unnecessary calories. There is no need to serve broccoli with a rich cheese sauce—a sprinkling of olive oil and/or grated cheese will do fine. Also, even if the rest of the family doesn't have a weight problem, refrigerators stocked with soda, donuts and gallons of ice cream are not good for anybody. If your daughter is on a special diet under a doctor's supervision, she should still eat her meals with the rest of the family. Try to have her meal contain as many courses as does the family meal. Take special care to make her cottage cheese look and taste attractive—top with a spoonful of chopped olives or walnuts and surround with fresh veggies. Add a healthy cracker or two topped with some hummus or guacamole to satisfy a carb craving. For desert allow her a sliver of the family pie—she is after all just a teenager and the focus of a weight-loss regimen should be on learning good eating habits and portion control, not dieting. Have apples in the fridge for snacks—they're healthy and filling.

The important thing for you to do is to get uninvolved with your daughter's eating habits. Give her some time to come to terms with her problem. If she has setbacks, don't make her feel guilty. Support her by saying that tomorrow is another day and by telling her how well she has done so far. Remind her about the meals she ate properly and the snacks she skipped. Tell her not to allow a day or two of bingeing to destroy all her hard work. If she wants to put reminder notes on the refrigerator or a full-size picture of herself in a bathing suit on the living room wall, let her but don't you suggest it or say anything should she later take it down.

If your daughter just talks about eating better but never does, don't make her feel guilty for not following through. You will only add to her lack of self-esteem. Remember that her poor eating habits and improper attitude about food were a long time in the making. It will be very difficult for her to change her ways. Be aware too that research has shown that fat and sugar are addictive. The body instinctively wants sugar for energy and to store fat against possible famine. Mother Nature wants us to be fat so we can reproduce and take care of our young. She cares little for us after that. It's our psyche that wants us to live past our child-rearing years. Thus, if we want to live a long healthy life, those of us that are fortunate enough to be able to take advantage of our food abundance must always do battle with Mother Nature.

If you do your part by adhering to medical advice and/or counseling, not nagging her about her weight, and being careful about the food you buy and serve (and improve your own eating habits if need be), your daughter should eventually take the initiative herself to control her appetite. Of course, there's nothing wrong with the gentle art of persuasion as long as you are not so subtle that you are cruel. It would be wrong for you to buy a cute mini-skirt two sizes too small for her to wear *when and if* she loses weight. If she wants to buy it for herself as an incentive, that's fine but if you buy the skirt, you would be putting her weight in your control and it isn't. However, if your daughter is grossly overweight and you can afford it, suggest she spend her summer at a weight-control camp. Such camps are pricey so take care to suggest same only if you can readily afford the cost and are mentally prepared for the possibility that any weight lost at the camp might return.

Good eating habits are mostly learned by example and knowledge. Regardless of whether your daughter is too thin or too fat, take her food shopping and have her read the labels. Let her discover the high sugar content in so much of today's foods, which foods are the best sources of protein, which food products contain mostly unpronounceable ingredients. Be aware of how relatively inexpensive box-store food has changed our eating habits. Foods that used to be exotic treats are now available in bulk at affordable prices. Trays of spanakopita fill our freezers and packages of chocolate covered dried fruit of every sort fill our pantries. Such abundance is intimidating for the poor eater and far too tempting for the overweight. It's hard not to take advantage of our good fortune in having so much bounty to choose from but keep it minimal if anyone in your home has an eating disorder or weight problem.

As stated above, obesity and anorexia are serious conditions. If, despite your best efforts, you do not see even a modest improvement in your daughter's weight within the time frame initially suggested by the doctor or counselor, make another appointment. Further professional intervention, different approaches to the problem, and/or medication may be necessary.

12. IT'S HER LIFE, BUT . . .

Choosing a Camp — Choosing a College
Free Time (Too Little/Too Much)
School (Homework, Grades & Dropping Out)
The Three R's

CHOOSING A CAMP

Summer camp, whether in-town or sleep-away, exposes your daughter to a variety of activities that may not be available in your hometown or gives your daughter the opportunity to enhance her abilities. And looking ahead, attending summer camp can also morph into summer counseling jobs during her high school years.

Your daughter has never been to sleep-away camp but has now decided that she wants to go, or perhaps she has gone to the same camp for years and now decides that she wants to go to a different one. Regardless, it's probably best that your daughter not spend summer as a "new face" at a traditional camp where the same campers have been going year after year. Cliques have most likely been formed and your daughter might feel out of place and isolated. She may be tempted to do things that she wouldn't normally do just to win acceptance.

Isolation and loneliness may cause unusual behavior in adults and adolescents are no less prone. Instead, if your daughter wants a change from her prior camp or wants to give camp a try for the first time, look for a special interest camp where campers are grouped by interest or proficiency rather than grade or age. There's tennis and other sports camps, acting camps, wilderness camps, travel camps, music and arts camps, weight loss camps and so on. Also, many colleges have special summer programs for high school teens. Should it be your daughter's first time away from home for a period of time and you're concerned about her being homesick, mail her a sweet and loving postcard a day or two after she leaves for camp with the suggestion that she put the card under her pillow.

Meryl Fishman

Generally, it's best if you're not the one to pick the camp, especially if your criteria for choosing the camp is because you would have liked to attend it when you were your daughter's age. Your role is to find the types of camps available that might be of interest to your daughter and that are in your price range and meet your standards with respect to health facilities, licensing, accreditation and certification. Let your daughter select the camp from those which you find acceptable. After all, she is the one who will be going. Besides, if the camp turns out to be a dud, she won't be able to blame you. Also, if the camp was her selection, she will more likely accept it even if it does not fully meet her expectations. After all, it's important not to lose face.

My daughter and her friend selected a wilderness camp for their first camp experience. I was amazed at the selection because their only contact with nature until then had been choosing a pumpkin to carve up for Halloween. I thought the idea terrific but I had plenty of doubts as to whether my daughter would like roughing it. I decided though not to intervene. The camp was accredited and had a good reputation. I did not feel it was my parental duty to describe outhouses and cold showers or "separation stops" (peeing in the woods). Neither did I feel it my parental responsibility to point out the discomforts of sleeping on the floor of a cave without the benefit of a soft mattress nor how uncomfortable it could be to hike with a full pack while dodging mosquitoes in 95° weather. All any such comments would do anyway would subject me to attacks for being negative, a party-pooper, or not knowing what I was talking about (likely all three) or actually dissuade her from going, in which case she would lose an opportunity to find out about herself. So off she went. She did seem a little hesitant though, when as she was leaving, I slipped a roll of toilet paper into her backpack.

My silence was wise. She loved the suffering. She was so proud of herself. She even wanted to return the following summer. She learned how to canoe, how to survive in the woods, how to get along with people she didn't like, how to handle fear and discomfort. And I learned that it would have been as wrong to impose my own doubts about her abilities on her as it would be to impose my own dreams for her on her.

Special Note. If your daughter is going away to camp or to school let her know about the possibility of advances from other girls or women as well as from any males she may encounter. Telling her that a female may make a pass at her should be no different than telling her that a boy or man may do so. (*See also* Chapter 14 at "Gender Identity.")

CHOOSING A COLLEGE

Applications. You and your daughter should be realistic when choosing a college. You both may want one of the Ivy Leagues or Big Ten but so do thousands of other high-schoolers and their parents. Realize that the competition for some schools is extremely tough and while your daughter may have all the qualifications, she still may not be selected. Colleges seek diversification—not only racially and ethnically—but geographically as well. If your daughter is hoping to attend a selective private or highly competitive public university, you may be more involved in the application process than you anticipated. While some high school college counseling services are terrific, some are woefully inadequate. Also, counselors may limit the number of applications that they will review because of the necessity to spread their time among many students. Thus, even if your daughter already knows exactly where she wants to apply or is extremely self-sufficient, be prepared to play college counselor at least to the extent of being a knowledgeable springboard for her thoughts and concerns.

The college application process is definitely an area where money helps. There's the cost of college entrance exams and preparation for same, application fees, and visits to college campuses. The SAT or ACT should be taken for the first time in the junior year so your daughter will have some idea of which schools will be within her reach academically. If improved scores are needed, consider signing your daughter up for a college-exam preparation course. The courses do not make one smarter but they do offer good test-taking tips. The confidence gained from being familiar with the process and taking practice tests is always worth a few additional points. Practice exams are also available on-line for free through The Kahn Academy. If money for the applications is a problem, perhaps you can induce a few relatives to each give your daughter the gift of a college application fee for Christmas or her birthday while she's still a junior in high school. Perhaps too someone in the family may be flush enough to treat your daughter to an SAT or ACT preparation course in your area.

Your daughter's high school and/or local library should have college guides by majors and other criteria. However, unless your daughter has a pretty definitive idea which colleges she'd like to apply to, I think a good way to begin choosing colleges is to first know what's available and where. To start, your daughter should browse through the college guide books at the local library or a major bookstore. Such books give descriptions of U.S. and Canadian colleges—size, admission standards, courses offered, costs, financial aid, student life, etc. While such information is available on the Internet, the advantage of looking through college guide books at leisure, particularly if your daughter is unsure of which direction she wishes to go academically, is that the books show majors that your daughter may not have thought of. Further, in my view, flipping through pages of a college guide book to compare one college to another is quicker and easier than doing so on the Internet not only in determining which colleges should be researched more thoroughly but also in eliminating some from further consideration. For example, your biggest concern may be distance from home while your daughter is honed in only on colleges that offer a junior year abroad.

Your daughter should select about fifteen colleges for further research via the Internet. In addition to a virtual tour of the campus, she should try to find answers to the following questions and anything else she feels pertinent. What's the graduate rate generally? What's the graduation rate for the major she's interested in? Are there any pending law suits against the school and for what? How large are the freshman classes? What's the student-to-teacher ratio? Is there a problem with campus crime? What about religious or racial discrimination or sexual harassment incidents? What's the boy-girl ratio? What student organizations, religious or otherwise, are on campus? What's the culture of the campus and town where the college is? Would it be difficult for her to go from her home town to a big city college or large college campus or to go from a big city to a small college in a small town? How accessible are the professors? How many classes are taught by graduate students rather than professors? Thereafter, your daughter should apply to the maximum number of colleges that her high school allows (usually five)—where she really wants to go, a "safe" school (e.g., a shoo-in for your daughter), and three acceptable schools.

If your daughter's school facilities regarding college applications are sparse or over-burdened, you might want to consider a private college counseling service company. Check with your daughter's high school counselor and parents of prior school seniors for recommendations.

Many colleges offer some type of early acceptance which may be binding on your daughter meaning generally that if she's accepted, her high school won't complete applications to other colleges on her behalf. Thus, even if your daughter wants to go that route and is sure of being accepted, she should still research other colleges before applying. Early acceptance applications usually have a November deadline so your daughter should get going on her research the latter half of her junior year.

Note too that not all college scholarships are based on sports or academic excellence. There's a plethora of scholarships based on various criteria such as the race, ethnicity or sex of the applicant, family membership in a particular organization, or for pursuing a special or unusual area of study. Also, various civic groups and many businesses, large and small, often have unique scholarship programs. Search the Internet and your local library and Chamber of Commerce for possibilities.

Generally, do not interfere with your daughter's selection of colleges unless she is completely off-track vis-à-vis her abilities. The cost of the school should not be a factor as most colleges offer some type of financial assistance (if needed) along with the acceptance. However, since the financial aid package offered by the school may not meet your family's needs, you should prepare your daughter that even though she might get into her first-choice or a particularly prestigious college, she may not be able to attend for financial reasons. However, since I believe that every child should go to the best college that he or she can get into, check again with the college and members of your extended family for further assistance. Like it or not, a Harvard graduate is always a Harvard graduate and in difficult times, prestige counts. Don't despair though if your daughter's choice of colleges is limited for financial reasons or less than stellar academic performance. Her keeping up with college alumni contacts will also pay off not only socially but in hard times. Remember too that our country's state universities offer an excellent education covering a multitude of majors and also may offer a leg up when job hunting in the state, particularly for graduates with majors that are particularly pertinent to the home state's needs and best interests.

After your daughter has made her choices, follow up to see that she and her school mail in their respective application sections on time. (Many colleges send acknowledgment of an application soon after its receipt.) Some teens may delay mailing the application to their first-choice or even to their "safe" school because of fear of being rejected. If your daughter is dillydallying, explain to her that rejection is always a possibility but encourage her to mail it in anyway. After all, if the application never gets mailed, she certainly will never attend that school.

Acceptance/Rejection. You must be very patient while your daughter is awaiting her acceptance letters. This is a very tense time for her. If your daughter is not accepted by her first-choice institution, don't drown her with your disappointment. Don't remind her that you told her to write about a different topic for her application essay or that she shouldn't have babysat the night before she took her college entrance exam. She feels bad enough as it is. If, however, your daughter is not accepted by a school that she really wants to attend and if she has the usual requirements for that school soothe her feelings by noting that her rejection was apparently random based on the number of similarly qualified applicants and geographical concerns. In such situations, though, have your daughter check with her high school counselor about the feasibility of contacting the desired college for reconsideration of her application.

Hopefully, though, one day the coveted envelope arrives and your daughter is ecstatic. However, soon afterwards your daughter seems in the throes of a major depression—the thought of going off to college has her traumatized. All along, she has been looking forward to going away but now that she realizes that the big day will actually arrive, it has dawned on her that going away to school means she won't be living at home anymore and *she's scared.* She realizes that soon she really will be grown-up and have to take care of herself. Reassure her that it is normal for her to feel apprehensive and that her home will always be her home no matter where she may live. Don't tell her you plan to convert her room into a sewing room for yourself or that you gave the OK to her sister to redecorate their shared room the moment she left. Such things shouldn't be done anyway until your daughter is really on her own and even then, you may have to go easy on any room conversions for a while. (Don't toss away any of her teddy bears either!)

If your daughter will be going away to college but has never spent any time away from home on her own such as at camp, try and arrange it so that sometime before she starts college, she will have an away-from-home experience. Perhaps she could spend part of her summer before college as a mother's helper in a near-by town or with a governmental funded group or not-for-profit organization such as America Corps or the Student Conservation Association that have civic and environmentally focused teen intern/volunteer opportunities. Also, as previously mentioned, many colleges offer summer programs for students entering their senior high school year.

While most teens enjoy the experience of being away from home for a week or more, some girls may be very upset by it. Going away to college is not for everyone. Your daughter should not be made to feel like a failure if she wants to stay in the nest a bit longer and attend a local institution. She will need to be on her own sometime though and it is part of your job to prepare her to do that. Some girls just need more preparation time than others. Thus, if your daughter attends college while living at home, give her as much freedom as possible but *do* for her as little as possible. Don't even think about reminding her to study. You shouldn't be doing her laundry either. You wouldn't be able to do it if she were away. However, while many colleges no longer have curfews, you are within your rights to set some. Such curfews though should not be couched as restrictions on her but on practicalities. For example, a 10:00pm or 11:00pm curfew is reasonable during the week since it would be unfair to the other members of the household to be woken up from the noise of a car door slamming shut or a door jamb unlocking just because your daughter is a college-age gadabout. I know you're still going to worry while she's out at night no matter her age but that's just the price we pay for the joy of having them around. While I empathize with your desire to keep tabs on your college-age daughter just as you did while she was in high school, you shouldn't burden her with your natural propensity towards worrying.

Alternatives. Recognize too that your daughter may not be college material, at least not right after high-school. She may need a year or two off to mature. Remind her, though, that a college degree (even a two-year degree or some type of vocational or technical training) is a must for almost any job paying more than the minimum wage. If your daughter is still reluctant to attend college, bring home some brochures for the local community college. Courses offered at these schools are generally of a more immediately practical nature and she might find something that interests her. Explain that since she is so eager to work, she may as well do something that she enjoys and that usually requires some training or education. Suggest she start out with a course or two while she's working at a part-time job. She may surprise herself and really enjoy learning.

Also, don't rule out technical or trade schools or on-line courses or colleges as alternatives to traditional colleges—just research any carefully to ensure that they are *bona fide* and accredited and deliver what they promise. Society will always need plumbers, welders, electricians, EMTs, police and firefighters, medical technicians, machinists, computer techs, yoga instructors, etc., etc. Personally, I think everyone, even Harvard grads, should have a marketable fallback skill whether it be landscaping, cosmetology, whatever. Also, your daughter might wish to consider military service. I know even mentioning that she enlist in the armed services might be scary for you but for some children it would be an excellent option. If it's you that mentions military service as an option and not your daughter, do so carefully since you don't want to take the chance that you are so disappointed in her that you're happy to send her off to war. Conversely, if your daughter is interested in military service, don't pooh-pooh her interest but let her find her way. The armed services have pre-enlistment tests to help potential enlistees decide whether a particular armed service is right for them and also have programs to answer parental concerns.

If your daughter thinks she is college material even if you don't, don't discourage her. Give her as much support and assistance as you would an A student. My cousin's daughter, for example, struggled all through high school earning only a C average, yet she was determined to be a teacher. After beginning her studies at a community college, she went on to a four-year state university (taking a year longer than usual to complete the program). Thereafter, she earned a master's degree in special education and she became an extremely effective and highly-regarded teacher of students with learning disabilities. One doesn't need to be a rocket scientist or a brain surgeon to be a successful and productive adult. Ambition and dedication takes one very far in life— often further than does scholastic brilliance.

FREE TIME

Too Little. During the school year, your daughter is involved in many after-school activities. She's on the swim team and she tutors Spanish. She works for her uncle on Saturdays and she's active in your church's youth group. Now she tells you she tried out for a supporting role in the school play. She has no time to think or to dream or to spend with you. Your life too is no less hectic. You feel like you're both stretched-out rubber bands—ready to snap at any moment.

These days, there's so much societal pressure on adolescents to succeed and parents are made to feel guilty if they don't sacrifice their golf game so as to be able to chauffer their children around from one activity to another. You're reluctant to say *no—enough is enough!* Besides, you want your daughter to experience life as fully as possible and don't want her to miss out on a single thing. Thus, if your daughter cannot cut out any activity, you'll both have to hunker down and keep home life as simple as possible. Be forgiving if your daughter doesn't always pick up after herself or clean her room; learn to live with sticky floors and dusty shelves; buy lots of socks and underwear in case the wash doesn't get done. Get help if you can afford to but don't expect too much from the other family members—they are just as likely to be as busy as you and your daughter.

While it's always important to get plenty of sleep and eat well, it's especially important for you both to do so during hectic times. You can also help the situation by structuring some down time. For example, no one in our house made plans for Sunday evenings. We used that night as a time to get ready for the week. It was our time to cook for the week, try green nail polish, discuss the coming week's schedule. This is when you will learn that your daughter volunteered you to coach her softball team and the first meeting is scheduled for Tuesday or that on Wednesdays rehearsals for the school play will end after the last school bus and you will need to pick her up. Or this might be the time when you discover that she has a conflict between competing in a swim meet and taking a much-awaited trip with a youth group and she's in a tizzy about how to handle the situation.

Planned weekly down-time gives everyone a chance to resolve these types of conflicts without the pressures of last minute immediacy. Also, it's a good time for bonding as it gives each family member the opportunity to offer and receive both moral and practical support for his or her individual endeavors.

Too Much. Your daughter announces she's not going to camp this summer—she's going to get a job. Terrific! But what if she doesn't get a job? Perhaps prospective employers might think her too young or there's an economic slump and that your daughter instead of being wooed by the local fast-food place or box store would be competing with laid-off workers for the same job. If your daughter doesn't find a job on her own and is adamant about not returning to camp, consider contacting friends, relatives, business associates, neighbors and whomever else you can think of to see if any of them might have a job for your daughter. Perhaps you can suggest a job that your daughter could do that they hadn't thought of. For example, a stockbroker friend of mine hired my fifteen-year old daughter to deliver proxy statements and wait around for them to be signed; a teacher I knew hired two students every August to help her prepare posters and similar materials for her kindergarten class. I believe it is a civic duty to hire teens during the summer and when my girls were at college, I "hired" my friend's stay-at-home 14-year-old to do some of my errands. I also referred her to some dog-walking and pet-care jobs offered by my neighbors. The point is that a teen-age girl should not be allowed to just "hang out" with no plans for an entire summer.

Your daughter need not have all her time filled, nor need it be filled unpleasantly. For example, this might be a good time for her to take a Driving Ed class or a college exam preparation course or help care for a community garden. Also, check into local intern and volunteer programs. The important thing is that your daughter has some focus to most of her days. Otherwise, her summer will be rife with opportunities for sloth and laziness or worse. Don't allow your daughter the opportunity to get into some real trouble.

Expect your daughter to balk at your setting up her summer for her. In such case, give her an ultimatum—camp, courses, a job, volunteer work—her choice. No buts about it. Explain that it is *your job* to see that her body and mind function twelve months a year, not just nine.

SCHOOL (Homework/Grades/Dropping Out)

Homework. Many parents seem to act as if their daughter's homework is *their* responsibility as well as their daughter's. However, it is my belief that a child's homework is his or her responsibility and that parental responsibility rests primarily with providing the tools, time and space for homework. Of course, you should be a sounding board for your daughter's opinions, essays, book reports, speeches, etc. as well as be around to quiz her for upcoming exams. You should also provide assistance with any assignment she finds difficult—not by answering the problems for her but by either teaching her how to do them herself or by helping her find the resources where she can find the information she needs on her own. Remember it is her homework, not yours.

Punitive threats are risky. *If you don't do your homework, you can't go to the dance* is an invitation to war. Are you really willing to let your daughter miss a big dance? If not, your threat is meaningless and if you are, you risk alienating your daughter over a homework assignment. Better to find out why she's not doing her homework—is it too difficult or is she too busy with Facebook or after-school activities. If the work is too difficult, take appropriate action like providing assistance as stated above. If insufficient time is the problem, help her prioritize her time so that there's sufficient time for homework even if it means dropping some after-school activities. Suggest too that she treat herself to social media time only when she's finished her homework—sort of like having a candy treat after a job well done.

Personally, I'm not against rewards (i.e., bribery) for homework since I believe that for most students doing homework reinforces retention of what was taught in the classroom. Parental rewards for school work should be based on realistically achievable goals, offered with a light touch, and given for a job well done. For example, I offered my daughter, who was a mediocre student and lackadaisical when it came to doing homework, $10 for every final B grade, $15 for a B+ and $20 for an A. I knew she had a chance of making such grades in some courses but that she would have to work hard to do so. She asked me if I would pay her a $100 for an A average. I told her no—that if she wound up with an A average, I would give her $200! At first, I wanted to swallow my words. Her chances of ending the semester with an A average were just about zero and I thought that I'd hurt her feelings terribly. Instead, though, she had a good laugh and said she might surprise me. I was thrilled to discover that she could view her own limitations with a sense of humor but that she also viewed her limitations as a challenge. My daughter earned a B or a B+ average that term and every term thereafter. I was happy to pay her the promised reward and considered myself lucky to having hit on a way to motivate her regarding homework and school work generally.

However, just because you motivate one child with money doesn't mean you need to do the same for your other children. I definitely believe that while parents should love their children equally, equal love does not mean equal treatment. I believe equal love means recognizing each child's individuality and treating them accordingly. For example, my other daughter, an honor student, wanted to know why I didn't pay her for good grades. I responded that she was already rewarded—that she was one of the fortunate few that never needed to worry that she'd failed an exam.

In general, when it comes to motivating your daughter, tread carefully since a teen's emotional maturity regarding her future is as variable as is a teen's physical maturity. Your job is to help your daughter realize that there is such a thing as life after high school and helping her to prepare for adulthood as much as possible keeping in mind her emotional maturity. Elizabeth Edwards (wife of a former vice-presidential candidate) had it right though—that the best thing we can do for our children is to give them wings. Just remember that your daughter's take-off time may be sooner or later than you would like or wish.

Grades. These days we all hear about grade inflation starting as early as first grade when every student who reads a book gets an A whether the book is a Dr. Seuss or a Harry Potter book. Further, these days in many middle and high schools, children who routinely participate in class and religiously hand in homework get A's while some children who are shy or lazy students but score very high on standardized tests may wind up with C's and D's. Thus, your daughter's grades may be as much a reflection of whether she has accommodated the teacher as of what she has actually learned.

If your daughter receives a C and complains that the teacher marks her down because she doesn't like her or because she doesn't hand in her homework, tell her only A students can afford the luxury of such whining and that she should get busy and get to work. However, consider any grade under a C as an indication that your daughter and her teacher are not communicating.

Your daughter should be learning enough about a subject to warrant at least a C no matter whether the subject matter is exceedingly difficult or the teaching exceedingly poor. If your daughter is having trouble with a particular course, check out on-line tutorials which are available in just about every subject at various levels. Visit your local library to see what programs and/or materials it may have to help a poor student. If necessary, hire a tutor; if you can't afford the cost, try to find the time to learn the material and tutor her yourself.

Be objective when it comes to grades. Perhaps you think your daughter is underachieving because you believe her a genius but her grades are mediocre. Is she really underachieving or are your expectations too high? Remember, she may have a lot of common sense and native intelligence and a mature understanding of human nature but that does not necessarily translate into scholastic A's. Also, don't tell your C or B student that if she worked harder, she'd get all A's. True, a little more work may earn her a C+ or a B+ or even an A occasionally but even hard work may not transform a mediocre student into an A student.

Unless your daughter is hoping to attend a highly competitive university, focus more on what she is learning than on what grade she is receiving. Allow her the right not to hand in her homework that she considers make-work and take a B instead of an A if she feels like it. If, however, your daughter has her sights set on the Ivy Leagues or some other top university, she cannot afford the luxury of standing on principle and not doing make-work homework if her grades will suffer as a result. In this case, support your daughter's *feelings* but encourage her to do what's best for her. Empathize with her about doing make-work. Explain that perhaps it may not be make-work for the other students but agree with her that it is unfair for her teacher to mark her down for not doing work she does not need to do. It is too bad that these teens are not challenged more instead. If you can, try to get the school to pay more attention to its bright but under-achieving students. In any case, your empathy and gentle guidance toward choosing that she does what's best for her in the long run will help your daughter learn to pick her battles.

Beware of any sharp drop in your daughter's grades. The drop may signal that she may be involved with drugs, having some social problems at school or with friends, or that some situation at home is causing her serious concern. However, if all else seems well, don't treat every slump in performance as a major catastrophe or as a signal that something awful is going on. Your daughter may just feel overworked or bored or both and want a few weeks off. If she is open enough to let you know how boring school is or what a waste of time she thinks it is, she is probably taking a break from routine. However, stay aware. If her slump continues for more than a month or so, you'll need to take some action. After all, she shouldn't be *that* bored. Assuming you've ruled out drugs and pregnancy, find out if she is being bullied at school or is in a controlling or abusive relationship with a boyfriend or girlfriend, and check out her overall health. Proceed from there as appropriate to solve the problem. Some counselling might be in order.

Dropping Out. All along your daughter has been a model student.

She always got straight A's and approached her school and social life eagerly. However, at some point during high school or college, she might think seriously about leaving school. What she is being taught seems meaningless. *What's the point of it all*, she will ask. People will always be starving somewhere in the world, man will always commit atrocities toward one another, her life has no meaning. It's the *"Why am I here syndrome?"*

Take your daughter's feelings seriously. Don't think that just because she's doing well in school, she has it all figured out for herself. Her feelings may seem a normal rite of passage to you but to her they are unique and new. You can help by mentioning that almost everyone feels that way at one time or another—even more than once or twice. Almost everyone has felt overwhelmed by Life and their small place in it. Almost everyone goes through feelings of futility and inadequacy and thinks of seeking refuge through some form of escape. Tell her you don't have the answers for her, but in time she will have them for herself. All she needs to do is hang in there a little longer. In the meantime, she can attack the societal problems piecemeal. She can't feed the world but she can help out in the local food bank; she can't change man's propensity to harm his brethren but she can look into conflict resolution as a career. And, if it's simple ennui she's suffering from, give her something to do that's future oriented. Perhaps she can start selecting the colleges she plans on applying to or you can give her the job of planning the family vacation. While she's a potential dropout, you want to get her past the present by looking to the future. In the meantime, try not to be too cheerful. That will only make her feel her melancholy even more. Treat her as if she were recovering from a bout with the flu—with patience and kindness.

If your daughter wants to drop out of high school because of poor grades or social problems, encourage her to attack the problems rather than walk away from them. Perhaps she will agree to tutoring. Consider also that her poor grades may reflect problems at home or in her social life. Professional assistance might be advisable. Or, she may want to drop out because it seems glamorous to work or because she wants more pocket money. If so, help her get a part-time job while she's in school.

You might need to release her from chores at home or pick her up at late hours from a job at the Mall, but it's worth it to keep her in school.

If your daughter feels finishing high school and then going to college may be too much school for her to ever endure, do what a friend of mine did. She prevented her sixteen-year-old from dropping out by taking her to the law firm where she worked as a secretary. She showed her daughter her boss's impressive office—river view, leather couch, marble coffee table, large antique desk, private bar, thick carpet— and said *This is where you sit if you finish graduate school.* Next, she took her daughter to a paralegal's office, which was simply and efficiently furnished with a desk, a wall unit and a side chair and stated *This is where you sit if you finish college.* She then took her daughter to her work station which was equipped with the standard secretarial desk/computer tucked behind a tiny cubicle and said *This is where you sit if you finish high school.* Next and last, they visited the mailroom. No carpet, no private telephone, not even any chairs—only noisy machines, musty odors, and lots of dust. She told her daughter *This is where you work if you drop out of school.* Needless to say, the visit was very effective. Make the most of your office's "take your daughter to work day." Better yet, try and bring her there when the atmosphere's not so festive. (Incidentally, don't try this with a six-year-old—the mailroom with its array of colored paper and fancy copiers is likely to win out!)

My friend's solution might seem simplistic nor is graduate school or college the only route to success. However, my friend's immediate problem was to impress upon her daughter the need to stay in high school and "a picture is worth a thousand words." As for a child who has either no interest in attending college or the ability to do so, community colleges offer two-year programs covering a wide range of vocations. Such programs are often geared to the needs of the community and current industry.

THE THREE Rs

With the advent of Siri and Echo and their ilk, Reading, Writing and 'Rithmetic may soon go the way of the horse and buggy. As far as your daughter is concerned, reading has already become a lost art. All she needs to do now for information is to talk to her smart phone. She doesn't even need to know how to read in order to send or receive text messages—voice command, emojis and abbreviations usually suffice. As for arithmetic, in her view it was a waste of time for her to learn all those multiplication tables and how to do fractions when even not very smart smart phones can quickly come up with the answers.

The foregoing does not bode well for the human race since I believe our brains face atrophy unless they are routinely exercised. This belief is reinforced by modern medicine since old folks are encouraged to do puzzles and learn a language or another new skill so as to ward off or delay dementia. Further, many good test-takers will tell you that just before an exam they don't spend time "cramming" the material. Instead, they do mental warm-up exercises such as reading a newspaper's op-ed and editorial pages or working a crossword puzzle. Both of these activities jump-start the brain's thought processes enabling the test-taker to more readily analyze questions and apply answers from their own knowledge base. Smart phones and such eliminate the need for the brain to even remember a phone number.

Reading. While tech gizmos and multi-media are great for such things as obtaining information, introducing us to exotic places and telling us how to get there, and how particles and atoms interact or not, I believe that scanning a computer screen or viewing a video is no replacement for reading hard copy. All those pop-up windows and the need to click and scroll or change screens and wait for the little icon to finish its dance every time a fact or thought needs to be verified or examined is distracting to the retention process. There are other practical reasons for reading too—reading develops vocabulary and helps train the brain to organize thoughts.

Some teens will not read a book unless it is in paperback. Others are only interested in glamour or sports magazines. Whatever your daughter gets out of reading is more than she would get if she did not read anything. Being supportive of what she reads and encouraging her to speak about it can help develop a reading habit. You can also foster your daughter's reading habit such as by asking her to read out loud from the op-ed page of your local paper while you cook dinner. You could also leave the best-sellers lying around after you've read them instead of loaning them to a friend. If your daughter recommends a book to you or asks you to read a particular article, do her the courtesy of reading it. If your daughter's school gives her a suggested reading list from which she is to read a few, show an interest in her choices but don't dis any. You could also read (or re-read) some of your daughter's choices and discuss them with her later taking care to respect her opinions.

Also, don't criticize your daughter for reading things that you believe are too easy for her or for not getting from her reading what others do in terms of a book's message. For example, my daughter chose "The Diary of Anne Frank" for a sixth-grade book report. I was concerned about her reading it because I wasn't sure I was ready to face questions about man's inhumanity to man. However, after my daughter read her report to me, I discovered she had no real understanding of why the Franks were living in hiding. To her, Anne was simply a teenager who was having issues with her mother. Additionally, don't fear or criticize your daughter's literary tastes. Many adolescents have rather macabre interests (as do adults) and devour books about vampires or anything written by Stephen King. Even if your daughter's tastes run to smut or cheap love stories, let her be. Stephen King does not go around chopping people up even though he writes about people who do. Your daughter will not turn into Lizzie Borden just because she reads about murderers.

A Word of Caution. Sadly, some children *do* get heinous ideas from movies, books and various other media and, unfortunately, carry them out. It is impossible, however, to protect your daughter, especially as she enters her teens, from this type of pollution. Often, all one has to do is turn on the news or read a newspaper to learn about atrocities against man be they wrought under the guise of a holy war or the result of individual human failing. In any case, it is far better for your daughter to be exposed to life's sordid underbelly in the comfort and security of her own home where the contact between the depicted horrors and her own life is so extreme. Forbidding exposure to literary pornography, violence, smut, fanatical ideas and other forms of media pollution merely gives such things more credence. Allowing your daughter to pick and choose books for herself gives you a better chance of knowing what she is reading and thus an opportunity to express your own thoughts on a particular matter. So, by all means, monitor your daughter's reading material but don't deprive her of the right to judge for herself. Step in only if her reading of such books, or her spending hours reading dark news on the Internet, appears to have changed her behavior in a negative way such as causing nightmares, increased belligerence or despondency, lower grades, less interest in friends, other changes in behavior, etc.

Writing. Writing is literally becoming a lost art. And I don't mean writing stories—I mean writing in script. Children still learn to write in script in the third or fourth grade but in many schools, students are not required to use it thereafter. By the time your daughter is in high school, she may have entirely forgotten how to write in script. I believe that allowing children to continue to print after being taught script results in a further dumbing-down of our society. In my view, there is something about the flow of writing in script that allows what's being written to make an imprint on the brain and stay there. Moreover, I think script is faster than printing for note-taking. To encourage your daughter to write in script, supply her with free-flowing pens in a few colors and suggest that she write notes in script to the grandparents or write-up fun family memories or your stories about the adorable things she did when a toddler to be put in the family album.

'Rithmetic. Basic math is also becoming a lost skill and not solely because of computers. It used to be a common sight at the local supermarket to see a parent explaining to an elementary school-age child why one box of tissues was less expensive than another. However, today's parents are often too busy to take their young children along when they go shopping so children often grow up with having little or no idea of what things cost. Use of charge cards for almost everything also adds to the dumbing down of our children. Even adolescents who do well in school and who are given $5 to get a meal at a fast-food restaurant often seem clueless as to how to pick out what they want from the menu for such amount or less and determine whether or not they receive the correct change.

Bottom line to this problem is to take your daughter food shopping from time to time so she can learn to assess the best value not only dollar for dollar but also considering the ingredient list and nutritional value. And when it comes to buying school supplies, assess what you think is the cost and give your daughter the cash and let her figure it out. I would suggest the same for clothing but these days things cost so much, it's probably not a good idea to hand over large amounts of cash to your daughter. Instead though if you're picking her up from school and realize that you've run out of milk, send her into the store with some cash and let her do the shopping while you wait in the car. Any experience with money that you can give your daughter requiring her to use basic math will not only help her to become savvy money-wise but will also help keep her brain fed with things other than the click of a mouse or directions from the likes of Siri.

13. EVERYDAY CRISES

But I want to see your school play!
Boy Crazy — Dating — Her Room
If She's an Only Child — Practicing
Siblings & Jealousy — Sleepovers
Where Are You Going?

BUT I WANT TO SEE YOUR SCHOOL PLAY!

Adolescents can be real party-poopers. You've played Romeo to her Juliet all fall. You've gotten all your friends and co-workers to buy tickets for her school play. The flowers are ordered and your new dress is hanging in the closet, already hemmed. The big night is two days away and you're crying. Your daughter has just told you she doesn't want you to go. Taken aback but thinking she's concerned about her performance, you reassure her that she'll do fine but then she told you flat out not to go, that she would be embarrassed if you were there. You're crying because you are angry and because it's not fair to you. Why doesn't she want you to go? Why does she allow her father to pick her up from school concerts or parties, but not you? You're right. She's not being fair. Or is she?

Before getting into an argument about the matter, think about the situation from her point of view. Is she embarrassed because you're much older than all the other moms or are so overweight that you take up two seats instead of one? Are you overly loud or a braggart? Do you dress inappropriately, perhaps too youthfully or too sexy? Are you too critical? Realistically, almost all parents embarrass their children at one time or another and, more likely, more often than that. In this situation, however, be honest with yourself. Does your daughter have a valid reason to object to your behavior? If so, acknowledge your flaw (you're entitled to a few!) and make whatever changes are reasonable and possible so as to assure your daughter that you will not behave in a way that will embarrass her. Even if you think she is being ridiculous, offer to sit in the back and leave right after the performance. However, if there's a possibility that you're being in attendance will negatively affect her performance—perhaps it's your nature to be "helpful" by being overly critical or whether her concerns are groundless—respect her wishes and don't go, particularly if this will be her first foray in overcoming shyness.

Whatever your daughter's reasons for not wanting you to attend her performance, you can of course express your disappointment but don't make a big deal out of it or make her feel guilty. Perhaps she'll be less uncomfortable the next time especially if you've made valid attempts to correct or downplay your daughter's perceived deficiencies of you. However, she might raise the same objections in the future about camp visiting days or college parent weekends. Quite often too, if you're divorced, she will apply different standards to you than to her father and willingly overlook his flaws, but not yours. This too is a tough pill to swallow but again consider your daughter's needs before your own. It just might take her until college graduation or her first full-time job or even longer for her to feel secure enough to stand separate but together with you. Some people, adults as well as teens, are so insecure that they don't want anyone close to them to be in a position to comment on their performances or achievements. I know a woman who volunteers her time by giving lectures at a local museum. However, she has asked her friends not to attend them because having a friend in the audience makes her feel self-conscious. Very few of us are ever fully grown up. I know being left out hurts but be patient.

Of course, some parents would be relieved never to have to sit through school band concerts or freeze while attending outdoor school sports events. However, Murphy's Law rules again as these are the parents who have children who insist their parents attend every play, every track meet, every camp or school function. Naturally, for these parents, there is always some sort of schedule conflict. The middle school concert is on the same night as the senior high play or an important business function is scheduled the night of your daughter's swim meet. Or your daughter told you six months ago that it would be okay if you missed her ballet recital—that she "understands." However, you'd better show up if your daughter (i.e., the martyr) told you ten times a week for the past month that it's OK if you don't attend. It's a difficult situation though if you *really* can't attend, even for part of the time, because of work-related responsibilities or a conflict with another child. In that case, appeal gently and calmly to your daughter's burgeoning maturity when explaining why you cannot attend something that is important to her and explain how disappointed you are. And as always, don't make promises about the future that you might not be able to keep.

BOY CRAZY *(In this section and elsewhere romantic relationships are presumed to be boy/girl for literary convenience but the situations discussed are also generally applicable to non-traditional gender relationships. See also Chapter 14 at "Gender Identity.")*

It seems that all your daughter and her friends do is talk and think about boys. Muffled giggles sail through the house interrupted only by various ring tones and beeps. And it was only last Halloween that your daughter and her girlfriends were childishly squealing with delight while they squirted each other with Slime.

During the beginning stages of your daughter's fascination with boys, very little boy/girl interaction actually goes on. However, because of her seemingly incessant preoccupation with boys, you are worried that you'll be looking at baby cribs the next time the two of you go shopping. Relax. Right now, your daughter is just behaving normally and is probably not even ready to date unless someone teases or pushes her into it. One young girl I know was invited out on a date a few times by a boy in her class. She always refused and one night her mother got a call from the boy's father wanting to know what was wrong with his son. *Nothing,* explained the mother. *It's just that my daughter would still rather play with the neighbor's puppies than go out on a date.* Be aware too that an older sibling's teasing might push your daughter into dating before she's really ready.

Some girls however are the ones who do the chasing. I know of two thirteen-year-old girls who paraded up and down a particular street hoping to "accidentally" run into certain boys. Their excuse for being on that street was that they were out walking the dog even though they were a mile from home and the dog, just a puppy, could barely stand. (They had taken turns carrying the puppy to their destination.)

Being a teenager and discovering boys should be fun. It shouldn't immediately bring an accusation of boy-craziness or an onslaught of lectures about contraception and promiscuity. However, if you have not already discussed the subject of sex, intimacy and STDs (*see* Chapter 14—SEX and Chapter 3 at "STDs & AIDS"), this is a good time to start. This is also a good time to tell your daughter the other facts of life—that it's best to let the boy do the chasing. This might sound quaint and old-fashioned but, unfortunately, except in unusual situations, girls do not really have equal rights when it comes to dating despite the media seeming to make it so.

While it has always been considered proper for a girl to invite a boy to be her escort to a party or to a concert if she provides the tickets, girls who constantly chase boys are still considered too forward and too "easy." However, your daughter might be a take-charge person and it would be out of character for her to wait for the phone to beep and if she acted at being demure, her relationships with boys would not be honest ones. Thus, if your daughter has an aggressive personality, let her know the pitfalls about making the first move but that while she may be subject to some ridicule and have fewer boyfriends, the ones she will have will like *her*, not someone she pretended to be. Also, as your daughter gains some experience regarding boy/girl relationships, she'll learn that some boys are so shy about girls, that she'll need to make the first move. An invitation to a group event might move the situation along.

Try to have a light touch and a light heart with respect to your daughter's hormone-induced silliness and don't make a major issue out of your daughter chasing a boy. However, make sure she knows not to make a pest of herself and that if she invites a boy out and he declines the invitation without suggesting an alternative time, she should not keep contacting that boy about a date. She should also know not to contact a boy to ask him why he hasn't returned her messages.

DATING

Group Dating. In many communities, teens don't really "date" until their last year in high school if even then. Instead they socialize in groups—at least on the surface. It's a good guess though that there's some pairing off here and there. It seems to me that this group dating thing has some advantages—there's less worry about not having a date on a Saturday night and the teens have a better opportunity to relate to each other as equals rather than feel pressured to fulfill stereotypical sex roles. In my view though because of the pairing up that occurs from time to time, girls are at risk of being labelled promiscuous if they pair-off with a different boy each time even if all they engage in is a few kisses and light petting. Also, another drawback of group dating is peer pressure to go along with whatever. All it would take for all the children in the group to get into trouble is one bad apple with some drugs, a bottle of alcohol and/or a really bad idea such as vandalizing a store or a place of worship. Remind your daughter that it's easy to get into trouble but hard to get out of it.

Make sure your daughter is aware of the pitfalls of group dating even if you have to follow her around while you continue your discourse about being easy and the pitfalls of peer pressure. She will be annoyed… she will smirk…she will cover her ears. Regardless, she *will* hear you. Further, just as if she were on a traditional date, make sure you know at least most of the children in the group, what the group plans to do, when she'll be home, and that she has a way of leaving the group and getting home either on her own or by contacting you.

Traditional Dating. There's no set age when to allow your daughter to begin dating though traditional dating is beginning at a later age than in the past. Nowadays, teens are taking longer to reach adulthood—they are starting to drive and drink later as well. There are probably many reasons for this—high gas and movie prices, parental hovering, difficulty of finding paid part-time jobs so as to have money to date, etc. but the consensus is that the main cause is what I call *Techitis*, the constant interaction with multi-media displacing face-to-face interaction. Whether this is good news or not only time will tell but extended adolescence is keeping pace with a longer middle-age and a longer life.

Look for cues from your daughter before you lay down the law as to when she may start dating. Remember, you don't need to take any position until she has been asked out. Find out at that time whether or not your daughter *wants* to date. It might well be that she really doesn't want to, but thinks she should. Also, before you take a position on dating, consider your values and community customs, as well as your daughter's needs. You might be able to keep your sixteen-year-old from dating but at what cost? Forbidding your daughter to date when all her friends do could cause a major breach between the two of you, something that you definitely don't want to do at this time in her life. You want her to hear you, not tune you out, when you talk about your values regarding sex and relationships and you certainly don't want her sneaking out to date. Thus, be realistic about when it's appropriate for your daughter to start dating.

The first time a boy asked my friend's daughter out, she refused— she just wasn't ready to date. She'd not even begun the muffled giggling about boys with her friends. That fall, when she started high-school, she still looked as if she were only eleven but that turned out to be a positive. The boys who had not yet started to develop physically flocked to her because she looked "safe." These late bloomers hung together and though they didn't date, they were able to develop friendships and learn how to get along with the opposite sex on an equal basis—knowledge that we all could use at any age.

When your daughter starts dating, you need to make sure that the boys your daughter is dating are teens (and not men) and that her dates are known to her (or you) through friends, school, extra-curricular activities, camp, church, or family and not someone she just met through social media. Nose-around, whatever, as much as you need to assure yourself of your daughter's physical safety (*see also* Chapter 3 at "Sexual Predators").

Before your daughter steps out the door on a date, be sure that you know who the boy is and where he lives. You should also know where they are going and approximately when she will be home. Afterwards, don't embarrass your daughter with too many questions about her date as she may be uncomfortable with her new feelings. Besides, since time immemorial, teens have kept their parents in semi-darkness about their boyfriends and all you need is to be assured of her safety. Thus, even if your daughter chooses not to share her social life with you, you should know enough about it to ease any worries you might have about her being or becoming involved with alcohol or drugs, engaging in sex, or participating in illegal activities. You don't, for example, want your daughter double-dating with teens who think a fun Saturday night is to shop-lift at the local Mall.

"Going Steady" may be the norm in some communities. Going steady limits your daughter's experience in interacting with dates with different personalities, interests, world-views, etc. but for some girls, it may be a type of freedom. Going steady may give your daughter enough security to freely pursue her studies or a special interest since she won't have to spend time cruising the Mall or worrying about whether or not she'll have a date for the Junior Prom. Don't intervene because you don't feel the boy is "good enough" for your daughter or just because you disapprove of the idea of going steady. But don't hesitate to intervene if you believe the relationship is putting too much pressure on your daughter sexually or if the boy is so controlling that she no longer participates in other activities that had been important to her. However, if you think physical abuse is involved, do not under any circumstances allow your daughter to be alone with the boy again and take appropriate action before someone gets really hurt. It is likely that if a boy physically abused your daughter, he will do the same to other girls. You will be doing the boy a favor by reporting him so that he could get some professional help before it's too late for him and some other girl.

If you prohibit your daughter from going steady or from dating a particular boy without reasonable grounds, you run the risk of her defying you by lying and sneaking out. If you disapprove of the boy and you have good reason to do so, certainly voice your concerns loudly and clearly, but don't forbid the relationship unless you actually fear for her safety. It is better for your daughter to go against your wishes openly than covertly. This way at least you will know where and with whom she is with. Also, *she did hear what you said* about the boy and your words will linger in her mind so don't be surprised if she ends the relationship on her own. If so, skip the "I told you so's."

The danger of absolute prohibition of a date with a particular boy without very good reason may cause your daughter to sneak about. If she snuck out for a date, she will likely be afraid to call you if she is in trouble. Also, it is highly likely that you will discover her sneakiness sooner or later and then you will be mistrustful of her. Your daughter will not feel good about herself for losing your trust either. When a major breach of trust occurs, while some children will work hard to earn back their parents' trust; others may choose to continue on a downward spiral to justify your feelings of mistrust and their own resultant negative feelings about themselves. It's far better to state your negative feelings about her date and let your daughter make her own decisions about people whenever possible as long as no danger to your daughter is involved. Don't be surprised that when left to her own judgment, your daughter will often reach the same conclusions as you about a particular boy.

I think it's natural for parents to want their children to date children with similar backgrounds, particularly with respect to race and religion. However, like it or not, the world is changing and America has become a hodge-podge of people of various colors, ethnicities, religious beliefs and backgrounds and will likely continue to become even more so. Consequently, your daughter will be entering an adult world considerably different from the world you entered as an adult. Such differences between your daughter and a boy she wishes to date is not a reason for you to disapprove of the date. Again, your disapproval of her date should be based solely on safety concerns.

HER ROOM

You've worked hard so that your family can afford a bedroom just for your daughter. You remember the joy the two of you shared picking out the paint colors and the furnishings. Nowadays though not only has the paint lost its luster but the walls are pitted with bits of colorful masking tape and the furnishings are barely visible under a week's worth of dirty laundry and discarded loose-leaf pages. And the floor? It's a complete disaster area littered with cotton balls smeared with nail polish, candy wrappers from left-over Halloween candy, loose change, hair bands of every color and shape, broken barrettes, a plethora of troll-like plastic creatures, and miscellaneous pieces from various building blocks. Further, the only way you know that the bed is still in the room is because there's a menagerie of stuffed animals atop a pile of blankets nestled against the back wall. You've tried bribery, withholding allowances, grounding, etc. to change your daughter's slovenly ways—all to no avail.

The truth is that some people are just sloppy or simply oblivious to a mess or work better amid one. Regardless, unless the Board of Health has issued a condemnation notice or bugs have become your daughter's roommates, go for the minimum. First and foremost, put your foot down really hard that she keep the floor, window area and stairs clear so as to provide safe exit in case of fire. Check on this every night and if she's already asleep when you do, wake her up and have her get up and do it. After doing some picking up before bedtime has become *her* habit, go for the dirty laundry being routinely put in the hamper or at least brought to the washing machine on a weekly basis. If she fails to do this, don't do her wash. As for the rest of her mess, rather than make an issue of it, set aside a once-a-month family clean-up day. Note that I say the foregoing as a neat-nick. My home may seldom pass a white glove test but it is always neat. Having had two messy daughters and looking the other way was a real challenge for me. However, it's always a good idea to pick one's battles carefully especially when teenagers are involved.

Some children don't like to stay in their room—they feel left out if they hear other family members enjoying themselves. For example, your daughter may have a desk, her own computer, good lighting, a comfy chair and a kitty for company but she does her homework sprawled in front of the TV. She says she works better with noise and clatter about. If she likes to do it that way and her grades are OK, it should be OK with you too even if you're relegated to a corner on the couch. Of course, it never hurts to suggest that she do her homework elsewhere but again, I don't think this matter should rise to battle level. What you can insist on though is that she pick up after herself since the living room is shared by the entire family and not her private domain.

If your daughter shares a room and she is the older sibling, she likely considers it *her* room. Younger siblings will usually accept the territorial rights of the elder sibling—sort of harking back to the days of yore when primogenitary (first-born son inherits all) ruled the land.

It certainly would be fairer if your daughter actually shared the room but it's probably best not to interfere with your children's perception of the natural order of things. Besides, it's easier for you to get used to the idea of having the younger child practice the violin or do homework in the living room than it is to hear your children squabbling all the time.

If the younger sibling has voiced concerns about his or her status as a second-class citizen in the shared bedroom, tell him or her that the time will come when the older sister leaves and he or she will then have the room all to themselves. Best to say this out of earshot of your teen daughter though since she will seethe about the younger child having his or her own room when she leaves the nest—something *she* never had! Pointing out that she had her own room before her sibling was born will only add fuel to the fire because *it didn't count then*.

IF SHE'S AN ONLY CHILD

Adolescence hits parents of an only child like a ton of bricks. Suddenly, their wonderful, devoted, cooperative, well-mannered, well-spoken, happy daughter seems to short-circuit. Now she wants to dress her own way; she spends hours locked up by herself text messaging with her friends; she is very secretive; she is barely civil to family visitors and relatives; and, worst of all, she doesn't think you're so wonderful any more. Unless the mother of an only child has many families around where she can observe the capricious behavior of other pubescent girls, she is going to feel that something is terribly wrong with her daughter. Remember, much of adolescent behavior is extreme. If your daughter seems happy tucked away with her Facebook buddies or is so engulfed in environmental concerns that she criticizes you for every drop of gas that you use, don't be too concerned. Most likely the answer is just to relax and stop pushing so hard.

Being expected to be perfect or to overachieve is often a special burden of an only child. Your daughter is retrenching for her passage from adolescence to maturity. She has had the benefit of lots of attention from you through the years and as long as she continues to feel your love and concern, more than likely she will make a safe passage. Too much intervention on your part though is going to slow such passage and make the atmosphere in your home unnecessarily stormy. It is often more difficult for the only child to become her own person because there are no other children around for her parents to focus on. This is a good time for *you* to develop other interests—perhaps to finish college, start a new business or career, or get more involved in your job or your community or find some new hobbies.

PRACTICING

Music lessons, dance instruction, gymnastics all cost a lot of money. You want to be sure your daughter is getting your money's worth so you push her to practice, practice, practice. However, if you constantly need to push and prod your daughter to practice and there is no progress, there is no point in continuing the lessons if it is causing unnecessary friction between the two of you or is any kind of burden on the family. By the time your daughter reaches her teens both of you will likely know if she has any talent or even decent proficiency in the chosen activity. It is ambition, not just talent, that gets the budding actress more than a few parts or the figure skater to the Olympics. While ambition in a youngster may be squashed, it's not a trait that's easily infused. If your daughter is a talented violinist but is satisfied to play only in the high school orchestra, you cannot force her to aim for Carnegie Hall. The desire to succeed, to be the best, must come from within. It's true that there are stories about many children who succeeded only because they were pushed by their parents. My guess is that these "pushed" children harbored ambitions as great as their parents but were just not outwardly aggressive in pursuing them. They let their parents do the pushing because underneath they wanted success as much as their parents did. Besides, it's often easier for an inwardly ambitious child to put the onus on their parents; e.g., *I can't do such and such because my parents already paid for the rink time* rather than acknowledge their own ambition.

On the other hand, be careful not to quash your daughter's ambition even if you feel she has no talent. That is for her to find out, not for you to determine. While it is only natural for you to want to protect her from hurt feelings or disappointment, your daughter needs to discover her own limitations herself. Thus, don't encourage her fantasies about being talented when she is not—just stay more or less neutral emphasizing that what's important is that she gets pleasure from the activity not whether she's a pro at it or not. (Check out "Florence Foster Jenkins," a highly acclaimed movie based on a true story of a delusional would-be opera singer.)

Allow your daughter to continue her lessons even if she never practices without being prodded if it's no financial strain and she enjoys them. In that case, don't even bother her about practicing and run the risk of hurting your relationship by spoiling something that she simply enjoys doing. Conversely, if she wants to stop lessons that you encouraged, let her. No lessons are wasted. Any skill that your daughter develops, even at a minimal level, will likely give her pleasure or be useful later in life in one form or another even if she seems completely turned off to the activity now.

SIBLINGS & JEALOUSY

Generally. Even if your children are close in age or of the same sex, they should always be treated as individuals no matter how much you might be tempted or how much easier it is to do otherwise. What you do for one child, you need not do for another. As a parent, your job is to see that each child's *needs* (not "wants") are met. Buying a guitar for Alicia, who is interested in music, does not mean that you need to buy a guitar for tone-deaf Cindy. As a matter of fact, you need not buy anything for Cindy just because you bought something for Alicia.

If your teen daughter accuses you of favoring her brother or sister over her, explain that you are only human and it is perfectly natural that at times you will favor one child over another just as sometimes you prefer cake to ice cream. Nobody can or should treat their children exactly the same because no two children are exactly alike—even identical twins may have some differences.

Remember too not to act as a referee if your children quarrel. You cannot win. Let them work it out for themselves as long as no blows are struck. If physical fighting does occur, intervene to stop the fighting but do not take sides. If one child always gets the better of the other, speak to each child in private. It takes two to make a disagreement. Don't automatically favor the "loser" either. It may be that the "weaker" child uses his or her vulnerability to get your attention. If your children are always at each other and often come to blows, or if one consistently takes advantage of the other, seek outside advice. For example, it's possible the anti-social behavior may stem from a physical problem such as a metabolic abnormality that is not readily apparent or you may be unwittingly provoking such behavior by always responding to the wants of the most verbal child.

For example, I know a family where the middle child, Wendy, who was small and highly sensitive, was teased and verbally bullied by her brother and sister. Wendy would run to her mother and tearfully tattle on her siblings. The mother would scold the siblings and sometimes punish them but the situation didn't change. The scenario repeated itself several times during the week and sometimes several times during the same day. The mom's sympathy for Wendy is understandable; however, it's a fact of life that children will take advantage of a whiny sensitive child. It's also human nature for the strong to take advantage of the weak and that's what civilized societies try to control.

Thus, in the above example, rather than attempt to civilize the siblings through threats and punishment, the mom and Wendy could help the situation along by changing their reactions to the siblings' actions. Families often get into destructive verbal communications that trigger arguments, threats, bullying and general unpleasantness among family members. If your family is in this type of unpleasant cycle, try changing your reactions and those of the "victim's." Altering routine responses may often reduce family friction. Get outside help if need be even if you think all children fight and tease. The victim needs help with self-esteem and you deserve a more peaceful household.

Remember too that it is healthier for your children to be in cahoots against you than against each other. Allow them to stand together and pull the wool over your eyes occasionally. Siblings are often so different that their only commonality is their respective irritation with their parents. (Fortunately, the infamous California Menendez Brothers who murdered their sleeping parents for money are an anomaly.) Be careful not to destroy what your children's only bond may be. Don't ask or force one child to tattle on the other and don't listen to any tattling. Obviously, however, you need to encourage your children to come to you if their sibling (or a friend) seems to have a serious problem such as using drugs or stealing. This is a tricky area and if you suspect one of your children is covering for a sibling (or a friend) who is involved in unlawful or harmful behavior or contemplating a heinous act, trust your instincts and take appropriate action immediately.

Special Needs Siblings. Being a parent of a special needs child, even one with minimal special needs, is not only physically demanding but extremely stressful. It is a day-in, day-out worry, 24 hours a day, 365 days a year plus the worry of who is going to take care of the child when the parent is gone. Add to the strain of caring for a special needs child, a jealous insolent teenager, and you've got one harried and likely very cranky parent. If your daughter has a sibling who is a special needs child, your daughter will likely have exhibited periods of intense jealousy toward her sister or brother, particularly if they are younger than she. Fortunately (or hopefully), however, she takes her feelings out on you rather than on the sibling.

There are a few things you can do though that will make life a bit easier for all. First, make sure you get enough rest and time for yourself. Take advantage of offers of help from family and friends. Find a hobby that you like that doesn't take too much time but gives you satisfaction—perhaps a few nights at the gym or a weekly night out with the girls. You deserve at least this. Next, empathize with your daughter that you understand that she often gets the short end of the stick and, if you haven't already done so, explain the sibling's specialness in a way that she can relate to.

Basically, let your daughter know the cause of the sibling's disability and the prognosis and the limits it places on the family. Take care not to tell your daughter how lucky she is not to suffer so—she can figure that out for herself. Instead try to find some way or time to make your daughter "special" too. Perhaps you can let her choose the family breakfast cereals or you can arrange with your employer to take a late lunch hour (or have a neighbor watch her sibling) so you can pick her up from school and have some private time together. Simply said, you *must* make some time for yourself and for you to be with your daughter even if it means mac & cheese every night for dinner or sticky floors forever. And lastly, *see* "Jealously" below.

Jealousy. It's common for siblings to be jealous of each other from time to time but jealousy of the attention given to a special needs or gifted sibling is likely to be intense and quite worrisome for the parent. Jealousy indeed is an ugly trait but one that you cannot talk or nag your daughter out of. Just like with bad habits, your daughter must cure her jealousy herself. I'm sure your daughter doesn't enjoy being jealous even if she has reason to be. Validate her feelings and acknowledge her reasons for jealousy while gently explaining that the reasons for her jealousy are not going to go away, not ever. Then explain that jealousy is like a green-eyed monster living in her body and that the more jealous she is, the larger the monster gets. Tell her that if she doesn't stop feeding the monster, soon there will be no room inside her for anything but the monster and that if she doesn't get a handle on the problem, her jealousy will rule all her actions. She may choose not to engage in a sport she likes just because her sister is a champ in it; instead of doing her math homework, she may spend her time plotting childish ways to get back at her sibling; or worse, she may do something really stupid or foolish just to get your full attention.

Challenge your daughter to find a solution to her jealousy. Even suggest a few. Maybe a chart on her bulletin board marking her jealous feelings aiming for a downward trend might be the way to go. One girl I know who had this problem decided to be as jealous as she wanted but only on one day a week. I don't know if she still has her "OK to be jealous day" but I do know that not too long after her solution the green-eyed monster rarely showed itself.

SLEEPOVERS

By the time your daughter is a teenager, sleeping over at someone's home shouldn't be a big deal. By now she and her friends should be responsible enough to get to sleep at a reasonable hour even if the sleepover is on a school night. And if they don't, one night without enough sleep won't cause your daughter any harm. Basically, sleeping over at a friend's home is a good experience for your daughter. She'll have a chance to practice good manners and converse with other adults. Also, sleeping out may give your daughter an opportunity to learn about another culture or lifestyle. She will come home and tell you, *yes, she remembered to make the bed*, and that she learned how to make *dim sum* (bite-size steamed dumplings with various fillings) and to play chess. Don't restrict your daughter's freedom unnecessarily by denying her the opportunity to feel proud of herself and for you to be proud of her.

Notwithstanding the foregoing, if you don't personally know the host family, check them out even more carefully than you would if your daughter were to babysit for them (*see* Chapter 10 at "Babysitting"). Having done so and if you have reason to believe that the other child or host family will behave in a way that is harmful to your daughter, or your instinct makes you uneasy, veto the sleepover. If appropriate, explain to your daughter why you nixed the plan. Most likely your daughter will argue that you don't know what you're talking about. Stay firm. Trust your instincts. The old adage that "*he doth protest too much*" may also be a good indication of how on-target you are about your unease. Be sure though to check out your misgivings at your earliest opportunity and explain or apologize to your daughter as appropriate. In the meantime, be prepared for a sulky daughter and a door slam or two.

There's a zillion reasons not to allow sleepovers at your house—the chosen night is inconvenient for you, the children were unruly at the last sleepover despite promises to behave otherwise, having over-night guests has become a physical burden for you, whatever. You don't even need a reason—you do have a right to be selfish from time to time. Just be honest with your daughter as to why you don't want her friends staying overnight. On the other hand, if you have the time and energy and an extra air mattress or two, it could be fun not only for them but for you too. Also, hosting a sleepover will give you some insight as to where your daughter and her friends are emotionally and socially.

Sometimes sleepovers between two friends means that the sleepovers are always at the same child's home even though both families would welcome sleepovers. Your daughter may be the exact opposite of a home-body and is always going out, never inviting her friends in or to sleepover. Don't look at it as a rejection of her home. More likely, she feels so safe and secure that she's never afraid to leave it. If you feel odd about her being at her friend's home all the time and there really is no reason why your daughter shouldn't invite her friends over for a night—it's not roach heaven, snacks are abundant, and family members do not behave as if they're from another planet—it may be because you're concerned about what the host family may be thinking about you. Don't waste your time—they know you're not an ogre. Remember, they have a teenage daughter too! You could though assuage any guilt you may have about your daughter's seeming preference for any place but home by sending along some simple goodies for the host family to enjoy.

Notwithstanding the foregoing, if you're feeling uneasy, rather than guilty, about your daughter always sleeping over at the same friend's house, trust your instincts. There may be some hanky-panky going on between the two girls. While such adolescent goings on are not abnormal nor are they indicative of your daughter's or her friend's sexual identity, it is not something that should be encouraged. Also, most likely your daughter and her friend feel some guilt over their nocturnal activities so it's best to put a stop to it by nixing future sleepovers between the two girls. As an explanation, you could say that you're concerned that the girls *might* become too physically close. You'll probably get a loud MOTHER! from your daughter implying that you don't know what you're talking about. That might be true but it doesn't hurt to be safe than sorry particularly if your gut tells you that your daughter is being exploited in some way. If the other parents want to know why the change, you can simply say that you read something that made you concerned that the girls *might* become too close and leave it at that. (*See also generally* Chapter 14 at "Gender Identity.")

WHERE ARE YOU GOING?

Some teens do everything at the last possible moment—whether it's cramming for an exam or letting you know that they volunteered you to chaperone a class trip that very weekend. I am sure that there must be some societal reason for this. Perhaps the underlying threat of domestic terrorism or today's economic uncertainty is the cause of their here today, gone tomorrow attitudes. More likely though, it's probably just their age. Whatever the reason, though, the result is the same. You are hereby forewarned that your older teen daughter will receive an 8:00pm call to go to a party which she will swear that neither she nor her friends knew anything about before the call.

I was brought up not to run out at the last minute. I never understood why I shouldn't though so when the situation arose with my daughter, I was unconvincing with my argument that she shouldn't go. I had no answer when she asked, *"Why not?"* I was, however, able to maintain certain parental rights, but only with a great deal of negotiation. The scenario was as follows.

SHE: *After putting her phone down.* I'm going to wash my hair.
ME: So late, dear? *Daughter already in shower.*
SHE: *After blow-drying hair.* Olivia and I are going to a party.
ME: Now? Tonight? You can't go. You can't just run out at the last minute anytime someone calls you.
SHE: Why not?
ME: It's just not nice—don't ask me why.
SHE: That's not a reason. What difference does it make if I was asked last night or now?
ME: *Silence.* Where's the party?
SHE: I don't know.
ME: *Incredulous.* You don't know?
SHE: *Following an eye roll.* Olivia knows…I'm meeting her downstairs.
ME: OK…I'll walk down with you and get the name and address.
SHE: *Hesitantly.* Olivia doesn't know either.
ME: *Astonished.* Wait a minute--how can you go to a party if you don't even know where it is?
SHE: *With a how-could-you-be-so-stupid look.* We know *where* it is—it's on 86th and Broadway—we just don't know the address.
ME: Well, whose party is it?
SHE: We don't know. We'll ask the doorman.
ME: *Counting to ten very slowly.* If the doorman tells you the apartment number without your knowing even the name, it's certainly not the kind of party you belong at.

SHE: *With another how-could-you-be-so-stupid look.* MOTHER! Don't you think Olivia and I have enough sense to leave if it is *that* kind of party?

ME: *Not really too sure, but very firmly.* You will have to call and let me know the name and apartment number as soon as you get there.

SHE: I won't…I'm not a baby.

ME: You're still my baby and when the man on the news asks, *Do you know where your children are?* I need to be able to answer…I need to be able to tell the police where you went when I send them out looking for your body in the morning.

SHE: *Sighing disdainfully.* Okay, okay, I'll let you know you as soon as we get there.

About a half-hour later, the phone beeps…*Hi, Ma…We found the building but the doorman wouldn't let us in 'cause we didn't know the name. We're going across the street for pizza. Be home in an hour or so. Love 'ya. Bye.*

If you want your daughter to stay home and she wants to go out, unless you have a reason for her to stay, allow her to go. Otherwise, it is like asking her to put on a sweater because you are cold. You should of course always know where and with whom she is going and when she will be home. If your daughter realizes that you need this information not because you don't trust her but because it's your job as a parent to know such things, she will likely be honest with you. Teenagers, like most adults, will rise to responsibilities given to them. If you treat your daughter mistrustfully or as if she were only eight years old, she will likely fulfill your negative expectations. If you give your daughter your trust as well as your care, she's less likely to misuse it.

14. SEX & SENSUALITY

It's Time We Had a Talk
Love and Intimacy — Gender Identity
Promiscuity — Date Rape
Pregnancy — Your Sexuality

IT'S TIME WE HAD A TALK

Discussing physical intimacy, pregnancy, date-rape and STDs with your daughter presumes that you can talk to her about sex at all. Most likely, she will roll her eyes and say she knows all about it. Besides, as far as adolescent girls are concerned, sex may be for the birds and bees but it is not for their parents. You're middle-aged or nearly so—too old to have sexual desires and even well beyond the memory of any! Don't presume that because of all the sexual innuendo and activity in the media that your daughter's views about sex are sophisticated.

My daughter would never let me discuss sex with her. Even letters delicately explaining life behind the bushes (which I thought were potential Pulitzer winners) sent to her at camp were mysteriously never received—of course, snacks and money had no problem reaching her. Generally, if your daughter is eleven or so, she may be too embarrassed to discuss anything about sex with you. Even when she's older, she still might be too embarrassed or she will proclaim that she has learned everything she needs to know at school or from her friends. Conversations with our daughters about sex usually start out as follows.

PHASE I—WHEN SHE'S ELEVEN.

YOU: Could you take off your head phones, please…now that you may soon become a woman, there are a few things we should discuss….

SHE: *The infamous eye roll as she removes the head phones.*

YOU: Seriously…we need to talk about a few things.

SHE: I know everything. *Fidgets with head phones.*

YOU: Sex? Babies? Disease? Contraception?

SHE: *MOTHER!*

PHASE II—WHEN SHE'S OLDER.

YOU: Now that you'll be dating…there a few things we should discuss…

SHE: I don't want a lecture.

YOU: No lecture, honey. I just want to make sure you know a few things…like that boys and girls view things differently…

SHE: **MOTHER!!** (*Leaves room to blow-dry hair.*)

PHASE III—A SATURDAY MORNING SHORTLY BEFORE HIGH SCHOOL GRADUATION.

SHE: I'm going to the beach today.

YOU: With who? (*The beach is two hours away.*)

SHE: Jerry, from history class—his father has a beach house—you know who he is.

YOU: Just the two of you? Is his father going? Will his father be there?

SHE: No, just his brother.

YOU: How old is this brother?

SHE: Nineteen.

YOU: (*Do you discuss a ménage a trois?*) Honey…there are a few things we need to discuss…

SHE: But Jerry and I are just friends! Besides his acne still oozes. Yuk!

YOU: True, but sea, sun and sand have turned lots of friends into lovers.

SHE: **MOTHER!!!** (*Disappears to find suntan lotion.*)

PHASE IV—WHEN SHE'S HOME DURING A COLLEGE SEMESTER BREAK.

SHE: Ma…where's your birth control pills? I left mine at school.

Don't let your embarrassment or your daughter's seeming sophistication put you off about discussions about sex. Keep trying. Likely it will be an uphill battle. But you cannot count on what she was taught in a school sex education or hygiene class. It may have come too early or be too late and say too little or too much. Besides, your daughter has a right to know your beliefs about sex and intimacy and what you expect of her and want for her. Regardless, depending on your daughter's age and maturity, you need to talk to her sometime about contraception, the "morning after" pill, and date rape (*see* this Chapter below at "Date Rape").

In discussing sexual feelings and behavior with your daughter, keep in mind that the rate of physical development varies from teen to teen. The Kinsey studies of the 1950s found that most young women became sexually active about five years after having begun menstruating regularly. Thus, a girl who physically develops at the age of eleven is likely to have different sexual feelings at the age of sixteen than a girl who didn't begin to menstruate until she was fourteen. Life today, however, is far different than it was in the 1950s when the average age for menstruation was thirteen and when it was common for girls to marry right after high-school. These days, life is much more complicated. Girls may start menstruating at eleven or twelve or even earlier but are not expected to marry until sometime in their twenties or later. Thus, many teens today may engage in pre-marital sex while still in high school despite your best admonitions. Don't despair though. Your goal is to help your daughter delay intercourse until she is mature enough to find out who she is and handle rejection and to at least get through high school without contracting an STD or becoming pregnant.

Some parents, however, are permitted to talk about all aspects of sex with their daughters. Their daughters come home from a date and tell them that they are sexually frustrated and they can't wait until they're old enough to try it out. They talk openly about the latest in contraception and feminine hygiene while all you've managed to do with your daughter is a bare bones discussion about AIDS and condoms.

Don't feel bad if all your attempts to discuss sex have not been as complete as you would have liked. It is not only discussions about sex that control your daughter's sexual activity but how she views herself. A teenage girl who is secure about herself will be less vulnerable to pressure from her dates. However, you must be realistic. You must realize that your daughter may become curious or be overwhelmed by desire—either purely sexual or the desire to be popular. Or she may be too timid to be assertive enough to say no. Thus, you must make sure she knows about contraception and STDs even if you believe that women should be virgins until they marry. Her virginity is her decision—you won't be there to decide for her. Your responsibility is to see that she has the information to make decisions about her sexual behavior safely and wisely.

You needn't rush the topic though by launching into a discussion of herpes-2 the first time you see your ten-year-old daughter with a boy and no soccer ball around. However, don't close your eyes to the possibility that your fifteen-year-old may engage in sex no matter your religious or personal beliefs. Look and listen for cues so you can make sure your daughter has whatever information she needs to protect herself as indicated by her age and physical maturity.

A face-to-face conversation between the two of you is not the only way to impart appropriate information and your feelings about sex to your daughter. Perhaps when she starts menstruating, you can write her a letter and leave it on her dresser with a few roses. Or you can place leaflets on her dresser that not only contain information about teenagers and sex but list places she can go for information or assistance. Also, make sure her doctor speaks to her about contraception and *her* body—that it's not someone else's playground—and it's up to her to take care of it.

While I'm totally for your daughter having complete sexual information, I don't want to imply that I'm in favor of teens being involved in sexual relations—just that if they do, they do so as safely as possible. When discussing sex with your daughter, also discuss the virtues of abstinence and chastity in a positive light and in accordance with your religious beliefs and values. Remind your daughter that she has the rest of her life to enjoy sexual relations but it's only during her high school and college years that she has a chance for a tennis scholarship or a chance to study abroad for a semester. An STD or a pregnancy can certainly mess things up.

Meryl Fishman

LOVE AND INTIMACY

Regardless of your success at getting past the basic facts, try to find an opportunity to discuss love and intimacy with your daughter explaining that sexual feelings are both normal and healthy. It's just that acting on such impulses as a teenager can be downright unhealthy. Keep telling your daughter that she's far better off being safe than sorry since there no such thing as 100% safe sex. (She won't believe you—after all, she's invincible—but persevere you must.) Don't be afraid to be open with your daughter and tell her that at its best, having intercourse is the best of times—it feels great, it's a beautiful way to express love, it can result in beautiful babies.

Also, don't be afraid to answer your daughter's questions. For example, if your 11-year-old daughter asks about oral sex, take a cue from my Aunt Fan who told my cousin and me that *when you love someone, every part of their body is beautiful.* Also, a friend of mine was asked by her college-age daughter about having an affair with more than one boy at a time. My friend was aghast at first but her response was blunt and to the point—*I don't want you to even think such things with all the STDs around. Besides, with two or three boyfriends, how would you ever get your classwork done or keep up with the Debating Society? Believe me, as good as it is, there's more to life than sex so don't screw yourself!*

GENDER IDENTITY

According to scientists, Homo Sapiens just like us have walked the earth for at least the past 200,000 years trekking through forests, crossing oceans and over mountains, traversing wide plains, all the while mingling their DNA with other humans through unprotected intercourse. Thus, it is reasonable to assume that along the way nature occasionally got mixed up and a majority of DNA traits ascribed to femininity or masculinity didn't always correspond to a person's sex chromosomes which dictate the person's sexual organs. Consequently, some children are born as girls in a boy's body or as boys in a girl's body while some other children languish somewhere in between.

If you believe that your daughter's true sexual identity is unclear, discuss the situation with her doctor and go from there. Dressing her girly-girly style or insist she take ballet is not going to change who she is. Support her but don't push her one way or the other. Be prepared to agree to any hormonal or physical changes recommended by medical specialists and wanted by your daughter and to the time frame suggested by them. If your daughter is just fine with being a girl but it is becoming obvious that she prefers girls to boys, you need to accept that too. I'm not saying any of the foregoing is easy but it's a lot easier nowadays than it would have been even five years ago. Consider yourself and your daughter lucky; you need not deprive yourself of being proud of your daughter because of embarrassment and she can be who she truly is with equal rights under the law and with far less angst than in the past. (If you're squeamish about the whole issue of gender identity, check out "The Danish Girl," a beautiful award-winning film loosely based on a true story.)

Homosexual and Transgender men and women are not a new phenomenon—what is new is that our laws, if not society as a whole, are recognizing that these people are just people, really no different than you or I in the same way that people have morphed into having a variety of skin, eye and hair colors. It's understandable if you feel uncomfortable about the issue of gender identity, particularly if your daughter has friends of questionable sexual orientation. However, you shouldn't prohibit such friendships unless you believe that a girl friend is pressuring your daughter for sex (*see also* Chapter 13 at "Sleepovers"). Keep in mind, though, that it is not abnormal for adolescent girls (and boys) to engage in some form of same-sex sexual activity with their friends. While you shouldn't condone or allow opportunities for such behavior, it's not a reason to become hysterical. Unless your daughter has a physiological bent toward homosexuality, by the time she is well into her teens, she will probably have broken off any sexual or pseudo-sexual intimacies with her female friends. That doesn't mean that she and her friends will not still brush each other's hair or text each other ten times a day.

Even if your daughter prefers girls to boys, your position should still be that she not involve herself in a sexual relationship until she is mature enough not to let it interfere with her finding out who she is as a person irrespective of sex and also mature enough to handle rejection. Moreover, she should understand that homosexuality is not an excuse for promiscuity—that the same rules about casual and promiscuous sex apply regardless of her sexual orientation.

PROMISCUITY *(see also this Chapter below at "Date Rape")*

Sexual promiscuity usually stems from a lack of self-respect and self-esteem. In addition to knowing how to protect herself against pregnancy and disease, your daughter should also know that some boys will play on her fears or lack of self-esteem in order to elicit her acquiescence to sex. Your daughter may be easy prey for the form of date rape that occurs when a girl's "consent" is predicated on threats such as *I'll tell everyone you're a bad date if you don't* or *I won't drive you home until you do*. Also, your daughter should know that a remark like *After all I've spent on you, you owe me* is not seduction but coercion. And these days, the basest bleat from a sexually aroused teenage boy is accusing a girl for not having sex with him because he's of a different race than she.

You can protect your daughter from these types of date rape by giving her love and acceptance at home. If your daughter believes that she and her opinions are valued and respected, she is more likely to have the courage of her convictions and not be as receptive to threats to her integrity or to any pseudo intimacy proffered by a Tom, Dick or Harry and is less likely to find herself in a situation where she could be taken advantage of. (*See also* this Chapter below at "Date Rape.")

If you suspect that your daughter is sexually promiscuous, there are probably other areas where it is apparent that she doesn't stand up for herself or think highly of herself. Is she fearful of participating in school discussions? Do you belittle her opinions with respect to music, religion, politics, etc.? Does she constantly seek assurance or acceptance from her peers? Perhaps she gives away her prized possessions so people will like her. Without accusing or admonishing your daughter about her sexual activity, reassure her of your love for her and find ways she can improve her self-esteem including obtaining counseling. (*See also generally* Chapter 11 at "Assertiveness Training.")

Accusations, punishment and admonitions to change won't work-
-all they'd do would cause your daughter to lie thereby increasing her
feelings of unworthiness. It is important that you allow your daughter
some dignity so don't cross-examine her about the how's and why's of
her sexual activity. Besides, your daughter's knowing that you know "all"
might make her feel even worse about herself and thus even more likely
to seek solace in sexual acceptance. On the other hand, a promiscuous
teen might want parental interference. Be aware of her cries for help.
For example, if she discusses her sexual activities with friends within
earshot, she may want you to interfere since she's aware that she can't
control herself. Regardless of whether your daughter tries to hide her
promiscuity from you or is sending you cues to interfere, ground her
for a bit—not as punishment but as an opportunity for her to change
course and find ways to increase her self-esteem. Your job is to do
whatever you can so she can believe in herself and say "NO" loudly and
clearly not only to sex but whenever she feels pushed to do something
she knows is wrong or not good for her to do. Some outside counseling
may be in order.

DATE RAPE

Instances of date rape are increasing. Whether it's because of
more occurrences or more reporting is of little consequence if it's your
daughter that's been taken advantage of. While your daughter has every
right to lie naked under a boy and change her mind at the last minute,
too many men and boys still believe that the mere act of a female going
to a secluded place with them is tantamount to a "Yes to Sex" from
which there is no retreat.

Rape is a crime yet in no other circumstance is provocative behavior
on the part of the victim considered as consent to the crime. A man
who strikes a fatal blow in response to a verbal attack, no matter how
foul the language, is still a murderer; a man who physically gives in to
his anger with a nagging wife is still a wife-beater no matter what she
may have said or done; and a boy who sees a carelessly unattended purse
and bounds out of the store with it is still a thief. It follows then that a

boy who cannot hold back his disappointment when his date protests, regardless of how provocative her actions, is still a rapist.

You don't want your daughter to think all boys and men are perverts but you do have an obligation to make her aware of the fact that just because someone is known to her or to her friends, or because a young man may be well-connected or well-regarded, that she may throw caution to the wind. She needs to understand that she should not risk putting herself in a compromising position trusting that her date will pull back should she have a change of heart at the last minute. Tell her that if she has the slightest doubt about a person or a situation, not to second-guess herself. Tell her too that anytime she finds herself making excuses for feeling even the slightest twinge of discomfort in the presence of a boy, even one she's heard well of, to not be alone with the boy. She also needs to be on guard about peer pressure, from girls as well as boys, urging her to go off somewhere with so-and-so, particularly when she's in a new environment like camp or college or on Spring Break. (*See also* Chapter 11 at "Assertiveness Training" and "Staying Safe.")

Your daughter must understand that if she is date-raped, she should immediately report it to the police and other proper authorities and to tell you no matter how embarrassed she might be for having put herself in a compromising position. The longer your daughter delays in reporting the rape, the more credence she gives to the boy's defense that the sex was consensual. Your daughter needs to forgive herself and you need to avoid any *I told you so's*.

Your daughter should also know to take a "morning after" pill as soon as possible so as to thwart pregnancy and to see a doctor so as to keep an eye out for possible venereal disease. Whether or not your daughter wishes to pursue criminal charges should be primarily her decision after discussion with an attorney. Regardless of your daughter's decision, also discuss with the attorney whether the boy's family should be notified particularly if there's any chance that a pregnancy may have resulted from the date rape and your daughter would want to continue with the pregnancy. At the least, the boy should be responsible for any medical costs associated therewith as well as financial support for any resultant offspring. (*See also* this Chapter above at "Promiscuity" and below at "Pregnancy.")

PREGNANCY

So many times your daughter has said, *I've got to tell you something. Promise you won't be mad?* In the past, the news has been nothing more than having flunked an exam or dented a car fender. This time, though, through tears and quivering lips, she tells you she's pregnant. You are stunned. How could this happen? She's only fourteen—or she's seventeen and should know better. After the initial shock, you become angry. *How could she do this to you! Especially after all you've told her!*

Before you do anything, look at the bright side. Pregnancy is not a fatal disease nor is it addictive. Your daughter made a serious error in judgment. Being pregnant as a teen is not a tragedy but an unfortunate problem. Tragedies seldom have solutions but problems almost always do. Your daughter obviously wants and needs your advice and help. Try to be objective and rational and discuss the options open to her. Don't focus on why or how she got pregnant—at least not now. This is not the time to lay a guilt trip on her or yourself but to assure your daughter of your love and emotional support.

Generally, the solution to the problem should be your daughter's decision providing that she's physically and emotionally mature. It's a fact that teen pregnancies carry greater health risks to the mother and the infant than do adult pregnancies and the younger the pregnant girl, the higher the risks. Your role is to guide your daughter's decision so that she makes the best possible choice for herself. The first thing you should do, of course, is to take your daughter to a doctor to confirm the pregnancy and to do all things necessary for her health and that of the fetus no matter what is ultimately decided. Next, you and your daughter (and with guidance from the doctor as appropriate) should consider her choices of which there are basically four.

1. Getting Married and Keeping the Baby. Marriage is feasible only if your daughter is an older teen and the prospective parents planned to marry anyway. Even then, unless you and the boy's parents are prepared to support the newlyweds emotionally and financially, marriage is not a wise solution. For example, if my daughter chose marriage in this situation, I would continue to support her as if she were still attending school and, in fact, do everything I could to help her finish high school and attend college or a job training program. I would expect the boy's parents to do the same for their son. There is no reason to punish nearly-adult children for a lapse in judgment by requiring them to quit school and materially alter the course of their lives any more than necessary. Adjusting to marriage and a baby is difficult enough. Don't make it more difficult by withdrawing your support.

2. Keeping the Baby as a Single Parent. This solution has become more prevalent nowadays since there is little stigma for bearing a child out of wedlock. However, keeping the baby is only feasible if you live in an area where flexible infant care and school schedules are available *and* you are willing and able to provide for your daughter's education or job-training post high school just as you would have had she not decided to become a mom. Also, make sure your daughter understands that if she decides to go through with the pregnancy (whether she decides to keep the baby or put the infant up for adoption) that there are health risks to her and the fetus associated with her pregnancy, that she must follow the doctor's orders and skip the French Fries, sodas and more, and that her social life will be greatly restricted not only during pregnancy but for years thereafter. Also, contact a lawyer as to financial support and visitation from the father-to-be.

3. Putting the Baby up for Adoption. I think adoption should only be chosen for religious reasons *and* the lack of family finances sufficient to ensure that your daughter and the baby will not become poverty-stricken. In my view, the combination of those two situations is the only reason for your daughter to go through the emotional and physical trauma of pregnancy while at the same time risking her health and that of the fetus. If, however, adoption is the only feasible choice for your daughter, consider whether your daughter would be able to live at home and continue school during her pregnancy or whether she should leave town to stay with "sick Aunt Louise" and complete high school while there.

Because giving up a baby for adoption is a loss that lingers even when it is believed that the adoptive parents would provide the infant a far better lifestyle than could you and your daughter, be as non-judgmental of your daughter as possible. She will need assurances of your love and emotional support not only during her pregnancy but for some time thereafter. Remember, a healthy pregnancy and infant require a great deal of involvement by your daughter—she's the one who'll need to switch from the typical teen diet to one suitable for a pregnant woman, she's the one who'll need to quit her cheerleading team, she's the one who'll feel viability of the fetus, she's the one who'll place earphones carrying soft music on her tummy to calm a kicking fetus. Don't think that all of this won't lay heavily on your daughter from time to time after the adoption process.

4. Aborting the Pregnancy. Abortion is an unpleasant choice but may be the best long-run decision for your daughter. It's true that she will feel some remorse after having an abortion but she will also feel remorse after giving a baby up for adoption. It's only human to feel remorse for a road not taken even when we know that the road we took was the right one in the long run. Thus, if your daughter chooses to have an abortion, support her decision. Even a staunch pro-lifer such as ex-President Bush let it be known that he would support a family member's decision to have an abortion if that were such person's choice. Moreover, former Governor Palin disclosed in an article that she had thought about having an abortion when she learned that the burgeoning baby within would be born with Down's Syndrome. After deciding that she had enough love and resources to handle a Special Needs child, she *chose* to go on with the pregnancy. Your daughter deserves the same right to choose.

Whether you are pro-choice or not, what is important is that you answer your daughter's call for help and help in the way that is best for her. Your daughter's well-being should be your priority. How strongly you push for one solution over another depends on your daughter's age, family finances, and religious beliefs. Obviously, your input should be stronger the younger your daughter's age. Whatever the decision, make sure your daughter finishes high school and continues on to college or to technical school as had been previously planned. Single moms, regardless of race or ethnicity, are the poorest segment of our society. Your daughter is likely to live well into her eighties—she shouldn't be relegated to a second-class existence because she said "yes" when she should have said "no" or, just as likely, didn't say "no" loud enough.

Special Note. If your pregnant daughter is a drug addict, it is my belief you should guide her toward having an abortion. It's far too likely that a baby born from an addicted mom will be born with serious mental and physical problems and suffer great and continuing pain—pain far greater than what an aborted fetus may or may not feel.

YOUR SEXUALITY

Teens generally give very little thought to what their parents or any adults do. They are much too concerned with themselves. To them, as long as all is well, parents and other adults may just as well be automatons who go to work, cook, clean house, watch television, coach their sports activities and chauffer them to and from their piano lessons. Adolescents especially do not like to think of their mothers as sexual persons. Walking in on you and your husband or boyfriend is going to shock your daughter into recognizing your sexuality. No matter that the movies and TV depict kids walking in on adult sexual activity—that's not the same as *your* daughter walking in on you during the act. Don't assume that because your daughter claims to know all about sex that she won't be bothered by the realization that you engage in sex especially if you are unmarried. If she just appears embarrassed by the incident, don't make an issue of it. She may be more mature than meets the eye. If, however, she accuses you of being disgusting or thereafter treats you with hostility, you will need to go on a fishing expedition as soon as the two of you have some privacy. Was she embarrassed for you or for herself? Does she think sex is revolting? Or only your engaging in it? Does she still deep down retain the little-girl fantasy that she's going to marry her father or is she still hoping that you and your ex-husband will get back together? Does she have a crush on your boyfriend?

There is however no reason for your daughter to find a strange man in your bed. She has a right to know who is going to spend the night in her home. It will be more than awkward for her to run into your room in her underwear and find a stranger sprawled in your bed. Absent a snowstorm or some such thing, unless you're involved in a serious relationship, your dates should not stay overnight, even on the couch.

You don't want to give your daughter the impression that men come and go, that they are unreliable or function only as sex objects. Having your steady boyfriend stay overnight occasionally should not threaten your daughter as long as she knows of your plans in advance.

If you and your beau decide to live together, give your daughter ample opportunity to get to know him before it's a *fait accompli*. Start by having him stay overnight more frequently and doing things as a family. The relationship between your daughter and your beau needn't start out as a love fest but they should at least be respectful of each other and be looking forward to a better relationship. If your daughter's attitude becomes a road-block to living with your beau, particularly if you'll be moving into his place or where a change of neighborhood or school is involved, seek outside counsel how next to proceed. Keep in mind that your daughter might be totally disrespectful of your beau because she doesn't want to change schools or leave her friends or she may be harboring the idea that you and her father would get back together. In any event, don't promise more than you can deliver about the advantages of your daughter having a step-dad. Assure her though that your love for the man will not in any way lessen the love you have for her. You could also tell your daughter that you will have more time for her since with your guy around, you will be going out less. Of course, that may be the last thing she wants to hear! (*See also* Chapter 15 at "New Marriage.")

15. OTHER TOUGHIES

Illness (Hers/Family) — Death
Keeping Things from Her
Divorce — New Marriage
Peer Pressure
Running Away — Moving Out

ILLNESS

Hers. Some teens will use illness as an excuse to stay home from school as much as possible; others will go even when they're feeling quite ill. The thought of being parted from their friends for even a day is too much for them. Absent any excessive excuses, let your daughter decide whether or not she's too sick to go to school. After all, she's the one that knows how she feels. Even if she's not sick in the traditional sense, she might need a day off once in a while as a "mental health day" just as we all do at times.

If your daughter often seems to be under-the-weather despite a thorough medical exam showing her to be in excellent health, you might want to check on the air at her school. For some children, going from over-heated classrooms to chilly and damp hallways or sitting under or near heat or air vents will cause chest discomfort and fatigue. Perhaps changing her classroom seat or her dressing in layers might help her feel ill less often.

If serious illness strikes your daughter, your biggest concern, assuming she is expected to make a full recovery, is how she feels about herself. For example, many teens suffer long bouts with mononucleosis and as a result may miss a summer or drop back in school. Their question is *Why me? I had so many fun plans for the summer.* Try to find some way to turn the discomforts of illness into some positives. When I was faced with this question, I responded *I don't know why you but I do know you will get better and that sometime in your life, knowing you had suffered and survived will help you out in a difficult situation.* Don't point out how much better off than others she is—she will counter with how much better off others are than she. Instead, empathize with her about missing out on a summer of fun. Let her know you agree it's rotten luck. Talk about the future—the clothes she plans to buy for the new school year or the colleges she might like to apply to. Also, don't let her feel guilty about the vacation days you've used to take care of her or the medical costs of her illness. Remind her that you've saved for a rainy day and now that a rainy day is here, you're well prepared for it—*so, not to worry.*

Be aware too that when your daughter is ill, no one else is supposed to have a good time. My daughter's friend, who had a serious operation, told me that she was annoyed at her mother because her mother laughed sometimes when she was visiting her at the hospital. My own daughter showed similar behavior when she was home convalescing after her hospitalization. Whenever she heard anyone laughing, I would hear this little voice, *M-o-m-m-y.* Poor thing, the world went on while she was sick. Be gentle. It is very tempting to feel exasperated or just laugh outright when she is so demanding, but she *is* sick. It's normal for her to feel left out and want some extra attention.

Unfortunately, a teen may suffer an accident or illness from which there is no recovery. This is the worst of situations and my heart goes out to any family dealing with such a crisis. Though your job as parent-in-chief will increase a hundred-fold, it is paramount that you keep a sense of humor as much as possible and that you take care of yourself as much as possible. Remove all clutter from your life so you can focus on your daughter's needs and the needs of the other family members. Siblings may feel especially jealous, guilty, or left out. Instead of reacting to their pettiness, appeal to their better angels by asking for their assistance in helping you cope and showing real appreciation when they do. Don't worry about bribing the little ones with cookies to get them to pick up their toys; on the other hand, doing the pick-up together might be the only time you have for them. Above all, don't give up hope. One never knows when a cure might be found or a miracle may occur. In the worst case scenario though consider organ donation so that a part of your daughter will continue to live on.

Family Member. It is hard when illness or disease strikes a family member. Even if the prognosis is good or the illness temporary, the entire family is under extra strain. As the mother, like it or not, you are the one who is responsible for any reorganization that is necessary. This is often true even if you are the one who is ill.

Some children react well under stress; others fall apart. When anyone is ill, conserve your energy for what needs to be done at the time, and worry about exhibitions of selfishness on your daughter's part later. As usual, Murphy's Law arises during times of crisis. Not only is your husband scheduled for a serious cancer operation, your youngest child is hobbling around on a broken leg after falling off a swing, your roof still leaks from a recent storm, your mom is being treated for Alzheimer's, and all your daughter wants to know is whether you've finished altering her costume for the school play. You feel like screaming at your daughter for her selfishness but don't waste your energy—instead get help. Take your daughter's costume to a tailor, ask a neighbor to chauffeur your son to school and back, put a bucket under the leak, have your brother deal with your mom, and go sit by your husband.

When you catch your breath, realize that no matter how ill you or your husband may be, it's likely that your teen daughter's selfish displays aren't just worry over a costume or some such thing but worry about what will happen to her if you or her father dies. If it's a sibling that's ill, your daughter's selfish displays may be to cover feelings of guilt for wishing it so. Take a moment to assess your daughter's fears and reassure her that she was in no way responsible for the illness or, if she was, explain that we all make mistakes and when we do, we take actions to correct them at our first opportunity to do so. Assure her too that whatever the difficulty presented by the illness, the family will get through it.

It's natural though for your daughter to feel resentful and deprived of attention because of all the time you now need to spend with your husband or her sibling. Your teen daughter may understand that you need to be by her father's or sibling's side day and night but that doesn't make her feel better. Explain to your daughter that there were and will be times when she's first in your attentions and they need not have anything to do with illness. Remind her of the time she starred in the school play and you took over her dog-walking business for two months so she could spend the time rehearsing or the time the whole family was put out of the family room for a week because she needed the space to build a school science project. Regardless, this is a time when you need to be "super mom." Make time to give your daughter some special attention—maybe the two of you can go for a pedicure or take the dog for a long walk.

DEATH

Death happens to all of us sooner or later. The closer your daughter is to her elderly relatives, the more you need to (or ask that they) prepare your daughter for their death even if they are in good health. Because I provided day care for my youngest grandchildren, I was always concerned about how my sudden death would affect them. I wanted them to understand that death is a part of life and that it would be OK for them to be sad but not for too long. It may seem macabre but it became a game as to what kind of cloud each of the family old folks would wind up sitting on after their death and what they would be doing. Unfortunately, I didn't fare too well—while my cloud was fluffy and pink, all I got to do was to remind everyone to eat their broccoli.

Your daughter's reaction to death of a non-parent family member, regardless of closeness, will in large part be determined by her emotional maturity and how involved she is with friends, school and other activities so you need to be prepared for a variety of reactions. If the death occurred during your daughter's intense self-absorbed phase, she may exhibit very little emotion even if she was close to the deceased. *Aren't old people supposed to die anyway?* You can't believe it's the same girl who only six months ago cried for days because her cat died. Don't be angry with her. Right now, she's just not aware of anyone but herself—it's a short phase (thankfully!) but very intense. Probably best to keep her out of sight when the other relatives arrive. Your daughter is too self-absorbed to be even slightly considerate of their feelings.

If your daughter shows little or no emotion about the death even if the deceased was her father, a sibling or a close friend or relative, she may be feeling too great a loss for her to handle or she may be harboring childish anxieties that her bad thoughts or something that she did or didn't do caused the death. It is important however for her to face her emotions. If your daughter is still depressed or appears in denial about the death and you cannot get her to open up after things have settled down, seek professional advice. You should also seek professional advice if it was a parent that died regardless of her obvious reaction to the death. Her feelings of grief, despair and anger at the deceased parent for leaving her need to be worked out. In this situation, you might also want to attend a Bereavement Group if one is available in your community.

If your daughter is fearful of attending a funeral for someone that was close to her, explain that funerals not only help the survivors accept the finality of a loved one's demise but allows them to share their grief rather than bear their sadness alone. If you cannot convince your daughter that it would be best for her to attend, have a friend or neighbor stay with her while you go.

KEEPING THINGS FROM HER

I know you want to protect your daughter but don't be afraid to let her know about death and dying even if she's not yet a teen. Tell her about her favorite uncle's battle with heart disease because if he dies without your daughter even knowing he was sick and knows that you knew, she will feel betrayed. Also, she should not be left with the guilt that had she known, she would have called him more often or perhaps written a poem just for him. I still smart at a family member for keeping me in the dark about the impending death of a childhood friend. Had I known, I know I would have been able to give him at least a few hours of happiness by reminiscing about our childhood adventures together. And as for me, such a conversation would have brought closure—instead, I still grieve.

Whether it's a death or serious illness in the family, the loss of a job, or an impending divorce, don't hide the situation. There are unpleasant aspects of life that we all have to deal with in one way or another. When you tell your daughter that Aunt Helen needs a new kidney, tell her too that while there are some risks, the likely outcome is a positive one. If your daughter puts her hands over her ears and doesn't want to hear what you have to say, let her be. She may want more info later but if not and Aunt Helen's result was an unhappy one, at least she will not feel betrayed by you.

It's perfectly OK to sweeten bad news but don't sugar-coat it. For example, a friend and major family bread-winner was recently laid-off shortly before her daughter and her daughter's father were to take a trip to visit out-of-town colleges. My friend had planned not to tell her daughter about her job loss until they returned since she didn't want to spoil a special trip with worries about money. However, the night before the planned trip, the girl's father learned he wouldn't be able to do the trip. It was the perfect opportunity for my friend to tell her daughter about her lay-off. *Honey, your father can't take you but I can. I've got plenty of time—I just got fired. What time do you want to leave?*

My friend presented something fairly ominous in a favorable way. The loss of the job would mean some extra time with the family even if it would mean considerable belt-tightening. Some good can be found in almost anything. Death often means the end of suffering; divorce, the end of arguing. There are, however, some truly tragic moments for which no adequate words or humor can be found—the death of a parent, a child, or a special friend. Don't hide the news or try to cover your feelings so your daughter won't know. It's best just to let the grief flow and allow her to be a part of your grief, and to grieve herself. As an example, to this day, I regret not bringing my daughter with me to Florida to pack up my mother's house after she died. My daughter and my mother were quite close and it was unfair of me not to let her grieve with me even if it meant she would miss some school. Not only that, my decision deprived us of an opportunity to bond not as mother and daughter but on an equal level simply by being human.

On the other hand, if your daughter seems disinterested or unaffected when you tell her of a tragedy or misfortune that has occurred in the family, don't be angry about her lack of feeling or complete oblivion about the issue of death. This might just be one of those times when she's totally self-absorbed with the usual teen pursuits and everyday worries. Some time later though feel free to share your feelings— perhaps when she's helping you clean up after dinner or when the two of you are stuck in traffic. Mention how much you still miss Uncle Al but remembering how excited she was about the doll house he had built for her still brings a smile to your face. Her response will probably be *Yeah, I forgot about tha*t and not much more. At the least though you've shown your daughter a positive way to deal with the death of a loved one.

DIVORCE *(see also Chapter 16 at "Fathers & Stepfathers")*

Divorce doesn't result in a broken home, only a broken marriage. Make sure that your daughter understands that the marriage is the only relationship that is severed. Her home is still intact, as is her relationship with her father. All divorce means is that a husband and wife have decided to live separate lives with respect to their personal needs. Explain that she will have two homes instead of one. Take care not to disparage her father even if for example the divorce resulted because he was an alcoholic or found another woman. In such case, skip the details and simply explain that you are disappointed and hurt but that you'll get over it. Reassure your daughter that her father loves her as much as always and always will. Assure her too, particularly if she has been a difficult or sickly child, that in no way is she to blame for the divorce.

Not only will there be emotional adjustments for you and your daughter but there may also be many adjustments with respect to the family life-style because of limited finances or because you may need to work outside the home for the first time or go from a part-time to a full-time job. Obviously, this will put you under additional pressure, particularly when it comes to time. Your daughter too will likely be under similar pressure if she needs to take on additional household chores or provide after-school care for her siblings. Also, you may need to disappoint your daughter by begging off a prior commitment to choreograph the Sophomore Sing because of a conflict with your job while your daughter may have to give up her dance lessons. This is definitely not an easy time for the family nor is it the time for you to try to be Super Mom. Keep family life simple—branching out as time goes by and when the time and money situation gets straightened out, restore what you can of what your children had to give up.

There will also be adjustments as to the amount of time your daughter spends with her father. Consider joint custody if you live in the same neighborhood so that she need not change her schedule regarding her school, friends and other activities. However, if such is not feasible, your daughter should not feel pushed to spend more time with her father than before the divorce just because you and he choose to live apart. Let them work out their time together. It seems that teen girls have little enough time for any parental interaction between band practice, homework, texting, babysitting and chores. Thus, during the school year, the most that your daughter may be able to see her father is a once-a-week dinner or after any of her weekend sports activities.

Occasionally, your ex may be able to lure your daughter away from her friends for a hike or a ball game but neither you nor he should be surprised if she more often opts for hanging out at the Mall with her friends. Hopefully, her father will be understanding and will not feel rejected. When she does spend weekend time at her father's, suggest that he sometimes invite your daughter's friends or his friends with children to visit as well. His friends (and yours) may often serve as substitutes for the numerous aunts, uncles and cousins that used to live nearby before we became such a mobile society.

Don't pump your daughter for information about her father's life or point out that he never spent $100 on dinner for you. However, while you certainly shouldn't bad mouth your ex-husband, you needn't be a saint. If he's late with child support payments, you don't need to make excuses for him. He is what he is and your daughter is entitled to have the right to accept him for who he is, despite his faults or defects, real or perceived. Difficult as it may be and even if you feel some jealousy because your daughter and her father are able to share some special moments while you are not because you're the one stuck with spending your days off at the orthodontist or making sure the book reports and class projects get done, you should encourage the relationship between your daughter and her father. A good relationship with her father is crucial for your daughter's development into a mentally healthy young woman.

NEW MARRIAGE *(see also generally Chapter 14 at "Your Sexuality")*

Your daughter may have some difficulty accepting your new marriage. She may have secretly harbored the hope that you and her father would get back together again; she may be angry with you for being attracted to another man; she may be jealous of your new husband's place in your life; she may even feel disloyal to her father if she likes her stepfather.

You can allay your daughter's fears and bewilderment by letting her get to know your fiancé before the marriage. Let your daughter know that your new husband will not displace her in your affections and that you will still have time to give her all the love and attention she needs. It's also important that you involve your ex-husband in ensuring your daughter's acceptance of her stepfather-to-be. Whatever animosity you and your ex have, if not already put aside for the benefit of your children, should definitely be put away now. Both you and your daughter's father should let your daughter know that her place in your hearts and minds will not change. Her father should assure your daughter that she's not disloyal to him if she likes her stepfather-to-be. He should explain that he doesn't see your mother's fiancé as a rival, only as another person who will love and care for her.

Involve your daughter in your wedding plans as much as possible. Take her with you if you're looking for a new home or an apartment, or at least let her see it before moving day, and let her have input into any new decorating plans. However, your daughter may also want everything to stay just as it was—in her room, the family room, or elsewhere—even if you'll be moving to a new place. As you know, some people thrive on change while others find any change abhorrent. You know which is your daughter and try to accommodate her needs as much as possible, particularly with respect to her room.

If you ask for your daughter's assistance with plans about your upcoming marriage and any resultant changes and she refuses to help or acts as if she doesn't care, don't push her. You've met her more than halfway. Besides, she may be secure enough about you and her father that she really doesn't care, particularly if her school, friends and home will not change. If there is animosity between your daughter and fiancé for which there is no reason other than when together they are like mixing oil and water, perhaps a truce can be arranged between the two until your daughter figures out that her stepfather's not such a bad guy and he gets more used to the mood swings of a teenage girl. If the animosity has another basis, seek professional advice as how to best handle the matter.

Regardless of whether your daughter is totally for or less than Gung Ho about your impending marriage, make sure she knows as much about her stepfather-to-be's family and background as you do. The wedding is not the time for her to discover that her stepfather has a college-age daughter with whom she'll have to share her room during school breaks. Actually, anything that she doesn't know beforehand that will come to the fore after the marriage could be fuel for any fears, resentment or guilt that she may be harboring about your divorce and/or your new marriage. Try not to give her an excuse not to like her stepfather or to be rude to you. Once remarried, make sure that your daughter's life continues as before as much as possible. Her friends should still be able to come for dinner or sleepovers. She should still be able to practice the tuba in the living room. Remember too, she has some tough adjustments to make. She needs to be able to adjust to not being able to barge in on you whoever she feels like it; she may feel the need to wear a bathrobe for the first time in her life; she needs to adjust to having less of your undivided attention. And, of course, your new husband must also be ready to adjust to the normal noise and clutter of a teenager.

PEER PRESSURE

Most peer pressure is trivial. There's no need to bring out the big guns if your daughter indulges in the fad of the day like wearing miss-matched socks because that's what her peers are doing. It's only natural for her to want to fit in, especially if she's new to the neighborhood or to the school, and following harmless fads is an easy way for her to do that. The going gets sticky though if, for example, her peer group decides to shoplift a bunch of socks from the local box store. Your daughter knows stealing is wrong—*but it's only socks* she might think and, besides, *it might be fun not to be a goody-goody all the time.* So she goes along with her friends and they all get caught. Hopefully the shame and fear of having been nabbed by a store security guard will end your daughter's foolishness for all time.

Regardless of whether or not you dole out additional punishment for your daughter's wrongful behavior, this *is* the time for the two of you to have a "conversation" about peer pressure if you have not already done so. Explain that there will be never-ending temptations to do wrong and when faced with a decision to join in or not she should ask herself the following: Is it something she wants to do? Will someone be hurt by the group's actions? What does she have to gain by going along? What does she have to lose? Is she willing to suffer the consequence of the group's wrongful act?

The more confidence your daughter has in herself, the better she should be able to withstand peer pressure. Understand, however, that your daughter's staying behind and not going along with what her peers are doing can very well lead to her isolation, particularly if she lives in a small town or goes to a small school. Take care not to harp on her about why she isn't friends with so-and-so or has no one to eat lunch with. She might be a natural loner or possibly just doesn't want any part of what this group or that group is doing and just feels safer staying away. On the other hand, if your daughter runs with a crowd that is constantly getting into trouble and despite your best efforts, you cannot wean her from them, seek professional guidance. Such crowds get rowdier and uglier as the teens age and you want to get your daughter out of their grasp before real trouble occurs.

RUNNING AWAY *(see also generally Chapter 3 at "Domestic Abuse" and "Sexual Predators")*

One day you come home from work or shopping and discover that your daughter has run away from home. Whatever the reason for her leaving—domestic abuse, pregnancy, feeling unloved or unworthy of your love, that you're too strict or unfair, that she's done something stupid media-wise, or she's relapsed into drug addiction—immediately make all efforts to locate her. Any delay will merely affirm her righteous indignation against you or any negative feelings about herself. Most importantly, remember it's a dangerous world for a teen girl on the loose and the longer she's on her own, the more likely the scum of the earth (human traffickers for sexual purposes) will find her.

Enlist the police, friends and family, and your community in attempting to locate your daughter. Once you do, bring her home immediately even if you have to drag her. Tell her how much you love and value her. Regardless of whether or not your words fall on deaf ears or how resistant she may be to being home, promise you will cooperate with her to help resolve whatever is troubling her—even if it is your behavior that is causing the problem—and make good on your promise. Often the introduction of a third party goes a long way in resolving issues between or among family members. Make whatever changes and compromises that are necessary to ensure that your daughter will not run away again even if it means boarding school or allowing her to live with a friend or other family member. Your obligations as a parent require that you place your daughter's safety first even when she breaks your heart.

You may feel that you've been the model parent—expressing love, care and concern—and feel not only heartbroken, but emotionally abused by your daughter because of her apparent lack of her appreciation of you. You have every right to feel that way. However, you must, at least temporarily, put your feelings aside in order to get to your daughter's troubles. She may have run away because she does not feel truly accepted by her parents. For example, a teenage girl I knew ran away from home because of her parents' constant criticism. The girl was well-behaved but espoused ideas radical to her parents who harped on her constantly about her vegan ways and views about religion and politics. When her parents were notified that she was a runaway, they immediately set out to bring her home. The girl was sensible enough to return with them because she knew her alternative as a high school drop-out would mean fast-food employment forever. She tried to explain to her parents that she ran away because they didn't love who she was but what they wanted her to be. Unfortunately, the parents, rather than accepting their daughter's values, continued to mock them as childish and insisted that she would outgrow such ideas. Their daughter did not run away again—instead she just left home when she became of age and is estranged from her parents to this day. If only the parents had accepted their daughter's right to her own views, though different from theirs but not harmful, a lot of heartache on both sides could have been avoided.

Runaway teens may often run away from their own behavior rather than from parental control because they are too embarrassed to face their parents. If your daughter ran away because she's involved with drugs, is pregnant or misused social media by sexting, spreading vile gossip, or posting nude photos of herself on U-Tube, when you find her, you must not be judgmental. The important thing is to move forward. Your daughter is in trouble and it is a time for you and the family to be rational and do whatever you can to help your daughter overcome or resolve the problem. If it's drugs, depending on the type and degree of dependency, counseling or a treatment center is the way to go. If it's pregnancy, there are options as discussed in Chapter 14 at "Pregnancy." *See also generally* Chapter 3 at "Bullying" and "Drugs, Alcohol & Cigarettes."

MOVING OUT

If your daughter threatens, *I'll move to Daddy's if you don't let me go to Louise's party,* counter with that she can move to her father's any time she wants but she still can't go to Louise's party. While your daughter may jump with glee at the thought of living with her father, stay calm and explain to her that changing households is a major decision and she cannot flit from one to the other on a whim just because she thinks she will have fewer chores or a later curfew. Also, it may dampen your daughter's enthusiasm for a move when you point out that her father is allergic to her cat or that she will have to train him to put up with her loud music, moods and vegan diet. Adolescents can be extremely practical. When given respect and a careful view of the options, your daughter will probably decide on the status quo.

Sometimes though, the tension between you and your daughter may reach a point that is intolerable. Even with counseling you and she simply cannot coexist at even the most basic level of civility. There are constant differences of opinion, spiteful actions by both of you and, worse, self-destructive acts on your daughter's part. Don't be afraid or embarrassed to consider alternative living arrangements for your daughter. If you are divorced or separated and your daughter has a good relationship with her father, she could live with him. If that's not possible, consider allowing her to live with friends or relatives. Boarding school might also be a solution if you can afford it and if your daughter is amenable to the idea. Perhaps, live-out arrangements even on a temporary basis might help to alleviate the tension between you and your daughter. However, if there is no other choice except for the two of you to continue to live together, you as the adult, must bend over backwards in thought and deed to prevent any further self-destruction on her part. Your priority should always be to act in a way to help ensure that your daughter reaches adulthood safely.

If you and your daughter don't get along, don't feel you have failed as a mother. Sadly, some personalities just don't jive together. If circumstances are such that your daughter can live safely and comfortably elsewhere, take advantage of that situation. Living apart may give you and your daughter a chance for a warm, loving relationship. Forcing the maintenance of a stormy situation because of false pride or your insecurity when there are alternatives will only make things worse between you and your daughter because she will now view you as a hypocrite. Your daughter needs to live in a positive environment to be able to develop her full potential. She cannot do that in an environment where she directs most of her energies, rightly or wrongly, toward taunting you or some type of self-destructive behavior. Seek professional advice about the matter before any final decision is made.

16. SPECIAL RELATIONSHIPS

Comparisons Between You & Her
Fathers & Stepfathers — Joint Custody & Visitation
Her Stepmother — You're the Stepmother
Relatives — Friends (Hers & Yours)

COMPARISONS BETWEEN YOU & HER

Almost every mother knows she should not make comparisons between her children. Much has been written or said about treating children as individuals. However, what hasn't been given enough attention are comparisons between you and your daughter.

When you daughter was little, she loved being told she was just like her mother. Now the same comment will make her cringe. The merest hint from you or someone else that she is similar to you will evoke expressions of disgust even if your daughter's friends think the way you look and act are terrific. Don't despair. You know you're not perfect but overall, you're pretty darn good. Your daughter is simply unable to treat comparisons between the two of you realistically so don't let your feelings be hurt. Instead, smile through it and know that once she feels secure, she will likely be more than happy to be like you in so many ways whether she admits it or not.

In the meantime, recognize that some adolescent girls go through an intense negative phase where everything is magnified out of proportion. If you are slightly overweight, your daughter views you as fat; if you still put your hair in curlers, you're hopelessly old-fashioned about everything.

Wait for your daughter's distortions to smooth out. She will often want to be like you if it's her choice. In the meantime, don't make direct comparisons between her present self and you at her age. Also, don't try to look like her or dress like her when the two of you are together. You may like hearing how young you look—but what your daughter hears is how "old" she looks.

If you happen to be a natural beauty and your daughter is not, take special care when you're together at a public function that your "look" is less fashionable than hers and perhaps even a tad dowdy. If you look so good, you shouldn't need to hear compliments at your daughter's expense, especially when it's her school concert, her party, or her graduation. Let her be the star she deserves to be. As she develops more and more confidence in herself, she will be able to accept lots of stars in her life, including you.

FATHERS & STEPFATHERS

Assuming your daughter's father or stepfather is not a fiend or child molester, you shouldn't interfere in conflicts between your daughter and her father or stepfather. Obviously, there will be times when you feel you must say *something* but avoid taking sides. It's fine to support your daughter (or the father or stepfather) *before* a potential conflict arises if your assistance was sought by such person but do not jump into the middle of a clash even if you are asked. Get busy or go to a movie if need be. If pressed to commiserate afterwards though, in most instances simple responses such as *it's just a phase she's going through* to the father or stepfather or *nobody said life is fair* to your daughter, should suffice even if annoyingly so.

It may be, however, that your daughter's father may be so adoring (either because or in spite of his feelings toward you) that he spoils her unnecessarily and overtly favors her over you or the other children. This is especially common with divorced fathers who see their daughter only on weekends or during school vacations. It's hard for them not to play Super Dad. As a result, you wind up being the "heavy," especially if you work outside the home. What usually happens is that on "his" weekends, your daughter has no responsibilities. On "your" weekends, however, you either pile on the chores or supervise the completion of school projects.

However, it's not necessary for you to be the mean one to counterbalance the father's actions. That's not fair to you or your daughter. You're entitled to your relationship with your daughter, not one that is merely a response to the relationship between her and her father. Speak to her father. Perhaps you can schedule the orthodontist appointments on his weekends instead of yours or suggest that he be the one to scour the libraries with her for a book on medieval witchcraft so she can finish her history project or some such thing. You are entitled to some time to spoil your daughter too and you should try to plan some time when you and your daughter can do something enjoyable together even if it is something as simple as painting each other's toenails or going for a leisurely bike ride.

On the other hand, your daughter's father or stepfather may be unduly harsh or strict. If so, try to change his mind, but do so in private. However, if you feel that his beliefs and actions are truly out of step with reality and he refuses to bend, seek outside advice on how you should next proceed. For example, if your daughter, a high school senior, always has to be home by 10pm on a Saturday night, she's likely going to have a very difficult time fending for herself if she goes away to college. While the foregoing curfew is not harmful to your daughter in the traditional sense, it is, absent any extenuating circumstances such as living in a dangerous neighborhood, hurtful to her as she is being deprived of learning how to make certain decisions for herself. However, if the father is adamant and refuses to relent, you could let your daughter know your feelings but explain that it is something that her father feels strongly about and his wishes therefore are to be respected. The point is that you can let your daughter know you disagree with her father without belittling or betraying him. Also, just as you and her father must love and accept your daughter for who she is, imperfections and all, give your daughter the opportunity to love and accept you and her father for the person you each are.

Some adolescent girls like to think of their father as The Great Protector. She likes the idea that her father is there as nay-sayer at a time when she is not ready to join the activities of her friends. It gives her an excuse not to take risks that she's not ready to take. However, make sure that your daughter knows that her father is not her only protector. Sometimes, instead of letting her father make all the rules, you should make a few too. You too could be the one to pick her up sometimes from her night-job at the Mall or do some of the bad-weather driving while on a family vacation instead of leaving it all to her father. You don't want your daughter growing up thinking that she always needs to look to a male for protection or to do the hard stuff. The more examples of your "know-how" or "can-do" you show your daughter, the more you give her the opportunity for inner growth and self-confidence.

JOINT CUSTODY & VISITATION

Whether or not you have a judicial joint custody agreement or merely a weekend/vacation visitation agreement, chances are that if you and your daughter's father live near each other, your daughter will often be shuttling back and forth between the two of you during her teen years. The key to all such arrangements is flexibility whatever your daughter's age.

You and her father should cooperate with each other regarding your daughter's living and visiting arrangements. The guiding criteria should be your daughter's well-being based on her school schedule and extra-curricular activities (as well as those of her siblings) *and* her father's and your work schedules. Personal convenience or preference, as well as the formal custody arrangement which may have been agreed-to well before your daughter became involved with seemingly every after-school activity in existence, might often need to take second place. Further, when it comes to visitation and any type of custody arrangement involving your daughter, there is no place for spite or vindictiveness between you and her father. You and your daughter's father should each provide a loving and caring home where she and her friends are always welcome just as if she had only had one home to go to.

Obviously, of course, you and your daughter's father should, as much as possible, have similar guidelines for your daughter. Though they need not be the same, they should be consistent when it comes to your daughter being responsible for her homework or carrying through a "grounding" or some other punishment imposed by either of you for poor behavior. Also, try not to compete with each other for your daughter's favor. She loves both of you. Assuming that any differences between you and your daughter's father do not revolve around things such as physical abuse, drug use or drinking, you and he should each explain that the differences between the two of you involve personal preferences and are reflective of different life styles and goals. There is no reason you each can't point this out to your daughter without belittling the other's choices.

If your ex uses drugs or drinks heavily in your daughter's presence, or is physically abusive to your daughter, keep your daughter home and seek professional advice about changing or ceasing visitation arrangements.

HER STEPMOTHER

If your daughter likes her stepmother, consider it to your credit. If she didn't think much of mothers she wouldn't think too much of stepmothers. If your daughter dislikes her stepmother though, it may be that she is having problems letting go of childish fantasies about being the woman in his life when she grows up or is still resentful about the divorce and blames the stepmother. It will do your daughter no good to be at odds with her stepmother so while being super-understanding of your daughter's complaints, put the stepmother in the best possible light. She will hear you even if she refuses to discuss the matter further.

If your daughter thinks her stepmother is the most wonderful person of all time, try hard not to feel jealous or threatened. Do not let the ugly head of jealousy or your insecurities rise to the surface even if the stepmother is younger, more talented, better educated or more successful than you. No matter how great any of us are, there is always someone who is better than us at every turn. Besides, you need not worry about your daughter comparing you to her stepmother. She will not compare her to you because she takes you for granted and assumes you have no identity other than as her mom and are therefore not worthy of comparison with *anyone*, let alone a glamorous stepmother. Remind yourself that even though you may think that one of your daughter's friends is absolutely terrific you don't want her for a daughter instead of your own. Your daughter's raving about her wonderful stepmother is no different from her ecstatic carryings on about her favorite movie star or singer and thus, even though it may be difficult, do not feel threatened if your daughter has a good relationship with her step mom.

If the stepmother's values are different from yours, let them be so as long as they do not cause your daughter any harm. However, her offering your daughter a joint or a beer to garner favor is definitely wrong. Not only do you have every right to criticize those type of actions, you should. Further, if they don't cease, you are within your rights to prohibit your daughter's visits until they do. Ideas, however, are not harmful. Your daughter is no longer a two-year-old. Consider the differences as part of your daughter's overall education. The world is full of all sorts of folks who act and think differently than she and different is not synonymous with better or worse. And as far as any truly weird or hateful ideas are concerned, let your daughter know your feelings in these areas and address your concerns with her father in private.

Your young teen daughter will also likely go through a sickeningly "cute" phase. She will adorn her room with stuffed animals and stuff her favorite in her back-pack. She will squeal at teenage rock stars, go gooey-eyed over stray kittens, and offer to do the dishes. She will also want you to appear together with Daddy and Step Mommy at her school play or some other school activity.

It's not that you dislike your ex-husband's new wife. You just feel awkward, especially if you don't even have a boyfriend. Also, why should *she* be there and share the kudos? She didn't raise your daughter—you did and you want the glory. You're the one who listened to her recite her lines at least a hundred times over and suffered through multiple readings of book reports and asked dozens of questions in preparation for pop quizzes so she could graduate middle or high school with honors. You're the one who chauffeured her to 6:00am ice-skating practice or to soccer matches and stood outdoors in freezing cold to watch her score a goal or two. You don't mind her father showing up to see her star in the school play—after all, he is her father but why *her?*

Of course, you feel petty and foolish explaining all of this to your daughter. As understandable as your feelings are though, you should not let them rain on your daughter's parade. Don't cave in to your weaker self! Have courage! Look at the situation as an opportunity to show the world how civilized and sophisticated you are. Upon arriving, sit together with your ex-husband and his new wife. Don't force your daughter to choose between two sides of the auditorium after her performance. Moreover, you would only feel hurt if you sat elsewhere because most likely she would choose to go to her father's side first. After all, you've brought her up to be polite and the stepmother qualifies as deserving of "guest" treatment. Besides she sees you all the time and feels more secure about your feelings toward her than anyone else's.

If you truly are a petty weakling about this, as understandable as your feelings are, don't threaten *If she goes, I won't.* It's unfair for you to put your daughter in the middle and have her chose between her father's wishes and yours. Instead, if you can't put on a brave face and go, simply don't go but recognize your daughter's disappointment in your decision. Explain that you have a right not to be perfect (just as she has) and that even people who love each other sometimes disappoint each other. The important thing to remember in this situation is that it's your problem not your daughter's. Don't make her feel guilty for wanting everything just right.

YOU'RE THE STEPMOTHER

Be yourself. See yourself as any mother. Don't be apologetic or defensive. Treat your stepdaughter as you would your own daughter—with love, patience and respect. If your stepdaughter is visiting you, of course it is natural to want to treat her "special" but don't overdo. If she wants to treat you as a friend, that's fine but don't become so chummy that you appear to be in cahoots with her against her mother or lose all right to authority. While you should not try to usurp her natural parents in any way, there may be times that you are left in charge. For example, you may be alone with your stepdaughter while her father's golfing and she wants to go to the Mall with a friend. If you have no idea who the friend is, you'll want to say "No" and you'll want your stepdaughter to accept your "No" without her feeling that you are betraying your friendship with her. Thus, it's best to preserve a little distance.

If your stepdaughter is generally always hostile toward you, don't be taken aback. She may feel disloyal liking you or believe that you are the cause of her parents' divorce. Give your relationship with her some time. She needs to come to grips with reality and your adding to her problems by trying to force some friendliness between the two of you will not dispel any of her hostility. You can and should, of course, insist on civil treatment and respect. If you are patient and consistent and do nothing to polarize the situation, she should come around.

Be aware too that there may never be any love between you and your stepdaughter. It may just not be possible for her to develop a warm, loving relationship with you. She may forever blame you for her parents' divorce even if her father didn't even know you existed until well after the ink on the divorce papers was dry. After all, in her mind, the fact that you exist is what prevented her parents from getting back together. Also, deep down, you may actually dislike your stepdaughter. That's a real possibility if you came on the scene as she was entering her teens. However, if you behave as the adult, a relationship based on mutual respect and even affection should develop over time.

If a serious problem arises with your stepdaughter about her behavior or concerning a major decision that has to be made with respect to her life, stay out of it unless you are her only mother (or if her father solicits your opinion in private but even then, tread lightly). Her natural parents must deal with these kinds of things. Don't volunteer your opinion even if you know the best drug therapist in the world or think that buying her a new car instead of a used one is a big waste of money. At best, you will be accused of meddling; at worst, of being selfish.

RELATIVES

If a verbal confrontation arises between your daughter's grandparents and your daughter and you can't stay out of it, take your daughter's side. The grandparent is already a grown-up. Your daughter needs to know she can trust you. As an example, a friend made a dinner reservation for herself and her granddaughter at a charitable function. However, her granddaughter refused to go even though the girl supported the charity in spirit. The girl had no homework or other plans. She simply did not want to go because she'd be bored. The grandmother was aghast. *How could [the mother] not insist that [the granddaughter] go? What would her friends think? How*

could she face them knowing that her granddaughter didn't want to go with her? A big
disagreement developed between the girl's mother and the grandmom
but the mother respectfully and firmly supported her daughter's right to
choose. Surprisingly, the results benefited all. The mom felt good about
standing up to her mother (my friend tended to avoid any confrontation
as much as possible), the grandmom gained more respect for her daughter,
and the teen girl was reassured that her mom was on her side.

Whether or not your daughter needs to be on hand when relatives or
friends arrive, or to stay around to entertain the cousins, should depend
on the particular situation. Let your daughter know who's coming and
when, and what you would like her to do. For example, Auntie and Uncle
are coming to dinner. Absent an important prior commitment by your
daughter, she should be present for the meal and, if she wishes, politely
excuse herself to do homework or needing to go to a friend's house to
study for an exam.

Also, if Auntie and Uncle always bring their six-year-old child along
expecting your daughter to babysit at the last minute while they go out,
give your daughter the courtesy of asking her whether she wants to sit or
not. Your daughter shouldn't become an on-demand babysitting service
for any relative whether or not she is to be paid for her services. Of
course, if the relatives are coming to town to visit Great Uncle Charlie
bedridden in the local hospital, you are well within your rights to insist
that your daughter provide any babysitting that is required. However,
if she has other plans which are special or where others are depending
on her participation such as a school trip or an important track meet,
unless Great Uncle Charlie's circumstances are imminently dire, she
shouldn't be expected to break her plans. Ditto if Auntie and Uncle's
teenage children are in tow. Unless there's some rapport between them
and your daughter, the cousins probably feel pretty awkward at being
"dragged" along. In any event, they probably don't want to interfere in
your daughter's life. Let the cousins work it out amongst themselves but
don't berate your daughter for being rude if she goes out and the cousins
stay. They may all feel more comfortable that way.

Basically, don't assume that your daughter's plans are always less
important than someone else's just because she's not an adult. Your
daughter's plans usually involve others and her canceling out may

cause unnecessary disappointment and inconvenience to others such as teammates and classmates and perhaps their families as well. For example, perhaps a friend was counting on your daughter to help her study for a next-day test or a friend's mother was counting on your daughter's presence at a Brownie Troop meeting because of her expertise in Origami.

Also, your daughter shouldn't be required to go visiting with you unless it's a special occasion like a wedding or Great Granny's 102nd birthday. Her cries of but *I'll have nothing to do...I'll be sooo bored* are probably right. In most instances though, a compromise might work. For example, if time and distance permit (e.g., the visit is within walking distance or accessible by public transportation or taxi), it should be okay for her to go along, make an appearance and then leave with a plausible excuse such as homework needing to be done. Remember, too, when you need to apologize for your daughter's absence, to make the same social excuses for her as you would for anyone else. Just say she had a babysitting job or a school paper to do but otherwise she would have loved to come along. Your hosts have a right to expect politeness from you and it certainly isn't going to make them feel good if you tell them that your daughter thinks they're stiffs.

Sometimes visiting relatives is a duty; more often it is fun. However, don't burden your daughter with the same duties as you or expect her to enjoy the same people that you do. If you treat these types of situations according to their respective importance, you will likely find your daughter reasonable and cooperative when you really need her to be. You never know—she may want to be around when you least expect it.

FRIENDS

Her Friends. Your daughter's friends are her friends, not yours. While you will probably like some of them, you will think some are too bossy, too timid, too whatever. However, there's no need to interfere in any relationship that your daughter has with a boy or a girl unless the relationship is destructive or dangerous to your daughter such as situations where your daughter is being taken advantage of or her physical safety is at risk. You should also interfere if your daughter is taking undue advantage of one of her friends since her learning "not to take candy from a baby" is also part of growing up.

If you notice that your daughter *always* does what her best friend Martha wants to do or that your daughter seems particularly upset after an evening out with her friends, it's an appropriate time for you to step in but take care to tread lightly. Your daughter may complain all the time that Martha doesn't want to do anything anymore except hang out at the Mall but telling your daughter to stand up for herself by insisting that she get her way sometimes or find new friends will not enable your daughter to do either. Your daughter may be suffering great pangs of adolescent insecurities and lack the confidence to give ultimatums to anyone.

Finding new friends is not always easy. Thus, instead of highlighting your daughter's timidity of the moment and making her feel even more insecure, help her find something to do that does not involve her friend. Suggest that she join the YWCA swim team or teen chess club at the local library. She may protest but don't be surprised if you hear her tell her friend that she *has* to join because you insist. Your daughter may actually need and want you to intervene because she's unhappy with her friendship but doesn't know how or is unable to change it. If your daughter does get involved with something new, she might find new friends and Martha will either join her or drop from the scene. If, on the other hand, your daughter refuses to get involved elsewhere, she may be as content as Martha to just "hang out" but feels guilty about it. Anyway, if your daughter and Martha are otherwise happy and not particularly troublesome, just boring for the moment, one of them will outgrow the other sooner or later. In the meantime, remember to nag them occasionally about wasting all that time just hanging out—this way, they can spend part of their time complaining about you instead of all their time giggling about boys.

If you suspect your daughter's peers are pressuring her into having sex, using drugs or alcohol, or taking part in some other inappropriate or unlawful activity, don't just forbid certain friendships or punish her by taking away certain privileges. While such actions by you may be then-appropriate depending on the circumstances, they are not the final answers to such problem behavior. Obviously, your daughter has lost her way. Best to pull back and involve her in a constructive time-consuming activity. Hire her to do the laundry, polish the silver, mow the lawn. Pay her to baby-sit. Spend a few weekends camping or visiting relatives. Do whatever you can to help her break destructive patterns. Perhaps she can work part-time for a friend or relative or volunteer at the local animal shelter or become involved with a church youth group. Even a girl who's only interested in makeup can put that interest to productive use. Perhaps she could volunteer at a nursing home and help elderly women with their makeup and nail polish.

If, despite your efforts, your daughter goes back to her old ways, seek professional assistance. Don't wait until it is too late by tolerating numerous cycles of alternating good/bad behavior. Also, beware of the temptation to blame your daughter's bad behavior on her so-called "friends" who may well have instigated your daughter's unwise instances of illicit, addictive or unlawful acts. Ultimately, your daughter is the one responsible for her behavior. A refusal to recognize your daughter's weakness will only make her problem worse. (*See also* Chapter 15 at "Peer Pressure.")

Your Friends. Your daughter doesn't expect you to hang out with her friends, you shouldn't expect her to hang out with yours. She should of course be polite to them but you shouldn't expect her to stay around just so you can show her off, at least not more than once in a while. And when you do, respect her desire to escape as soon as possible.

If she wants to join you, and your friends have no objection, that's fine on occasion. She may want to be with you because she is under too much pressure from her friends or at school. Being with adults can give your daughter a chance to relax and recharge herself. Things may not be well though if your daughter always prefers being with you and your friends rather than with her peers. If your daughter is seeking safety from the foibles of the teen world on a more than temporary or occasional basis, try to find out what it is that she's having difficulty with. Sometimes the problem might be very real—perhaps it's a bully who always makes fun of her looks or lack of athletic ability.

Adolescents, especially girls, can be very cruel toward one another. Most schools have rules prohibiting bullying. However, bringing this to the attention of the proper school authorities can also have consequences. Also, your daughter may feel being bullied is far better than being embarrassed (*but see* Chapter 3 at "Bullying"). Perhaps too your daughter is more comfortable with your friends because they accept her totally, particularly if she's socially, emotionally and physically a year or two younger than her chronological age and has nothing in common with girls her own age. If this is the case, consider having your daughter repeat a grade in middle school *if* it is OK with her and recommended by the school. (Note that it's not uncommon for boys to be held back a year so they can bulk up for sports.) Alternatively, your daughter may just really like your friends or be a home-body.

If you are single and date, do not regard each and every beau as a potential stepfather. Of course, some situations call for "family fun" such as a day at the beach or a visit to an amusement park. However, even on such occasions, if your daughter joins you, ask her to bring a friend along. However, if it's a boyfriend that she brings along—don't turn it into a "double date." Ensure that the chosen activity is family friendly and doesn't involve pairing off in cozy places by either of you.

Generally, it's not a good idea to invite comments about your dates from, or let your dates get too chummy with, your daughter. Keep all your dating relationships casual as far as your daughter is concerned. Your daughter is likely to view any man in your life, even platonic friends, as prospective fathers. Thus, it is best to play it safe and unless it's been a relationship of some length or a strong likelihood that you and the man in question will ultimately live together, keep him at a reasonable distance from your daughter. In any case, whether a broken relationship was long or short, your daughter may feel the loss of the relationship as much as or even more than you do. Regardless of who instigated the break-up, your daughter may view the end of the relationship as a rejection of her and she may already feel rejected by her father. This is not a pattern that you want repeated.

17. ADULTHOOD

Senior Year — Freshman Year
Quitting College
Leaving the Nest — Living at Home

SENIOR YEAR

Much of what your daughter has read and heard may have led her to believe that wonderful things would happen to her during her senior high school year but in reality, it may be a big let-down for her. She never made it to a varsity team or became first violinist and not even one of her stories ever appeared in the high school newspaper. Definitely sympathize with her disappointment but remind her that nowadays a successful senior year is no longer the be-all that it was in the past. Often the prom queen or class valedictorian never reached comparable heights as adults and after being launched into adulthood with so much fanfare, they became bitter because of their disillusionment. Explain that for her and many of her classmates, high school graduation is just a step, albeit often bumpy and sometimes steep, to a full and satisfying life.

These days, by the time many teen girls reach their senior year, they are simply too mature to still be in high school. Many turn eighteen before graduation. Yet while they can vote, marry, work, sign contracts, and join the army without parental consent, they might still need a note signed by a parent explaining a school absence. Furthermore, many of today's teen girls are more worldly than their counterparts in the past. They have been exposed to cultures their parents may never have heard of and have mastered technology that would have befuddled Einstein. As a result, parents are often faced with a bored, mature teenager who is in a year-long holding pattern.

As a parent, you are worried about your daughter's ennui. She is so full of life and impatient to start her chosen path. She's so eager to be out in the world that it is difficult for her to simply attend high school and be told not to chew gum in class. In the past, school and extra-curricular activities excited her and gave her joy but now she just goes through the motions and just waits. She waits to hear from the college of her choice, she waits to see where her friends will be going, she waits for the school-year to end. You fear that as an alternative to the status quo, she may become pregnant or experiment with drugs or alcohol. You fear that the impatience of youth will overpower her reason.

During this time, be understanding and supportive. Perhaps she can take a course or two at the local college or become active in community affairs at an adult level. In other words, help get her started on her life as an adult even though she's physically still in high school. This may perk her up a bit. Explain to your daughter that knowing she survived what to her was a long period of boredom will give her strength to meet the challenges of life after graduation be it college, work, marriage or the armed services. Any success often involves long periods of tedium or persistence whether it was walking across the continent alongside a wagon on The Oregon Trail or, as Thomas Edison succinctly put it, *"Genius is 1% inspiration and 99% perspiration."*

FRESHMAN YEAR *(This section also applies to technical and vocational schools and other special training courses.)*

Freshman year at college whether spent out-of-town or locally, should be treated as the official beginning of your daughter's adventure as an adult. By the time your daughter starts college wherever its locale and regardless of her age, she should be well aware that people come in all colors, sizes, shapes, attitudes and beliefs and be looking forward to learning about their differences as well as learning about her chosen field of study. She should also know how to do her own laundry, take care of her basic health, manage her expenses whether it be via a charge card or checking account, care for her car if she has one, stay away from drugs and alcohol and the students who offer them, and how to stay safe on campus. The latter is usually thoroughly addressed at a college Freshman Orientation but she may have to check the safety issue on her own if she's at a vocational or technical school. And if she wants to avoid gaining "The Freshmen Ten," she should also know to get sufficient exercise and be wary of over-eating at the campus cafeteria or over-indulging in pizza while studying.

Further, your daughter's financial aid package may be based on her working part-time, even if only 10 hours a week. You know your daughter and if the cash to be earned is a must for your family, discuss with your daughter whether her freshman class load should be 12 credits instead of the usual 15 or 16. Even if your daughter won't be working part-time, the number and type of courses that your daughter believes she'll be able to handle during her first semester should also take into account the amount of additional outside or lab work the chosen courses will require. Check with the college too about dropping a class. Usually, it's OK to do so without any academic penalty before midterms.

QUITTING COLLEGE

If your daughter arrives home from college during a school break and doesn't want to return because of the *"Why am I here/what does it all mean syndrome,"* insist that she at least finish the semester so she doesn't waste your hard-earned money and her time. Together you can plan what she might like to do when the semester is over—keep your fingers crossed though that she will decide to return. If you handle her despondency with tact and understanding and do not turn the situation into a major battle, it is likely that she can be persuaded to return to college (perhaps a local one). Also, if you are tactful and understanding, you should be able to convince her to resume her education even if her proposed exodus from college was prompted by poor grades. Perhaps, after discussing the issue, all she needs to do is to take a smaller course load. Missing courses can be taken during summer school or perhaps she'll need five years to finish college instead of four. (This is not the time to worry about where money for the summer session or fifth year will come from—these things have a way of working themselves out.) Maybe she can switch roommates at the end of the semester. Pride might be at stake too. She may have been high school valedictorian but discovered that at college, she's just one of many such stars and she's had to struggle just to keep up. Perhaps a return to a less prestigious college might be the answer. Loneliness might also be the problem whether it's for her family or her cat or perhaps being from a small town, she finds the large campus overwhelming. Conversely, a big-city girl might find a small college in a small town boring. In any case, find out what the problem is and see if it is solvable, at least in part.

If despite your best efforts, your daughter still wants to take a year off to travel or even stay home, that's fine too. The important thing in such case is not to let your daughter feel like a failure. Failing a course or even running away from a problem is not tantamount to failing at life nor does it mean that she will always run from problems. Of course, the goal is to have your daughter return to college and complete her education. While a few people succeed and succeed grandly without formal education, such instances are rare. Explain that another advantage of a college degree, even if she doesn't want to be "anything" now, is that it will give her the option to be "something" when she's older. At the least, a college degree will offer her a choice.

It may be that your daughter needs some freedom before she can settle in somewhere or perhaps she wasn't ready to leave home. If she chooses not to return to college, let her know that you hope she will finish college at some point and that whatever financial assistance you had intended to give her will still be there for her when she's ready. (Or you might say if she goes to college now, you're paying for it but if she goes later on, she'll have to pay for it.) In any event, advise your daughter that whatever she chooses—travel or home--she should have a plan. If it's travel, perhaps she could arrange to get a student visa and work/study abroad. A friend's daughter did that for a while. She'd thought about going to grad school after college but hadn't a clue about what she wanted to be or do after college. So, rather than work at some job in which she had no interest, she used her savings and graduation gifts and went to central Italy for six months and studied Italian. While there, she met people from all over the world—people whose socio-political views were far different from a typical American's. She also learned the joys of unrefrigerated packaged milk, to appreciate the benefits of central heating, and discovered the many ways to flush a toilet.

If your daughter's reason for wanting to drop out is because she's pregnant, see Chapter 14 at "Pregnancy." Regardless of her decision, do all that you can to see that she finishes college whether at home or elsewhere. If her reason for wanting to drop out is due to problems with physical abuse, date rape, drugs or alcohol, report the incidents to the school and seek professional guidance as to what your next steps should be. Your daughter should not have to drop out of college or even switch schools because of another student's abusive or illegal actions nor should your family have to suffer financial loss at least to the extent that your daughter is unable to physically or mentally complete the current semester.

If, though, your daughter's return from college is more of a return to the womb, by all means welcome her but don't treat her as a child. If she won't take independence, you'll have to give it to her. Make sure she gets some type of job and that she's responsible for her laundry, her expenses, her dental appointments, etc. You get the picture—don't baby her. Give her a chance to develop confidence in herself.

LEAVING THE NEST

Some teens leave home right after high school without going away to college or technical school. They marry, travel, get their own apartment with a friend or by themselves. If your daughter has left the nest, whether or not you agree with her life-style (assuming it's not dangerous or illegal) you shouldn't treat her as if she is still living at home nor should you expect or ask your independent daughter to keep you apprised of her comings and goings. When she does call or visit, don't complain that she isn't giving you enough attention. Let her know how much you love hearing from or seeing her. If you don't hassle her, she is likely to call or visit more often and maybe even let you in on her life.

Don't fault your daughter for repeating your life even if you have often expressed how sorry you were that you married too young or didn't finish college. Don't feel you've failed. How she lives is her choice and you must respect your daughter's decision. If she and her boyfriend decide to live together, don't disown her even if you disapprove. You need to accept her decision. Remind her, though, that while you have adjusted to her living with her boyfriend, Thanksgiving Dinner, with all the relatives gathered 'round, is not the time nor place for her to announce her new living arrangements or that she's about to become an unwed mother. No point in giving old Aunt Betsy a heart attack.

Absent a specific financial commitment to help your newly independent daughter as a result of an unplanned pregnancy or to buy a house or a car, keep your purse closed. Your daughter needs to learn how to manage money and shouldn't be able to come to you to be bailed out. You will be helping her more by directing her to a budget counselor. Of course, helping out in an emergency is a different matter but the rent or car payment being due are not emergencies—they are foreseeable events.

LIVING AT HOME

Consider your working daughter as having left the nest even if she still lives at home. She's probably living at home to save money for her own apartment, a car, or perhaps an upcoming marriage. Perhaps too you live in a city like San Francisco or New York where rental costs are so astronomical that your adult daughter might live-in for quite some time. Regardless, don't make life so comfy at your place that she'll never want to leave or make her feel guilty when she does.

Our society expects adults to live on their own and your daughter should want to be on her own as soon as she is financially able. For as long as your daughter is living at home, though, you still have the right to know when she will be home but as a courtesy, not as a controlling parent. Your daughter is a young woman now and should be treated as such. Your working daughter should contribute part of her salary for household expenses and food, do her own laundry, clean up after herself, make her own meals, and do a household chore or two. She should not expect you to, nor should you, wait on her hand and foot. Your working daughter should not need any money from you except perhaps for help in buying a car. If you do buy her a car, she should be responsible for the car's upkeep, insurance and gas.

Should the arrangement with your live-at-home daughter be one where she is expected for dinner, she should timely let you know when she'll be eating elsewhere. If the call comes in at the last minute, don't nag that you've prepared her favorite food. You'll only make her feel guilty but if it happens often, suggest she be responsible for cooking her own dinner. Similarly, your daughter shouldn't complain that there's "nothing to eat" in the house; instead, she should shop for her own goodies.

While your daughter should always be expected to be considerate of others, this is even more true if she's living at home when she's reached adulthood. As an adult, she no longer occupies a childhood position where inconsiderate or insolent behavior can be passed off as an adolescent phase that she's going through. She can't have it both ways. It may be difficult for both of you at first, particularly for you as you will be called upon to alternate between being a mother (upon news of her being laid-off) and a friend (she tells you about her latest boyfriend). You'll know all's well though when she invites you out to a movie—her treat!

ENJOY!

ADDENDUM

There are no guarantees in life but it's a good bet that children who are given consistent and loving guidance and opportunities appropriate to their age and mental maturity to use the values they were taught have a better than average chance at a productive and fulfilling life.

Children learn best from example. Some simple guidelines — Treat your daughter as an individual and appreciate her for who she is, not as you would like her to be. Don't lie to your daughter or put her in a position of lying to you. Forbid as little as possible. Let your daughter know you trust her and act as if you do. Keep your word, and when you cannot, explain why you cannot. Admit when you are wrong. Trust your instincts and don't be embarrassed to seek professional guidance if you feel something is awry with your daughter—better safe than sorry.

Let your daughter put as much emotional space between the two of you as she needs to be able to stand on her own and grow to maturity. If you don't, she will spend a good part of her adult life still trying to separate herself from you and to prove herself to you—and you will have denied yourself the pleasure of her adult friendship.

And most of all, always remember to
let your daughter know how much you love her.

ACKNOWLEDGEMENTS

Thanks to my family for their love and inspiration,
to my friends for their patience and assistance, and
to the many acquaintances who shared their stories with me.

Printed in the United States
By Bookmasters